CONNECTING VISUAL LITERACY TO THEORY

This volume seeks to close the gap between education systems across the world that remain systematically devoted to understanding our world through text rather than images.

Through an exploration of the contributions of well- and lesser-known visual thinkers from across disciplines and geographies, the contributors offer contemporary appraisals and modern re-conceptualizations of the subject. The book illuminates how experts from various disciplines ranging from art, communication, education, and philosophy laid the foundations for what we know today as visual literacy. These foundations and innovative ways of thinking and understanding images have been disruptive, but until now, have been relatively understudied. As such, the chapters examine the context of individual thinkers, expanding upon famous theories and providing new insight into why these visual and cognitive processes are imperative to learning and education and to disciplines spanning art history, museum studies, philosophy, photography, and more. The authors, all members of the International Visual Literacy Association (IVLA), are committed to advancing the study of visual literacy by raising new questions and proposing new routes of inquiry.

A unique and timely exploration of the way we derive meaning from what we see and how we interact with our visual environment, it will appeal to researchers, scholars, and educators from a range of interdisciplinary backgrounds across art, art education, art history, design, information science, photography, and visual communication.

Ricardo Lopez-Leon, PhD, is a lead researcher-lecturer at the University of Aguascalientes at the Design Sciences Center in Aguascalientes, Mexico.

Dana Statton Thompson, MLIS, MA, MFA, is the assistant dean of libraries and a research and instruction librarian at Murray State University in Murray, Kentucky, USA.

CONNECTING VISUAL LITERACY TO THEORY

Revisiting the Disruptions of Visual Thinkers in Education and Beyond

Edited by Ricardo Lopez-Leon and Dana Statton Thompson

Routledge
Taylor & Francis Group

NEW YORK AND LONDON

Designed cover image: © Getty Images/George Peters

First published 2024
by Routledge
605 Third Avenue, New York, NY 10158

and by Routledge
4 Park Square, Milton Park, Abingdon, Oxon, OX14 4RN

Routledge is an imprint of the Taylor & Francis Group, an informa business

© 2024 selection and editorial matter, Ricardo Lopez-Leon and
Dana Statton Thompson; individual chapters, the contributors

The right of Ricardo Lopez-Leon and Dana Statton Thompson to be identified as
the authors of the editorial material, and of the authors for their individual
chapters, has been asserted in accordance with sections 77 and 78 of the
Copyright, Designs and Patents Act 1988.

ISBN: 978-1-032-65176-7 (hbk)
ISBN: 978-1-032-65174-3 (pbk)
ISBN: 978-1-032-65178-1 (ebk)

DOI: 10.4324/9781032651781

Typeset in Galliard
by MPS Limited, Dehradun

CONTENTS

CONTRIBUTORS

Geri A. Chesner, PhD, associate professor, serves as the Strategic Educational Leadership Program Chair at National Louis University in Chicago, Illinois, USA.

Michele Colandene is a PhD candidate in Science Education Research and Teaching and Teacher Education at George Mason University in Fairfax, Virginia, USA.

Margaretha Häggström, PhD, is a senior lecturer in visual art and didactics at the University of Gothenburg in Gothenburg, Sweden.

Jacqueline Huddle, MSLIS, is the visual literacy and resources librarian at Indiana University-Bloomington in Bloomington, Indiana, USA.

Brian P. Kennedy, MA, PhD, is the president of Brian P. Kennedy Arts Consulting LLC, based in Salem, Massachusetts, USA.

Ricardo Lopez-Leon, PhD, is a lead researcher-lecturer at the University of Aguascalientes at the Design Sciences Center in Aguascalientes, Mexico.

Gary McLeod, PhD, is an assistant professor in the Faculty of Art and Design at the University of Tsukuba and is based in Tokyo, Japan.

Marty Miller, MLS, MA, is the art and design librarian at Louisiana State University Libraries in Baton Rouge, Louisiana, USA.

Ashley Pryor, PhD, is an associate professor of the humanities in the Jesup Scott Honors College at the University of Toledo in Toledo, Ohio, USA.

Diederik W. Schönau, PhD, is an art historian and psychologist who is currently retired but still active in the domains of both art education and art history in Beuningen, Netherlands.

Nikolai Selivanov is the creative manager of the not-for-profit organization Studio of Art Designing and teaches for the Russian State University for the Humanities in Moscow, Russia.

Dana Statton Thompson, MLIS, MA, MFA, is the assistant dean of libraries and a research and instruction librarian at Murray State University in Murray, Kentucky, USA.

INTRODUCTION

Ricardo Lopez-Leon and Dana Statton Thompson

The visual image has always gone hand in hand with human communicative practices. Even before the development of writing, images were present. We still preserve countless pieces of evidence in visual messages, such as petroglyphs and cave paintings, Mayan codices, or Egyptian hieroglyphs. However, in the history of mankind, there have been some important events that have undoubtedly boosted the use of images as forms of communication. In the invention of language, that is, the Western alphabet, visual thinking played an important role. The characters of the alphabet are visual representations of sounds, that is, an image replaces an oral expression. Words are visual representations of consecutive sounds, which also represent concepts. Likewise, character-based writing (Chinese, Korean, Japanese), contains visual representations that sometimes even imitate real-world references. The alphabet systems that emerged around the world in ancient civilizations have their own visual language, all of them with different references and associations – some of which are preserved to this day. Thus, we can consider the invention of language as the first impulse of mankind to communicate through images.

This development of writing culminated with the invention of the printing press, through which written pages could be reproduced much faster and in greater quantity. Printed books also began to include other types of images for other purposes, such as those that were merely decorative and others that were illustrative. The proliferation of written language, even though it is ultimately a set of images that represent sounds, became pivotal for visual communication. It seemed that the produced images that more and more included visual references by imitation had been relegated to privilege

DOI: 10.4324/9781032651781-1

the written word. Verbal language began to be conceived as a separate entity from the image, as if word and image belonged to different worlds. In addition, distrust in the visual image increased because of its open interpretation; instead, written language seemed a more precise and reliable communicative form.

As mankind was becoming literate, artists began obsessing with reality and truth. It is not a coincidence that by 1855, a Realist Manifesto emerged by the hand of Gustave Courbet calling to paint only what was observable, hence using image representation as an imitation of reality, leading the realist movement in visual arts. The imitative practices of the plastic arts that sought to represent reality culminated with the invention of photography. The emergence of this technology became another event that contributed to establishing a relationship between the image and the communication practices of human beings.

Photography came to liberate the plastic arts from their imitative practices. It was thought that a painting could not present a more faithful copy of reality than a photograph. For this reason, the plastic arts sought other forms of expression, other languages, non-imitative, which would lead artists to produce countless images that were increasingly difficult to understand (ahem, Cubism). Photography was the technology that boosted visual production by scientists and technicians at first, but when mass production at low cost was possible, people around the world could take and print a photograph within seconds through the Polaroid brand technology. Photographs, and therefore visual images, became a part of everyday life.

In the twentieth century, several events consolidated the importance of mass media and, with it, the use of the image as a protagonist. Newspapers and magazines increased their circulation thanks to technological advances in printing techniques, which soon had to face the technical challenge of including images in their pages. For this reason, it is understandable to observe a more faint presence of images in newspapers and magazine pages at the beginning of the twentieth century. As the decades went by, the presence of images with advertising intentions in print media became more prominent, increasing both their size and sharpness.

In addition to the technological aspect, the commercial impact of visual advertising also led to a rapid acceptance and demand for images as a means of promotion in mass media. Faced with a stagnant economy during the interwar period in the first half of the twentieth century, different products and brands had to develop various strategies to make themselves known and stimulate consumption, among which the use of images for such purposes played a significant role. Thus, advertising practices would soon find in images the expressive possibilities to make their products more attractive, giving another important impulse to using images in communication.

Another event worth mentioning was the proposal of the International System of Typographic Picture Education (ISOTYPE) in Austria by Otto Neurath in the early 1920s. Artists and scientists explored the communicative capabilities of the image, and from that moment on, communicative practices found different ways to include images in their messages. The communicative possibilities of ISOTYPE, due to its ability to communicate messages to speakers of different languages, soon gained notoriety and became the language par excellence for signage, at least in Western countries. Today we can relate to it when using emoticons.

In the middle of the century, the emergence of television would make it possible for moving images to become a part of everyday life. People had access to visual information every day and at all hours, causing new generations to spend an unprecedented amount of time in contact with images. With this, those children who grew up interacting with images demanded at the same time that communication become more visual, an aspect that was evident with the emergence of video games, the Internet, and, at the turn of the century, with mobile devices. Visual images penetrated all social spheres, from education to politics, from art to entertainment. For these reasons, it is necessary to turn to the reflections of experts from various disciplines, in order to understand the importance and implications of the image as a support of meanings and messages.

This book brings together those people who, through their practices and the dissemination of their way of thinking, have contributed to our understanding of the role that images play in our ways of communicating and thinking. From various disciplines ranging from art, communication, education, and philosophy, these experts laid the foundations for what we know today as visual literacy. Their way of thinking and understanding images has been disruptive from different points of view, and, in our opinion, they have not received the attention they deserve. As members of the International Visual Literacy Association (IVLA), we consider it essential to revisit the work of these great thinkers to understand them in greater depth and identify their contributions so that they can serve as a starting point for building and advancing the field of visual literacy. Visual literacy, as we understand it in the twenty-first century, can best be described as "an interconnected set of practices, habits, and values for participating in visual culture that can be developed through critical, ethical, reflective, and creative engagement with visual media" (Murphy, 2024).

This book is a compilation of ideas about the image. In each chapter, an author introduces us to a visual thinker. We recognize visual thinkers as a person who, regardless of the origin of their discipline, has contributed to question, investigate, or promote different ways of understanding and appropriating images by different societies. Thus, although even these personalities do not identify themselves as visual thinkers, we have categorized them as such, since, in our opinion, this is a characteristic that all those who appear in this work share. The authors of these chapters, all members of the IVLA, are committed to advancing the study of visual literacy by raising new questions and proposing new routes of inquiry.

As a starting point for these new routes of inquiry, we proposed a thinking tool to the authors. We, as editors, presented a premise that would provoke new questions and would promote a different way of looking at visual thinkers. The premise we used as a thinking tool proposed the existence of a *visual conspiracy*. The premise assumes that the explosion of printed media established the use of written language as the primary form of communication, a protagonist role maintained until the first half of the twentieth century. This written word's privilege was then replaced by the use of images in the second half of the twentieth century. What would happen if we thought there was a deliberate conspiracy? As if a group of artists, educators, and philosophers had come together to say enough is enough, and then designed a strategy to remove the written word's privilege of communication through their artistic, educational, and reflective practices.

The twentieth century was a century of manifestos. The different artistic currents that emerged in response to technological changes, social movements, and even in opposition to the same artistic movements, delivered various publications to declare their way of thinking. Different artistic groups considered it important, through a manifesto, to specify the objectives and boundaries of their movement. However, although some of them indirectly promoted the use of the image, there was no movement that generated a manifesto regarding visual practices. There was no clear set of objectives and goals declaring that it was necessary to promote the use of the image as the main form of communication, seeking to overthrow the hegemonic power of the written word. But if it had existed, who would be the people who could have developed it? What would be its statutes? Through what means and practices would they have sought to fulfill their objectives? The questions presented here and the concept of visual conspiracy are merely tools of thought proposed by the editors of this book to provoke reflection and inspire different ways of looking at the visual thinkers who make up this collective work. The result, from our point of view, is enlightening and thought provoking.

The 11 chapters included in this volume are divided into three thematic sections: Theoretical Ways of Seeing, Pedagogical Ways of Seeing, and Diverse Ways of Seeing. In the first section, Theoretical Ways of Seeing, chapters are devoted to several theoretical underpinnings of visual literacy including visual thinking, notions of trust and truth in relation to photography, as well as a mistrust in the very concept of a reality mediated by images. The second section, Pedagogical Ways of Seeing, focuses on how visuals have been used in teaching, both in educational and museum settings. Chapters focus on how art is used in social communicative processes, how illustrations in children's picture books have as much to teach us (and the children reading them) as the text, and how individuals develop an understanding of artworks encountered in a museum setting. Finally, the last section, Diverse Ways of Seeing, introduces the reader to the early twentieth-century avant-garde idea of 'expanded vision'; the need for, and recognition of, divergent thinking processes in education; cutting-edge sensory studies and multisensory literacy; and how to conceptualize visual literacy within the context of Modern Arab art. These chapters include overlooked and forgotten points of view and serve to challenge prevalent and prominent reliance on neurotypical and Western understandings of visual information.

Theoretical Ways of Seeing

The section begins with Diederik W. Schönau, a Dutch art historian and psychologist, who writes of his mentor, Rudolf Arnheim (1904–2007), a German-born writer, art and film theorist, and perceptual psychologist. In his chapter "Rudolf Arnheim: The Power of the Image," Schönau informs us that to Arnheim, visual thinking is the basis for understanding, imagining, and researching reality and that visual perception precedes and informs language-based thinking. He notes that, according to Arnheim, visual thinking should be taught in every field, without exception.

Next, Gary McLeod, a British photographer, writer, and professor based in Tokyo, introduces us to Vilém Flusser (1920–1991), a Brazilian Czech-born philosopher, writer, and journalist, in his chapter "Vilém Flusser: Play/ Read/Write/See." McLeod examines Flusser's idea of the camera as apparatus, a device to help one not only create photographs, but also decipher the meaning created by and mediated by that same apparatus. He reminds us that although visual literacy starts with reading (understanding) and writing (creating) visually, Flusser's philosophy ultimately directs camera users to question the very act of creating; for how true can a representation of reality be if all of the controls are predetermined?

Ashley Pryor, an American collage artist and professor, expounds upon the ideas of Guy Debord (1931–1994), a French Marxist theorist, philosopher, and critic. Her chapter, "The Conspiracy of the Spectacle: Guy Debord's Relevance for Visual Literacy Today," also wrestles with how images shape our understanding of the world, especially in a capitalist society. Pryor elucidates Debord's concepts of détournement and dérive, illuminating how we can, and should, evaluate images, especially in a world of misinformation mediated by visuals. In Debord's world, images have usurped the very reality that they purport to describe.

Finally, Ricardo Lopez-Leon, a Mexican art and design researcher and professor presents the work of Joan Fontcuberta (1955–), a Spanish conceptual artist and photographer, writer, editor, teacher, and curator. In his chapter "Fontcuberta and Postphotography: Unveiling the Border between Fiction and Reality," he explains, for Fontcuberta, photographs are, and can only be, fiction masquerading as truth, especially in the digital era. In addition to considering the technical capabilities of the camera, Fontcuberta focuses on the cultural and ideological intentions of the photographer. Lopez-Leon notes Fontcuberta's contribution to the notion of 'post-photography' which focuses on technological advances, possible through tools in software like Photoshop and filters on social media, and the immateriality of the photograph in the twenty-first century, divorced from any physical photography processes.

Pedagogical Ways of Seeing

This section starts with Margaretha Häggström, a Swedish professor in visual art and didactics, who focuses on the work of June McFee (1917–2008), a visionary American professor of art education, in her chapter "Visual Literacy Foundations in June King McFee's Art Education Philosophy." Häggström informs us that McFee's theory is rooted in the core belief that visual art is a primary way we can communicate and thus visual literacy can be developed through these social interactions. Not only does art provide a way we can communicate, but McFee also believed students should be taught how to use art as a communicative medium. Importantly, Mcfee called for cultural understanding through the arts.

Next, Geri Chesner, an American professor in educational leadership, presents John Stewig (1937–), an acclaimed American author, educator, and educational scholar. Her chapter, "Visual Literacy Development through Picturebooks: The Contributions of John Warren Stewig," high-lights Stewig's pioneering work. Chesner investigates Stewig's belief that the visual information included in children's picturebooks is just as important as the textual information. Stewig believes picturebooks can serve as a primary way to teach children visual literacy skills in an organic yet systematic manner. Notably, Chesner explains, he argued that illustration and design are essential teaching and learning tools in K-12 education and can contribute to a more critical understanding of the stereotypes prevalent in picturebooks, especially sexist representations of women.

Finally, Michele Colandene, an American PhD candidate in science education research and teaching and teaching education introduces us to Abigail Housen, an American professor of art education and co-founder of Visual Understanding in Education and co-author of the Visual Thinking Strategies curriculum (1945–2020). Colandene's chapter, "Abigail Housen: Visual Thinking from Museums to the Classroom," explains Housen's theory of an individual's aesthetic development, especially within the context of viewing art. Colandene describes the crucial development of the Visual Thinking Strategies curriculum, used worldwide in museums today, as well as her own alignment of Housen's visual proficiency with Bloom's taxonomy. She also underscores how, at the pinnacle of Housen's aesthetic levels of development, individuals can transfer their visual thinking skills across domains and disciplines.

Diverse Ways of Seeing

Nikolai Selinanov, a Russian artist and educator, leads this section with his chapter on Michael Matyushin (1861–1934), a Russian painter, composer, and leader of the Russian avant-garde. In his chapter, "Unleashing Perception: Exploring Michael Matyushin's Expanded Vision," Selivanov leads us on an exploration of Matyushin's inventive and experimental ideas, especially those related to how we see. He describes Matyushin's psychological and pedagogical methods of developing active visual perception and expounds upon how Matyushin's ideas radically expanded current understandings of perception, especially within the context of the historical evolution of visual art and synesthesia. Matyushin's work, Selinanov informs us, was meant to teach individuals how to develop creative perceptual skills for observing the world around them; he viewed visual perception and artistic thinking as the pinnacle of evolution for sighted individuals.

Jacqueline Huddle, an American academic librarian and scholar, presents us to Temple Grandin (1947–), an American academic and animal behaviorist in her chapter "Thinking in Pictures: Temple Grandin's Contribution to Visual Literacy." Huddle outlines Grandin's advocacy for visual thinking. As a person with autism, Grandin extolls the importance of visual thinking abilities and makes connections between it and neurodiversity. Huddle explains how Grandin's work emphasizes a desire for the acknowledgment and acceptance of multiple intelligences as well as the need for educators to address the needs of diverse learners in elementary and secondary schools.

Next, Brian P. Kennedy, an Irish arts and community leader, former director of multiple museums, and scholar based in the United States, introduces the work of David Howes (1957–), a pioneer of the anthropology of the senses and theorist of sensory studies, in his aptly titled chapter "David Howes: Pioneer of Sensory Studies." Kennedy details the development of sensory studies and sheds light on how visual literacy can, and should, be incorporated with sensory studies in order to escape its current silo. He explains Howes' idea of sensory literacy and how it has tremendous potential to open the doors of visual perception.

In the final chapter, Marty Miller, an American academic librarian and scholar, introduces us to Nada Shabout (1962–), an American art historian born in Scotland and based in the United States. Her chapter, "Nada Shabout: The Challenge of Visual Literacy in Modern and Contemporary Arab Art," explains that since Arab art does not conform to Western notions of what is modern, learning to 'read' it cannot rely on traditional visual literacy approaches. She explains how Modern Arab art has traditionally been devalued and marginalized. Shabout, Miller explains, has spent her career teaching students in Western institutions how to understand this gap in contextual knowledge.

As a collective, these chapters serve to disseminate the contributions of well- and lesser-known visual thinkers from across disciplines and geography. Their work spans disciplines such as art, art history, education, history, museum studies philosophy, photography, and psychology. By discussing and explaining the ideas of artists, philosophers, educators, and other authors that have contributed to understanding images, this book aims to spike interest in visual literacy as well as the different ways we can think about and understand visual media. This edited volume examines the context of these individuals, expanding upon famous theories and thinkers, and provides the reader with the reasons behind why these visual and cognitive processes are imperative to learning and education.

Reference

Murphy, M. (2024). Introduction in M. Murphy, S. Beene, K. Greer, S. Schumacher & D. S. Thompson (Eds.), *Unframing the visual: Visual literacy pedagogy in academic libraries and information spaces*. Chicago: ACRL.

1

RUDOLF ARNHEIM

The Power of the Image

Diederik W. Schönau

Cito Institute for Educational Measurement; ArtEZ University of the Arts

Biographical Sketch

Rudolf Arnheim (1904–2007) was born in Berlin, Germany, in 1904 in a secularized Jewish family. His father had a piano factory, and although Rudolf was expected to take over this family business, his interest lay elsewhere. In 1923, he became a student in psychology at the department of philosophy at Berlin University where he majored in music and art history. During this time period, the philosophy department of the university was the cradle of Gestalt psychology, a new approach in perceptual psychology research. After publishing his dissertation in 1928, Arnheim left academic life and spent five years as a writer and journalist, working for several German leftist magazines, commenting on what was taking place in cultural and intellectual life in Berlin and Germany in general.

In 1933 Arnheim left Germany, as his critical view was not appreciated by the Nazis who came to power in that year and because his Jewish ancestry made his future insecure in Germany. He moved to Rome, where he became a collaborator at the League of Nations to work with a team on the compilation of an encyclopedia on the history and theory of film. In 1939, he had to leave Italy, as in 1938 the fascists adopted anti-Jewish laws. Thanks to the help of the art critic Herbert Read and his wife, he was able to move to London. In 1940, he was given permission to enter the United States, a place where he had longed to live but that was inaccessible until that moment. While in New York he received several fellowships and in 1943 he was given a position as psychologist at Sarah Lawrence College in New York City. That same year he also took over the lessons of Max Wertheimer, his

DOI: 10.4324/9781032651781-2

mentor who had fled to the United States earlier, at the New School for Social Research in New York. In 1969, he became the first professor in the psychology of art at Harvard University. After his retirement in 1974, he moved to Ann Arbor where he taught at the University of Michigan for another ten years. He remained very productive in later life and his hundreds of publications cover eight decades. Arnheim died in June 2007 at the age of 102.

Introduction

Rudolf Arnheim's book *Art and Visual Perception*, first published in 1954, presented the first systematic research on what can be considered the foundation of visual literacy: understanding the dynamics in visual perception and their relationship with human-made imagery (Arnheim, 1957, 1974). This publication is still a point of reference for any discussion on the role of the visual in visual literacy. In later research, Arnheim elaborated on many related aspects in art, art history, architecture, and design and came forward with a plea for the importance of visual thinking as an independent and more fundamental way of thinking prior to language-based thinking.

Arnheim's view on perceptual processes was firmly rooted in the findings of Gestalt psychology. Gestalt psychology took its name from the German word "Gestalt". Although of an older origin, it was introduced in the psychological domain by Christian von Ehrenfels in 1882, who came to the insight that the form of a melody has qualities that cannot be deduced from its constituent parts. This observation found its famous summary in the maxim that the whole is more than (or different from) its component parts. An example of the unique qualities of the Gestalt principle, which Ehrenfels called *Gestalt Qualität*, is the possibility to transpose a music score to another key, through which all constituent parts change character but the melody remains intact.

In 1912, Max Wertheimer gave a follow-up to this principle in the visual domain. He presented subjects with a visual field with two stable bars of light. By then presenting these bars separately and in a specific tempo of alternation the bar seemed to move from one side to the other, the so-called phi-phenomenon. He assumed that this phenomenon can be explained by taking the overall perceptual quality of this phenomenon as an expression of its Gestalt quality. Here it is this overall quality that in its turn defines the role of the constituent parts. This explanation shows a holistic approach to the way the perceptual system works: not by association at cognitive levels, but by organizational processes taking place in the perceptual system itself.

This insight was one of the basic tenets of the Gestalt psychologists in their criticisms on perceptual research by the earlier 'structuralist' generation of psychologists like Wilhelm Wundt, Wilhelm von Helmholtz, and Edward Titchener. The Gestalt psychologists rejected their atomistic approach, in which what is sensed is supposedly based on distinct elements or atoms that are then combined in the brain by association into larger concepts and ideas. Wertheimer's research on the phi-phenomenon traditionally marks the beginning of the research school of Gestalt psychology. The two other co-founders were Wolfgang Köhler and Kurt Koffka.

Two major concepts, developed in the Gestalt approach of mental processing, are of special relevance for the domain of visual literacy: figure-ground and "Prägnanz". Figure-ground perception relates to a basic propensity of the visual system to see objects as distinct from their surroundings, being this a three-dimensional space or a two-dimensional surface. This phenomenon was extensively researched in the early days of Gestalt psychology. Arnheim came to the insight that a figure-ground relationship is not static but dynamic. "So I began to talk about figure and ground as having a reciprocal relation: the figure expanding outward and being compressed by outer forces" (Kleinman & Van Duzer, 1997, p. 117). This observation fueled his approach to art in terms of expression of meaning through visual forms.

Prägnanz is a German word that is mostly used to describe the phenomenon that we tend to see a figure or object as regular or simple as possible, correcting for small deviations from this optimum. Prägnanz thus results in a "good" Gestalt. Arnheim adds the following observation:

What Max Wertheimer had in mind when he spoke of the prägnanz (clear-cutness) of the 'good gestalt' was not only the effect of the basic gestalt law, which I call the simplicity principle, but that optimal state of perceptual form of which successful works of art are the finest examples. (Beardsley & Arnheim, 1981, p. 222)

So already in the early days of Gestalt psychology, there was the notion that the laws of spontaneous and optimal organization in visual perception find their best and most interesting expression in works of art.

Following this line of research, Gestalt psychology researchers proposed so-called laws of 'good Gestalt': the different dynamic mechanisms of the sensory system to organize perceived things, objects, and figures in the simplest way possible. For instance, objects that are seen as near to one another are seen as a group (law of proximity) and objects that look like one another also tend to be seen as a group (law of similarity). Additionally, the law of closure (incomplete figures are experienced as complete as the gaps are perceptually completed by the intrinsic dynamics of the figure), the law of symmetry (symmetrical objects are seen as belonging together around a center point), and the law of good continuation (an object that is seen as overlaid by another object is still seen as an integrated whole, not as two separate parts). Although often described in terms of laws, it might be better to describe these phenomena in terms of organizational principles. These perceptual phenomena are very powerful and it is almost impossible to look at these types of grouping without experiencing their visual organization. These organizational principles active in perception are widely used by artists and other image-makers in all kinds of visual representation, being these graphs, maps, artworks, typography, or technical drawings. They play a role in both the production and the perception of visual imagery.

Arnheim elaborated on these findings. The subject of his dissertation (Arnheim, 1928), under the guidance of Wertheimer, was on how observers "read" spontaneously the visual expression inherent in the muscular dynamics of the human face and the strokes of a writer's pen (Cantú, 1988, p. 248). It shows already his approach to visual phenomena: not as illusions, nor as organizational principles per se, but as carriers of desired or spontaneous expressive qualities. It was a short step for him to approach works of art as a special and even most effective form of Gestalt formation. According to him, artists have always applied Gestalt principles when making art. "Artists, of course, know intuitively all the things people like myself figure out in theory, but they often have no clear intellectual concepts of what they discover in the studio" (Cantú, 1988, p. 252). To him, the goal of art is to give visual form to observed and intended meaning. The works thus made retrieve their power from the same visual principles as objects in direct observation, but they do so in a more concise, abstract, fundamental, and purposeful way.

During the period when he was a writer and journalist in Berlin in the roaring 1920s, Arnheim was witness to the early development of German film. He started to write reviews and essays on film and film theory, and in 1932 he published *Film als Kunst,* translated and complemented with later essays as *Film as Art* in 1957 (Arnheim, 1932, 1957). This book became a classic in film theory. Its title is a program: Arnheim looked at film as an art form, with a specific interest in the way filmmakers give form to meaning by using the dynamic possibilities of their medium. At that time, films were made as silent movies in black and white. To him, both of these characteristics should be seen as tools to arrive at a new, artistic reality, bringing forward the essence of what is shown in a new and more generic way. Arnheim's artistic approach to contemporary film in the 1920s explains his discomfort with the introduction of sound and color in film in later years. What he experienced as a tool for new artistic explorations gradually became a tool to generate more illusionistic representation of reality and an instrument for entertainment. With the same artistic interest, he approached the then new media of radio and television, concluding that the artistic potential of these media became soon subjected to commercial and, to him, superficial goals.

In 1943, Arnheim published *Gestalt and Art*. This article may be considered his first text on the psychology of art (Arnheim, 1943). It can be read as a research agenda on how to make use of the insights of Gestalt psychology to analyze and understand the power of visual art and of visual perception in general. It was his conviction that Gestalt laws not only refer to organizational principles in human perception, but that the dynamics underlying these types of organization also have an expressive quality. His interest in the expressive qualities of visual objects, being these real or man-made, can be seen as one of the basic notions in his work. In line with the Gestalt tradition, he states that these qualities must be understood as characteristics of the visual organization of the object itself, not as an added value based on mental associations.

Arnheim devoted a decade scrupulously investigating all aspects of visual perception in relation to their role in the perception of art. He brought psychology to art, using artworks as the result of intuitive and sophisticated use of Gestalt laws by artists. The outcome of this work was published as *Art and Visual Perception* in 1954 and became an instant classic text (Arnheim, 1954). The revised edition of 1974 is still in print (Arnheim, 1974). Its subtitle, *The Psychology of the Creative Eye*, underscores Arnheim's point of view: the first step in any meaningful visual experience takes place in the eye and the perceptual system. Visual input is processed, unconsciously in the perceptual system, bringing forward what matters in the object observed. This process does not produce an image of reality the way a camera does, but must be understood as an active organization of visual information that not only represents what is seen, but in organizing visual input generates dynamics that are experienced by a viewer as expressing meaning. In *Art and Visual Perception*, Arnheim systematically investigates the contribution of the most important aspects of human-made imagery: balance, shape and form, space, light, color, movement, dynamics, and expression. Each aspect is discussed and elucidated with many explanatory drawings and examples from art. Through the purposeful combination of all these aspects, an artist can generate an image that not only (re)presents a reality, but at the same moment expresses its intrinsic or intended meaning. The dynamic character of visual information processing contributes to the experience of what is seen: which is an image in which meaning and formal qualities cannot be separated. Artists make use of all these aspects, as they look for the best way to give form to what they see and make this visible. The artworks discussed throughout the book serve as examples of certain principles of visual organization, both in their perception and in their production. Arnheim turned to the work of great artists, like Michelangelo, Henri Matisse, and Wassily Kandinsky, but also to non-Western artists, because these works provide the best examples of the application of visual dynamics.

This exemplary use of artworks to demonstrate certain principles of visual organization might run the risk of neglecting the iconological, historical, and cultural aspects of the works involved. Arnheim was very much aware of this. Artists do more than apply visual tricks: these only form the basis as they contribute to the overall visual effect and expression and, thus, to the meaning. Culture provides the content through themes, symbols, stories, conventions, and style, but what makes an artwork really interesting and valuable is the way use is made of the perceptual processes constituting the intended meaning as well as the experience of the work.

Although Arnheim made extensive use of examples of what is considered great (Western) art, his definition of art is much broader. Art can be summarized as describing "the capacity of an object or event to elucidate significant aspects of human experience through its sensory appearance by evoking constellations of forces characteristic of those human experiences" (R. Arnheim in his lectures, 1977). This is a very broad definition of art, in which traditional museum-related art represents only a sub-domain, albeit a most important and illustrative one. According to Arnheim, art is not limited to what artists make. All man-made products, when made with a good use of the intuitive insights in the expressive power of image making, can be seen as 'art'. "Art is not a criterion to separate some objects from others, it is a quality that is present in any object, natural or man-made" (Pizzo Russo, 2005, p. 261). At the same he also adheres to a view that refers to what are normally called artworks: art as an interpretation of life.

To demonstrate the many layers of art, Arnheim decided to make an in-depth analysis of what to him may be the most important work of art made in the twentieth century: *Guernica* by Pablo Picasso (Arnheim, 1962). It is fortunate that Picasso had made a lot of preparatory sketches and studies, all exactly dated, while working on this immense canvas. This gave Arnheim the opportunity to make a close examination of all artistic and visual decisions taken by Picasso to arrive at his final product. This book provides a classic analysis of this painting, presenting many insights in the way of thinking and working of Picasso – as well as of Arnheim. It also makes clear that a good and complete understanding of an artwork as a cultural statement includes a thorough knowledge of the themes used, the cultural background, and the historical situation, not to mention the tradition of art itself. But the compositional visual structure will always underscore the intended meaning, not only by guiding the eye of the viewer to what is most important, but also by generating dynamics in the perceptual experience that appeal to basic emotions and forms of direct understanding.

By this time, in the 1960s, Arnheim had become the most prominent voice on both the psychology of art and the tradition of perceptual psychology in the Gestalt tradition. His writing became influential in artistic and educational circles, and many of his observations were recognized and seen as helpful to understand how artworks 'work'. He wrote many essays and articles, took part in discussions with opponents, and tried to gradually work out the underpinnings of his insights and convictions. As a consequence of his intimate relationship with all kinds of arts – classic and contemporary, Western and non-Western, prehistoric and modern media based, visual and musical, literature – he was able to elaborate on both branches of his trade: psychology and art.

Visual Thinking and Art

Further investigations on psychology resulted in what may be considered his most innovative work, a plea for visual thinking, presented in his book *Visual Thinking* (Arnheim, 1969). This book can be seen as a follow-up to the only book written by Max Wertheimer on productive thinking (Wertheimer, 1945). Arnheim's position was more outspoken than Wertheimer's. Arnheim, through his in-depth experience with the visual qualities in the work of artists, solidified his conviction that visual perception is a cognitive activity. His perspective was that the form of truly productive thinking first takes place in the realm of imagery: "... images do not imitate reality, they hint at it. They have the ability to make the essential part visible, and are thereby a fundamental principle for understanding the world" (Grundmann, 2001). This view is a fundamental comment on the split in Western thought between perception and thinking. According to Arnheim, taking distance of an object, by following rational arguments or contemplating reality from a philosophical stance, neglects the contribution of the senses, not as channels of information processing, but as tools that directly generate meaning of the observed reality. Perception generates mental imagery. Thinking is, first of all, based on concepts that refer to perceptual images. Arnheim introduces the notion of 'perceptual concepts' that underlie any further conceptualization at linguistic level. The perceptual system first organizes the information seen immediately, thus making it possible to bring this information into memory. Put differently, memory is informed by perception, not the other way around. Perceptual thinking, however, does not take place in an isolated mind. Experience and knowledge play an important role, but they come second.

The relationship between perception and so-called higher-order thinking processes is dynamic and reciprocal.

The second track of research, on art, resulted in two books on architecture and on composition in art: *The Dynamics of Architectural Form* (1977) and *The Power of the Center* (1982, 1988). In these publications, architecture and artworks are not used as illustrations of visual phenomena but are approached as objects and images that in their totality express the artist's intentions and address the perceptual and cognitive understanding of the viewer. Creator and viewer share the same physical world and experience the same influence of gravity, distance, nearness, and spatial organization. Verticality and horizontality are very strong forces known to everyone who looks at a leaning tower or at painting that is not hanging perfectly horizontal: they are part of our natural sensitivity for directions while at the same time they express meanings like openness, robustness, and spirituality.

Where in his *Art and Visual Perception* (Arnheim, 1982) artworks were used to exemplify the visual effects of elements and principles in art, in the *Power of the Center* (Arnheim, 1982, 1988) Arnheim looked at artwork more holistically. This was also to counteract the assumption that artworks are composed of elements and principles that add up to a 'complete' artwork. On the contrary, the whole (the Gestalt) and the parts (the constituent elements and principles) define one another. The parts convey meaning, but that meaning only makes sense in the context of the whole, as the context of the whole comes across through the formal relations of the parts. This brought Arnheim to investigate the role of composition in art. Arnheim looked for compositional principles that apply to all art, of all times and all cultures, and the underlying dynamics that define the role of both the parts and the whole. He concluded that the perceptual field as we experience it plays a fundamental role in organizing what we see. He described this as the spatial system of perception based on horizontals, supported by our horizontal view of the world, and the vertical, as supported through the pull of gravity. This results in a basic grid on which all compositional decisions are taken. He called these the centric and the eccentric systems, respectively. He specifically introduced a psychological aspect to this geometrical approach:

> The centric tendency stands for the self-centered attitude that charac-terizes human outlook and motivation at the beginning of life and remains a powerful impulse throughout. (…) The eccentric tendency stands for any action of the primary center directed toward an outer goal or several goals or targets. (Arnheim, 1988, p. 2)

Secondly, these visual forces generate fundamental psychological experiences of equilibrium and dynamics, that is, being bound to one's place or being invited by the work, to open up, referring to oneself or to others, respectively. He systematically discusses the main characteristics of composition: the role of the center and the borders, the form of the borders (square versus tondo), bipolar compositions in which two parts of an artwork act as centers of attention, compositional nodes, generated by a combination of masses and directions of lines, and three-dimensional organization in space. Paintings are normally limited to a rectangular field within which a story is told. This generates organizational principles that keep what is shown inside the frame. As soon as an artist neglects or even contradicts the borders of the frame, like Piet Mondrian did in his geometric canvases or Jackson Pollock in his drip paintings, these choices must be seen as representing views on eternity or endlessness that reject the limitations of the artwork itself.

Paintings are a special category of representation as they represent reality in two dimensions only. To do so, different ways to suggest the third dimension can be applied. Western art has been dominated in the last five centuries by a search for realism and illusionistic representation, overcoming the limitation of a flat surface, by means of central perspective. But looking with one eye, as central perspective technically demands, is fundamentally different from looking with two eyes. Already, Leonardo da Vinci discovered that two-dimensional perspectival rendering has its limitations, as distortions appear when things that are out of focus in the perceived field, are rendered on a flat panel. So-called correct use of perspective includes all kinds of artist's adjustments that contradict the underlying geometrical construction. The development of central perspective reflects a tendency to represent reality from the point of view of the observer. This approach was brought to perfection in Renaissance art up to (hyper-)realism in contemporary Western art. It has led to the notion that (Western) art is about a search for perfect illusion, a point of view presented by Ernst Gombrich in his highly influential book on *Art and Illusion* (Gombrich, 1960). To Arnheim, art is not about the striving for illusion. Art is about abstraction, to represent the essence of (a) reality, idea, or emotion. To him, the development of central perspective in canonical western art is only one way to represent a reality. "(T)he picture of a world converging toward a center presupposes a very particular psychological and social conception, not suitable for just any world view" (Arnheim, 1989, p. 22). Other systems are also valid in their own way, like in classical Egyptian art, so-called 'primitive' art, or in the drawings of young children. "The discovery of central perspective bespoke a dangerous development in Western thought. It marked a scientifically oriented preference for mechanical reproduction and geometrical constructs in place of creative imagery"

(Arnheim, 1974, p. 284). Also Gombrich's view that art history is made by the adaptation of schemes does not do credit to the imaginative powers of the eye and mind. It also (re-)introduces the associationists' view on learning, leaving open the question how associations are possible in the first place, when the characteristics of input are not taken into account.

A third aspect of art, next to its relationship with visual thinking and the application of visual dynamics in architecture and visual art, is the deeper psychological meaning of the visual forces thus organized and experienced. Being so fundamental in all art, the underlying visual dynamics reflect the universal characteristics of human perception. Artworks can therefore generate meanings that work in a generic way that relates to understanding at a basic and common human level. Therefore, according to Arnheim, art is at its best when it addresses issues that surpass the moment and even the culture represented, when it relates to universal human emotions and insights. "(A)rt makes us experience what it means to be a human being and to love in this world" (Arnheim, 1971, p. 239).

Impact and Contribution of His Work

The publications of Arnheim reflect his lifelong quest to understand why artworks work the way they do. However, the principles he used and discussed do not apply to 'high' art only, but are valid for any form of visualization, being these geographic maps, logos, architectural drawings, advertisements, or informational charts. The findings and explanations given by the Gestalt psychologist on how perception (i.e. the creative eye) generates meaning were his main analytical tools. By historical coincidence, Arnheim was an eyewitness to the birth of Gestalt psychology, as well as a new medium: film. He looked at film as a new tool for artistic production, using the findings of Gestalt psychology as an instrument to discover the artistic potential of film. Although he was critical about the introduction of sound and color in movies and he might be considered old-fashioned, his many essays on film have in the past two decades gained a new interest.[1] His findings and ideas met criticism, to which he responded as thoughtfully as possible in many interviews, letters, and book revisions, always trying to make himself more clear or adapting his opinions.

As to the findings of Gestalt psychology, concepts like Gestalt and Prägnanz are still discussed and investigated. Much of this research finds its way through the Society for Gestalt Theory and its Applications and in the related multidisciplinary international journal *Gestalt Theory*, founded in 1979. More recently, thanks to technological innovations, research on visual perception has turned to brain research and to sophisticated types of quantitative measurements underlying perceptual phenomena. Arnheim himself was skeptical about the contribution of brain research to understand psychological phenomena, because this approach looked for explanations outside (psychological) experience. "(T)he brain part is the least important. I'm concerned with principles which govern the psychological processes, to understand what's happening in experience" (Galassi, 1974, p. 4). On the other hand, he still adhered to the original view of Wolfgang Köhler that processes at physical, organic, and psychological levels have dynamic organizational processes in common (Köhler, 1920).

Arnheim's own theoretical explanations have been subjected to practical scrutiny as well. For example, Ellen Winner and others investigated Arnheim's claim that location in the two-dimensional picture space affects perceived weight (Winner et al., 1987). Arnheim states that an object appears to have more visual 'weight' when it is located on the upper rather than the lower portion of the picture. Next to this up-down balance, there is also a left-right balance: an object appears to have more visual 'weight' when it is on the right side of the picture than when it is on the left side. The researchers found evidence for the first type of balance, but not for the left-right balance.

Another fundamental discussion is on the contrast between 'seeing' and 'knowing,' between perceptual concepts and intellectual concepts in the development of child art (Wilson & Wilson, 1977). Does a young child draw what it sees or what it knows? Arnheim defends the view that a child is trying to give form to what it sees, not in an illusionistic way, but based on perceptual concepts (Arnheim, 1978). At the earliest level of a child's development in drawing a circle is a basic perceptual concept representing oneness – or, more practically, an object or person. Drawing a circle has nothing to do with minimal physical drawing skills. Drawing what one knows is also begging the question of how this knowledge is generated in the first place. The use of schemes and examples does enter artistic development in a later phase, when the cultural environment gets greater influence on how a person communicates within a cultural setting. Arnheim defends the role of creative and meaningful perception before what is perceived is put into words. "The notion that the visual characteristics of an object are incapable of being distinguished and remembered unless they are associated with sound and thus relate to language, I propose to call the myth of the bleating lamb" (Arnheim, 1966, p. 141). Linguistic analysis comes second, both in cognitive development and in learning. Language can describe what is experienced but never replaces experience itself, which is direct and based in perception.

Arnheim's Legacy to Visual Literacy

With regard to the domain of visual literacy, the work of Arnheim can first of all be seen as a plea for visual thinking. To him this is the basis for understanding, imagining, and researching reality. Arnheim introduced the notion of 'perceptual concepts,' the grasping of the overall structural features of what is perceived. The underlying processes take place in the nervous system itself. The term 'concept' has a striking similarity between the elementary activities of the senses and the higher-order ones of thinking or reasoning. Any human-made image derives its meaning, power, and effect first of all on the way these perceptual concepts are visualized. This insight can also be helpful to take distance from the traditional Western approach to thinking and the role of language and open up our mind to look at other traditions as well.

Another aspect of Arnheim's approach to images is the notion of quality. When art and imagery in general are discussed in terms of quality and when selections are made of what is worth using or exposing from an artistic point of view, it is inevitable to look at the image as a visual statement in the first place, not as a representative of a style, idea, oeuvre, culture, or economic value. What makes an image – being this an illustrative scheme or an artwork – so powerful or qualitatively successful? How does an image express meaning through its visual structure and quality? Artworks are a special manifestation of imagery, in which several functions are combined and deeper meaning is intended, but the way any image 'works' is based on the same perceptual principles. It is impossible to negate the immediate impact of an image in the perceptual system. In his books, Arnheim has offered many tools to look at images from a perceptual point of view, like the elements of form, color, dynamics, and expression, but also the principles used by artists and architects to organize visual forces into a composition. These tools help to discover how an image 'works'. Arnheim's insights are still fundamental, also for approaches that concentrate on the more intellectual, social, and cultural aspects of art. It is also important to realize that by making use of the universal dynamics of the perceptual system and the relationship of this system to the biological make-up of all human beings, the impact of imagery can address insights and emotions that are universal. In this way, art and imagery affect common human understanding.

Finally, any discussion on the need for the enhancement of visual literacy must address the issue of education. What fundamental aspects of visual literacy should be part of the school curriculum? What are effective approaches in the classroom? What are the visual literacy competencies that professionals must acquire? In 1989, Arnheim wrote his only book upon request: *Thoughts on Art Education*. He was asked by the Getty Foundation to present his insights and view on art with regard to its role in education. The Getty Foundation was very active in those days to give a new country-wide impetus to art education in the United States. Getty advocated so-called discipline-based art education (DBAE), in which art in education is approached through four professional lenses: of the artist, the art critic, the aesthetician, and the art historian. DBAE was also intended to counter the one-sidedness in American education with its importance on making learning efficient. It addressed the issue that too little attention was given to invention and emotions. In *Thoughts on Art Education,* Arnheim did not follow the approach suggested by DBAE, but presented the issue of learning to make and to appreciate artworks from a holistic and developmental point of view. It is a summary of his thinking and research, brought forward at a more instructional level. In general education the approach by professionals should not be the point of reference, but the psychological and developmental approach of the child. Children must learn to develop their own curiosity and discover ways of visual thinking. This supports the notion that learning to look for complete structures is more effective than starting from disembodied elements, as is normally the case in education. At a practical level, learning to make art is to learn to manipulate materials, visual information, and the dynamics of perception. Art education is first and foremost learning to think in a medium and in visual terms. This is both broadening and limiting the possibilities to give form to what is intended, as it adds specific qualities to what needs to be visualized, while leaving out what is not relevant.

> Visual thinking has to be basic in education in every field without the exception, whether it's natural science or mathematics or geography or history, and the training for this capacity of thinking in images has to be accomplished principally by people in the arts. (Ecker & Madeja, 1979, p. 49)

Note

1 Especially in the German context and on the occasion of his 100th birthday. See: https://www.hhdiederichs.de/arnheim-forum/medienschriften/

References

Arnheim, R. (1928). Experimentell-psychologische Untersuchungen zum Ausdrucksproblem. *Psychologische Forschung, 11,* 2–132.

Arnheim, R. (1932). *Film als Kunst.* Rowolt.

Arnheim, R. (1943). Gestalt and art. *Journal of Aesthetics and Art Criticism, 2*(8), 72–75.

Arnheim, R. (1957). *Film as art.* University of California Press.

Arnheim, R. (1962). *The genesis of a painting: Picasso's Guernica.* University of California Press.

Arnheim, R. (1966). The myth of the bleating lamb. In *Towards a psychology of art* (pp. 136–150). University of California Press.

Arnheim, R. (1969). *Visual thinking*. University of California Press.
Arnheim, R. (1971 [1964]). What is art for? In R. A. Smith (Ed.), *Aesthetics and problems of education* (pp. 231–242). University of Illinois Press.
Arnheim, R. (1974 [1954]). *Art and visual perception: A psychology of the creative eye*. The University of California Press.
Arnheim, R. (1977). *The dynamics of architectural form*. University of California Press.
Arnheim, R. (1978). Expressions. *Art Education, 31*(3), 37–38. 10.1080/00043125.1978.11651923
Arnheim, R. (1982). *The power of the center: A study of composition in the visual arts*. University of California Press. Revised edition: 1988.
Arnheim, R. (1988 [1982]). *The power of the center: A study of composition in the visual arts*. University of California Press.
Arnheim, R. (1989). *Thoughts on art education*. The Getty Center for Education in the Arts.
Beardsley, M. C., & Arnheim, R. (1981). An exchange of views on Gestalt psychology and aesthetic explanation. *Leonardo, 14*(3), 220–223.
Cantú, J. C. (1988). An interview with Rudolf Arnheim. *Michigan Quarterly Review, 27*, 346–362.
Ecker, D. W., & Madeja, S. S. (1979). *Pioneers in perception: A study of aesthetic perception*. CEMREL.
Galassi, P. (1974). Rudolf Arnheim: An interview. *Afterimage 2* (November), 2–5.
Gombrich, E. (1960). *Art and illusion*. Princeton University Press.
Grundmann, U. (2001). The intelligence of vision: An interview with Rudolf Arnheim. The development of perceptual terms. *CABINET, 2*. https://www.cabinetmagazine.org/issues/2/grundmann_arnheim.php
Kleinman, K., & Van Duzer, L. (Eds.). (1997). *Rudolf Arnheim: Revealing vision*. University of Michigan Press.
Köhler, W. (1920). *Die physischen Gestalten in Ruhe und im stationären Zustand. Eine naturphilosophische Untersuchung*. Vieweg und Teubner.
Pizzo Russo, L. (2005). *Rudolf Arnheim. Arte e percezione visiva*. Aesthetica.
Wertheimer, M. (1945). *Productive thinking*. Harper.
Wilson, B., & Wilson, M. (1977). An iconoclastic view of the imagery sources in the drawings of young people. *Art Education, 30*(1), 4–12. 10.2307/3192209
Winner, E., Dion, J., Rosenblatt, E., & Gardner, H. (1987). Do lateral or vertical reversals affect balance in paintings? *Visual Arts Research, 13*(2), 1–9.

2

VILÉM FLUSSER

Play/Read/Write/See

Gary McLeod

University of Tsukuba

Biographical Sketch

Vilém Flusser (1920–1991) was a media philosopher who knew the difference between coming and going. Born in Prague to an intellectual family (his cousin was Israeli scholar David Flusser), he and his wife Edith were lucky enough to flee to London when Prague was occupied in 1939. When the opportunity came for refuge in Brazil, they would then stay there for many years until regretfully leaving for Europe again in view of more political upheaval. From their base in Robion in the south of France, Flusser's reputation grew in academic and art circles. While he always retained some privilege as a foreigner, translating his writing between languages became Flusser's primary means of developing his thoughts on the role of technology in society. As neither luddite nor technophile, he sought discussion of the freedoms left open to those using technology. That was best achieved by drawing attention to structure, but not by projecting; rather, Flusser sought a systematic study of communication, which he called 'Communicology.' In later years, his thinking was taken up by artists, while Flusser himself reflected upon and wrote about art and artists, notably for *Leonardo* journal. While discussion of Flusser often places emphasis on technology, it is worth remembering that translation and freedom of movement (derived from being a foreigner) are also fundamental concepts underpinning his work. Though retaining privileges in ways that many foreigners crossing borders today do not (e.g. money, education), it still mattered that he experienced the world as a foreigner for most of his adult life and rarely took that for granted, calling out his roots and holding his upbringing to critique. It might

DOI: 10.4324/9781032651781-3

even be said that he had a continual sense of how he was perceived and an understanding that perceptions can model learning. Since tragically losing his life in a car accident in 1991, Flusser's thoughts persist because they continue to be prophetic.

Introduction

Wearing two pairs of glasses might seem odd. Images of Czech philosopher Vilém Flusser doing just that are easily found on the Internet. As Figure 2.1 asks, try an image search for these terms: "Vilém Flusser" and "glasses." What might seem eccentric is also a symbolic gesture of intent conveyed in full knowledge of how such images are shared. Flusser was well aware of how gestures communicated. In a video by Fred Forest, made in 1974, Flusser talks to camera (operated by Forest) about his action of smoking a pipe, but he also goads the camera – and subsequently the viewer – into a game of looking and not looking. Frequently, Flusser mentions Forest and even holds a mirror up to the camera. As such, the viewer becomes acutely aware that they are an observer in this relationship. Like a so-called fourth wall-break in movies where a character breaks from a conversation to address the viewer directly, Flusser is addressing an audience in a lecture and then breaking away from that to show the audience how they are being kept

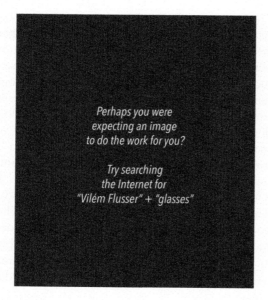

FIGURE 2.1 A photographic print by the author of a text prompt replacing an image of Vilém Flusser with an instruction to search for such an image on the Internet.

in the relationship by Forest operating the camera. But unlike a fourth wall-break that gives a feeling of inclusion, Flusser's presentation of Forest's gesture defamiliarizes the viewer and invokes a voyeuristic response. Although the film informs via text as spoken word, it is the image's construction that does the main job of communicating.

In photography education, Flusser's name is well-known, if anything for difficulty in understanding the book *Towards a Philosophy of Photography* (2000), which is often the entry point for many photography students. Even Nancy Roth, who has translated three of his books into English, acknowledged in her essay *Out of Language: Photographing as Translating* (2019) that his terminology was 'difficult to remember and apply' until encountering the book *Writings* (2002), an anthology of works edited by Andreas Ströhl and translated by Erik Eisel. Coincidentally, that same volume made it easier for this author to get a handle on Flusser's philosophical project, but not directly through the writing (that still took time); rather, my copy of the book, picked up in a bookstore in Shinjuku in 2007 had a peculiar feature. As Figure 2.2 shows, upon

FIGURE 2.2 A photograph by the author of the author's 'glitched' copy of Vilém Flusser's Writings (2002), picked up at a bookstore in Shinjuku, Tokyo in 2007.

opening the book, the frontispiece was clearly upside down. Rotating it to compensate meant that the book's spine was now on the right and not the left. Ordinarily, this would be 'wrong' for languages that read left to right, but being in Japan where a majority of books are written and bound right to left doubted the possibility of it being an error. Could it be that this book was intentionally bound so as to jar the reader from the publishing system from which it emerged? While still reading each page from left to right, I would find the 'last' page of each essay and start there, working back toward the cover. This disorienting effect meant that essays were not read in a set order. Somewhat fittingly (and freakishly given how this copy even made it to the shelf of the bookstore in a culture where items are impeccably packaged), the 'glitch' that was this copy of the book became an entry point for considering Flusser's contribution to the study of photography. While it did not make his writing easier to read per se, it encouraged me to understand his work through making images rather than writing text.

It was in that glitched copy of *Writings*, that I came across Flusser's philosophical 'self-portrait': an autobiographical account that even begins with a curriculum vitae, a word most familiar to readers as associated with job hunting. In this essay (which was now toward the front rather than the end depending on how you looked at it), Flusser was fairly transparent about his life, conceding that he came from 'well-to-do' intellectual Jewish parents and that this upbringing occurred in a 'spiritually and artistically inebriating atmosphere' in Prague between two world wars (Flusser, 2002, p. 198). He talked about three major influences: the first was Marxism, although a particular bourgeois form; the second was a structuralism associated with that of the Prague school, the Vienna circle, and Ludwig Wittgenstein; the third was existentialism espoused by José Ortega y Gasset and a re-reading of Friedrich Nietzsche. These influences would be tested, however, first as a fleeing refugee to London and then as a voluntary exilee in Brazil and later France. As a phenomenologist, the experience of being foreign in an unfamiliar place marked much of his thoughts on media. For instance, it is impossible to think about Flusser's concept of program – which so relies on discussing probabilities – without acknowledging the role that familiarity plays in experiencing the world. It is for this reason that it is hard to dismiss the doubly bespectacled photo of Flusser or Forest's film as being anything other than communicated gestures. They rely on having a particular visual understanding of media that is saturated; that is to say, they only jar if you have seen enough imagery for them to be jarring.

It has taken this author many years to pluck up the courage to summarize Flusser's philosophy. Studying Flusser not only requires interpreting own intentions but also those of translators and editors involved, translation being a key methodology. The editors of this book have given the opportunity to make clear what is felt to be a project akin to visual literacy embedded in Flusser's work: no longer a unique suspicion. Ströhl asserted via Flusser that:

> As many people as possible should learn to code and program. And everybody should be enabled to criticize, to understand the programs that are trying to manipulate them. There needs to evolve an awareness that every perception is subjective and indirect, and that this medial trait of our perceptions may surrender us to programs and programmers alike. (Ströhl, 2022, p. 9)

Ströhl here is not referring to computer programming but to cultural programming. He goes on to add that 'it can be tedious and challenging to acquire visual distrust' (i.e. develop a healthy doubt toward what is seen). For Ströhl, education is understood to be emphasizing skills and thus content production rather than critical thinking, but teaching students to be critical of images alongside acquiring a large range of technological skills to make eye-catching images is difficult (at least within visual design education) because it is time intensive. There is a very real pressure to 'get skilled' in accordance with set periods of time (e.g. graduation), and new technologies become complicit in such pressures (e.g. Wajcman, 2016). For Flusser, critical awareness of the program and its role 'depends on how fast we learn to play: we can become players of the game or pieces in it' (Flusser, 2014, p. 26). In other words, those that learn how to create faster are more empowered than those who struggle to keep up. As a slow-learner myself, this point is alarming, but cameras do offer means for us slow-learners to get a handle on what we are seeing and participating in. It's just that it isn't often understood outside of photography education. The following sections organize Flusser's relationship to visual literacy in accordance with four keywords: *Play* describes aspects of Flusser's thought; *Read* describes the impact of that thought; *Write* describes how Flusser's thought transforms visual literacy; and *See* points to Flusser's relevance to visual literacy's future.

Play

It would be unwise to convey the aspects of Flusser's thought without considering first what he understood work to be. Work was done first by tools and then by apparatuses. Tools took things from the world and turned them into information. Such information was then used by apparatuses. Whereas tools changed the world, apparatuses changed the meaning of the world through symbols. However, Flusser explicitly stated that photographers did not work. Rather, what they did was 'create', 'process' and 'store' the symbols that change the meaning of the world (Flusser, 2000, p. 25). Creativity, for Flusser, was something else. In an essay titled *Creativity and Exile*, creativity was put across as a means of making sense of noisy surroundings (Flusser, 2002). Noise, in this case, was the opposite of information; if information was familiar, noise embodied the unfamiliar, particularly in the case of getting to know new surroundings. Making sense of that noise was to survive it, to make those surroundings livable. If creativity was a mechanism of survival and neither a talent nor skill, it therefore can be said that anyone is capable of it.

Creativity as survival mechanism is hardly cheerful, but Flusser's initial thoughts on a philosophy of photography were stark. Cameras are metaphorical black boxes, which are operated by the pushing of a button by a functionary (i.e. any camera user) without knowing or worrying about what is happening inside. For many, the camera might seem a tool but for Flusser it was an apparatus, which he carefully described in his glossary,

> Apparatus (pl. -es): a plaything or game that simulates thought [trans. An overarching term for a non-human agency, e.g. the camera, the computer and the 'apparatus' of the State or of the market]; organization or system that enables something to function. (Flusser, 2000, p. 83)

Using a camera was to play along with a particular kind of game (i.e. a program) that was the sum of all probable photographs that could be made with the apparatus via its settings and then choosing between them. A crude example of this would be a digital camera with a fixed lens having 8 aperture stops, 8 shutter speeds, and 8 sensitivity settings, and therefore having 512 possible settings for making a photograph. If having never seen a photograph before, each of the 512 settings would produce a photograph that could be considered new information. In a life-world example, however, we are very familiar with photographic images, and cameras facilitate many more possibilities, expanded further not only by additional apparatus (lens, lights, tripods, etc.), but also by the photographer's movements, positions, and angles taken up to achieve a photograph that can be considered 'new' information. Every time the photographer 'succeeds,' the probabilities for new information decrease. For most camera users, however, this matters little, as the probability of the settings is centered only on *their* situation and *their* experience of it. This is apparent when enjoying wildlife photography as a hobby: one might set the camera to a fast shutter and a bright aperture because that is what most wildlife photographers do.

It is worth noting that the kinds of cameras that allow photographers to play with the settings can also be switched to automatic. There is then also the decision to possess or relinquish control of the camera settings. For instance, if the camera user is taking family photos at the zoo, they may let the camera decide all the camera settings (i.e. 'Auto' mode) so as to allow them to enjoy the moment. While some photographers (e.g. hobbyists) might like to play with the settings of the camera, everyday camera users are quite compelled to let the camera do its job in return for providing what they want. This is where smartphone devices with camera applications have become such a common sight.

The kind of playing that Flusser advocated, however, was not playing *with* the apparatus but *against* it. This was achievable by working to outwit its stupidity, smuggling human intentions into it, forcing it to do what it is not designed to do, or turning away from it and concentrating on information (Flusser, 2000, p. 80). In each of these, the camera user is aware of what the camera represents in their relationship. Flusser offered experimental photographers as examples of this, but even they were not aware (at least to him) that they were engaging in a conversation about freedom (Flusser, 2000, p. 80). It is also important to note that not even 'playing against the apparatus' is enough to guarantee new information. The game is ultimately absurd if seeking new forms of expression. This is seen anecdotally when camera enthusiasts embark on learning photography in higher education and in turn resort to conclusions such as "it's all subjective" or "everything's been done before." Clearly, they have evolved awareness of subjectivity as plentiful, but again, as Ströhl noted, it is the 'medial trait' that surrenders us to programs (Ströhl, 2022, p. 9). The only option left at such a time is to evolve awareness about how information is mediated.

Read

Visual literacy might be described like that put forward by John Debes as "a group of vision competencies a human being can develop by seeing and at the same time having and integrating other sensory experiences" (Williams & Debes, 1970, p. 14). Unfortunately, Debes' full definition does not age well, but points to deep issues within visual literacy, notably the power to "discriminate and interpret" not only images but also "visible actions, objects, and/or symbols" that "*he* encounters in *his* environment" (Williams & Debes, 1970, p. 14, emphasis added). The goal for such visual literacy was embarrassingly only to "comprehend and enjoy the masterworks of visual communication". Visual literacy has since broadened albeit with a need to end debate about definitions while moving onto assessing visual literacy skills (Kędra, 2018), as well as the need to start critiquing effectiveness of methods and methodologies in search of answers to visual literacy questions (Brumberger, 2019, p. 12). To take on Flusser's thinking requires at the very least to follow Brill and Branch (2007, p. 55) in accepting that visual literacy definitions will commonly incorporate ability to both read and write visuals.

Flusser acknowledged literacy when he talked about textolatry (the inability to read concepts from texts despite being able to read the words) and idolatry (the inability to read ideas from images despite being able to recognize image elements). Writing was a historical struggle against idolatry, but photography is a post-historical struggle against textolatry (Flusser, 2000, p. 18). With photography comes the emergence of what Flusser called 'technical images' (images produced by apparatuses). If the function of texts was to explain images, the purpose of technical images was to make texts comprehensible again (Flusser, 2000, p. 13). However, technical images are not the lowest common denominator between art, science, and politics as promised; rather they replace things with images of things, essentially complicating the problem of communicating by adding more layers to decipher. Technical images therefore remain difficult to decode, and crucially criticism toward them is not an analysis of their production but an analysis of the world they represent (Flusser, 2000, p. 15). If every photograph is the result of co-operation and conflict between the camera and photographer, then as long as criticism is unsuccessful in unraveling these intentions, photographs will continue to stand for what they depict in the world and viewers will continue to be programmed by them (Flusser, 2000, pp. 46–48).

For Flusser, anyone living a life prescribed by programs experienced the world magically (Flusser, 2014, p. 97); that is to say, they lived according to situations as events occurred. Transcending this magical state was possible, but it would not come through conceptualizing or historical critique, which conceived the problem as text. Rather, Flusser proposed a "new faculty" which he called '"technical imagination": the capacity to decipher technical images' (Flusser, 2014, p. 98). Through Roth, we can infer that this technical imagination was a kind of visual literacy. In her afterword to *Into the Universe of Technical Images* (2011), Nancy Roth considered Flusser's use of the German verbs *imaginaren, vorstellen,* and *einbilden* to refer to "a capacity to communicate visually for which no one word suffices" (Flusser, 2011, p. 176). This 'new imagination' established a qualitative difference between being able to read the world and not. As Roth continued:

The rising force of technical images breaks imagining into (at least) two, that is, into a before and an after, into an imagination that can read the world and one that sees it only as illegible whirling particles. Those who can read the world can picture it; those who cannot must envision it, confer a meaning, and rely on apparatuses and keys to do so. (Flusser, 2011, p. 176)

This is perhaps problematic when photography education has become either learning about what photographs symbolize or learning how to operate them to obtain desirable results. Nowhere are everyday camera users encouraged to think about the co-operation and conflict between camera and camera user. If picturing and envisioning involve imagining in two very different ways, then there is a need to learn how photographs come to exist without referring to photographs just as symbols. Those that can only envision the world need to start reading the world somehow. Thomas Spoerner noted as much when asserting that including photography in classrooms provided "an effective avenue to visual literacy" (Spoerner, 1981, p. 38). Thus an aim of projects such as Literacy Through Photography (Ewald et al., 2012) is teaching photography as form of expression. But, as Flusser would assert, there is a greater need for learners to challenge how the camera is used – to play against it.

Write

According to Roth, Flusser's last book *Gestures* (2014) was unique in how it came to exist and how it positioned the reader like a photographer moving around a scene (Flusser, 2014, p. x). In particular, the chapter "The Photographic Gesture" provided a clue to reading the rest of the book without concluding that photographic gestures were the best solution in a book describing 15 other gestures of equal importance (e.g. the gesture of video). For Flusser, a photographic gesture comprised all actions between the moment a camera is picked up until the point where its shutter is released. Things that happen after that have 'a decisive influence on the result of the gesture and were fascinating to analyze' but were not relevant to the situation (Flusser, 2014, p. 77). Without worrying how the resulting photograph is received, photographic gestures are a matter of learning how to 'write' with the camera, much in the same way as learning to form Chinese characters with ink and a brush.

In *Towards a Philosophy of Photography*, Flusser initially likened the gesture to hunting for new kinds of images and possibilities, but in *Gestures* considered it an active role in an optical process. While a photographer had an initial goal (e.g. to capture a moment with a particular angle and framing), they were also free to change that goal (i.e. to edit and rewrite). Flusser's example (again) was when photographing a person smoking a pipe, the behavior of trying different angles and possibilities was a kind of searching that revealed a gap in understanding between the goal and the experience, which in turn highlighted another gap between their decisions and the many possibilities available to the one with the camera. Such gaps can prompt questions: how did they deviate from their initial intention? And why choose one possibility over others? For Flusser, such questions could communicate doubt to the person being photographed while also having possible causal effects (e.g. the subject losing confidence in the photographer or looking away).

Yet Flusser's photographic gesture was notable for also considering that it was apparent to observers, of whom the camera user may or may not be aware. Assuming observers have familiarity with photography, they can therefore relate to the camera user's and subject's interactions and either ignore, align with, or oppose the camera user's intention. Any discrepancy between an intended gesture and its interpretation by an observer becomes a problem if criteria is a matter of right or wrong, or true or false. If considering familiarity (i.e. a scale whereby familiar is uninteresting, new is exciting), the observer's interpretation forms alliances between those that 'get it' and those that do not. Because gestures either communicate little information well, or a lot of information poorly (Flusser, 2014, p. 8), much therefore depends on camera users having similar experiences. If a learner has attempted the same kind of photograph, there is a likelihood that they understand it better.

Flusser's dialog with the artist Fred Forest took place around the time that Flusser was developing his thoughts about gestures. Of Forest 'almost automatically' recording Flusser's hand and body gestures, Flusser recounted:

> The camera that Forest had in his hands obligatorily followed my gestures with corresponding 'gestural movements.' But these gestures obliged, in turn, my own gestures to modify themselves in response. It is in this way that a dialog established itself, and of its multiple levels, neither Forest nor I were even fully conscious of, since not all of them were deliberate (…). In this example, the method followed by Forest is the observation of a social phenomenon (in this case: myself observing Forest) accepting, ever more consciously, the fact that this observation changes both the phenomena observed as well as the observer of the phenomenon. This is, indeed, a variation of the phenomenological method. But with this difference: in philosophy and in science this method is 'contemplative' (a look), while in the case described, becomes

active participation. A 'technique,' an 'art.' It is in this way, that the instrument (the video equipment) imposes, due to its structure and its function, an active attitude. (Flusser, 2006, cited in Arantes, 2009, pp. 4–5)

To be exact, this was a gesture of video, which Flusser described later in the book as similar to photographing but different in that photographers needed to be "objective" and video makers could be "intersubjective"; their decisions being made in relation to the scene as well as within the scene (Flusser, 2014, p. 144). Crucially, however, it should be noted that the distinction Flusser gave between the photographic and video gestures is potentially rendered moot by technological progress in the form of digital photography, whereby digital cameras are essentially video cameras. More specifically, the "live view" offered by such cameras is a video representation of the subject in a shared present moment, which the software pauses at the time of the user's preference in order to make a "still" image. Yet Flusser's reflections remain relevant. When I am using a digital camera to make photographs, I am essentially merging Flusser's photographic and video gestures, as Flusser anticipated:

Video can also be manipulated with gestures borrowed from other media, for example, gestures from films, texts, musical compositions, sculpture, or philosophical speculation. They will have a new quality, however. This new quality will come from the dialogic structure of video. To put it briefly, we will be dealing with a gesture that no longer attempts to produce a work whose subject is the maker but rather with one that attempts instead to produce an event in which the maker participates, even if he is controlling it. (Flusser, 2014, pp. 145–146)

The gesture here is now what we might call the digitally photographic gesture, but we would be wise to remember the emphasis on the photographic gesture, which arguably lays at the heart of both the filmmaker's gesture and the video gesture. Flusser was no luddite, and would probably not be surprised to think of these gestures merging, but he would likely also be sensitive to their differences and the fact that analog photographic gestures remain crucially different to digital ones. This is why a photomedia literacy is necessary. When experiencing affordances of different photomedia, it becomes possible to see how one tool obfuscates other possibilities for expression (McLeod, 2023). This is particularly the case when scholars employ digital cameras as a faster and more convenient avenue to visual literacy, and in so doing ignore qualities developed when using other photomedia (e.g. patience).

All this said, the digital photograph remains a technical image. If technical images are events, this is not immediately apparent when seeing photographs, which can be described as things, even when in digital form presented on screens. On the contrary, the gesture of the digital photograph *is* explicitly the event, particularly to an observer. While we may no longer be amazed to see photographs being made digitally, there is still curiosity if the gesture appears different when compared to the standard smartphone snapshot, or indeed, disdain if we disagree with such an action. The experience of seeing photographs being made professionally is either for student access (e.g. higher education classes), behind a paywall (e.g. online personal development courses), or the learning curve of a photographer's assistant or intern. Seeing that gesture 'in the wild,' so-to-speak, can still anecdotally trigger conversations with passers-by. My point here is that this observed gesture of the digital photograph remains instructive: it not only models how to write with digital photographs, but also how to exist with them. The challenge is not needing effort but having enough time to learn what to look for.

See

Following James Elkins (2008) in noting visual literacy as a problematic term, A. R. Werner (2015) suggested recognizing visual literacy as a 'metaphor of interformativity,' which is to say that it's just part of a general competence. Making an image thus becomes an entry point into that general competence. The great conspiracy is thinking that photography furthers visual literacy, but photographs are technical images, which ultimately cannot be deciphered without text: visual literacy through technical images will ultimately rely upon textual literacy. The digital photographic gesture, however, as a descendent of the analog photographic gesture, initially forgoes textual literacy by first modeling behavior; it readily distinguishes the visual as a practice alongside text, rather than supplanted by it. What is learnt through it can then be shaped by other gestures and the gestures of others. For those of us less skilled with words and cursed with slowness, Ströhl's 'visual distrust' can form when reflecting upon and evolving discussion about our own everyday digital photographic practices. There is no doubt that this happens: countless communities both online and offline exist to support camera users with evolving curiosity in terms of methods and techniques, while photography higher education programs remain popular for thinking philosophically about images made. Yet, the pivot required is in becoming an observer of one's own digitally photographic gesture. Everyday camera users can, I think, tap into the braveness that Flusser's conception of photography is said to offer artists and philosophers (Zielinski, 2010, p. 23).

Seeing yourself photograph a subject might seem strange but is fairly common, particularly in elite sports where improvement is the goal: in football, game footage is played back by coaches to evaluate player awareness and performance, and in cricket, batters study gathered footage of bowlers so as to anticipate changes in technique. Why not then invite everyday camera users to record themselves photographing with improvement in mind? Flusser's philosophy I think opens doors to this possibility. Of his four options for playing *against* the apparatus, we can think of each of them as building confidence in self-reflection. In outwitting the apparatus's stupidity, one can feel a sense of empowerment; in smuggling intentions into the program, one can get a sense of freedom; in forcing the apparatus to do what it is not design to do, there might be a feeling of control; and in turning away from the apparatus, there might be a feeling of peace; all of which almost vanish when shared and made aware that others had done something similar – an often soul-destroying criticism/realization. The goal of visual literacy, however, is not to seek originality in creative expression or outputs, thus becoming a life-transcending artist; rather, the goal is to relate to photographic expression (e.g. 'writing' images) so as to arrive at a more common means of communication where shared language may not be possible.

Conclusion: Visual Translation

Flusser's experiences of being a foreigner are key here. An overarching method of Flusser's broader work is translation: he would translate his own writing into different languages so as to better reflect upon the etymology and nuance of word choices. Following Roth (2019), I also think this is a central aspect beneath Flusser's philosophy of photography. Not everyone can be a polyglot, but what Roth makes explicit is the importance of understanding how a photograph is created: the role of unfamiliarity, the experience of being an observer, and then engaging in conversation with that experience. This does not mean that camera users must concentrate on the message of specific images as somehow different to other images; rather it means that camera users must learn to convey how they and others translate their surroundings visually. A good instance of this would be the practice of collecting images and rephotographing their locations in accordance with specific criteria (McLeod, 2019). It matters not as to whether collections are more significant or original than others; it matters more that camera users describe criteria for how the images came into existence.

Photographs as statements could never be universally understood, but that is not the aim of Flusser's philosophy of photography; rather it is a visual literacy project that asks any camera user to explore and then subsequently question their role in creating images through a gesture of seeing manifested against and not just via apparatus and its programs. Such a visual literacy project starts with everyday camera users, but they need encouragement in learning to read/write visually without a pressure to be creatively original. Although Flusser's thoughts remain jarring for some (particularly commercial photographers), the message is not that everyone with a camera is a mere button pusher; rather, the message is that the creation of photographic images does not have to be the preserve of a visual literati who get to choose what is good or what is not. Ströhl's visual distrust is perhaps easier than it seems.

References

Arantes, P. (2009) Media, gestures, and society: Dialogues between Vilém Flusser and Fred Forest. *Flusser Studies*, *18*, 1–10.

Brill, J., & Branch, R. (2007) Visual literacy defined – the results of a Delphi study: Can IVLA (operationally) define visual literacy? *Journal of Visual Literacy*, *27*, 47–60. 10.1080/23796529.2007.11674645

Brumberger, E. (2019). Past, present, future: Mapping the research in visual literacy. *Journal of Visual Literacy*. 10.1080/1051144X.2019.1575043

Elkins, J. (2008). Introduction. The concept of visual literacy, and its limitations. In *Visual literacy* (p. 232). Routledge. 10.4324/9780203939574

Ewald, W., Lord, L., & Hyde, K. (2012). *Literacy & justice through photography: A classroom guide*. Teachers College Press.

Flusser, V. (2000 [1983]). *Towards a philosophy of photography*. Reaktion Books.

Flusser, V. (2002). *Writings*. University of Minnesota Press.

Flusser, V. (2011 [1985]). *In the universe of technical images*. University of Minnesota Press.

Flusser, V. (2014 [1991]). *Gestures*. University of Minnesota Press.

Flusser, V. (2015 [1983]). *Post-history*. Univocal.

Kedra, J. (2018). What does it mean to be visually literate? Examination of visual literacy definitions in a context of higher education. *Journal of Visual Literacy*, *37*(2), 67–84. 10.1080/1051144X.2018.1492234

McLeod, G. (2019) Rephotograph. *Philosophy of Photography*, *10*(1), 89–99. 10.1386/pop_00008_7

McLeod, G. (2023). Slow glass: A case for photomedia literacy. *Journal of Visual Literacy*, *42*(4), 287–308. 10.1080/1051144X.2023.2277029

Roth, N. A. (2019). Out of language: Photographing as translating. In M. Durden & J. Tormey (Eds.), *Routledge companion to photography theory*. Routledge.

Spoerner, T. M. (1981). Look, snap, see: Visual literacy through the camera. *Art Education*, *35*(3), 36–38.

Ströhl, A. (2022). Flusser's take on media pedagogy. *Flusser Studies*, *34*, 1–14. https://www.flusserstudies.net/sites/www.flusserstudies.net/files/media/attachments/strohl-flusser-take-on-media-pedagogy.pdf

Wajcman, J. (2016). *Pressed for time: The acceleration of life in digital capitalism.* Chicago University Press.

Werner, A. R. (2015). Visual illiteracy: The paradox of today's media culture and the reformulation of yesterday's concept of an écriture filmique. *IMAGE. Zeitschrift für interdisziplinäre Bildwissenschaft, 22*(11), 64–86. 10.25969/mediarep/16480

Williams, C. M., & Debes, J. L. (Eds.). (1970). *Proceedings of the first national conference on visual literacy.* Pitman.

Zielinski, S. (2010). Interview. *Flusser Studies, 10,* 23–24.

3

THE CONSPIRACY OF THE SPECTACLE

Guy Debord's Relevance for Visual Literacy Today

Ashley Pryor

University of Toledo

Biographical Sketch

Guy Debord (1931–1994) was a French writer, filmmaker, provocateur, and, for some, a master conspiracy theorist. Born in Paris, France in 1931 into a well-off, middle-class family, there is relatively scant information about Debord's childhood, except that his father died when he was four, and shortly after that, his mother sent him off to live with his grandmother in Nice. The outbreak of World War II forced the family to relocate several times (Merrifield, 2005, pp. 16–18). The experience of perpetual disruption, his de facto alienation from his mother, and his general feeling of being disconnected from society profoundly affected Debord's worldview and, by most accounts, his personality. In his monograph, *Considerations on the Assassination of Gérard Lebovici*, Debord offered a compendium of the many nasty traits that had been attributed to him that defined his public persona:

> Mastermind, nihilist, pseudo-philosopher, Pope, loner, mentor, hypnotizer, bloodstained-stooge, fanatic of himself, devil, eminence grise, damned soul, Professor of Radicalism, guru, second-hand revolutionary, agent of subversion and destabilization in the pay of Soviet imperialism, third-rate Mephistopheles, noxious, eccentric, hazy, enigmatic, angel of darkness, ideologue, mystery man, mad sadist, complete cynic, the dregs of non-thought, bewitcher, fearsome destabilizer, enragé, theoretician. (Debord, 2001, p. 75)

DOI: 10.4324/9781032651781-4

His penchant for heavy drinking, belligerence, and a tendency to dogmatism made collaborations with him difficult and often short-lived (Jappe, 2018, p. 55; Lefebvre, 1997, pp. 69–71).

Arguably, Debord is best understood as an autodidact. A voracious reader, his education was informed primarily through independent readings of social and political theorists (especially Karl Marx, Friedrich Engels, György Lukács, and Friedrich Nietzsche) and conversations with contemporary theorists and artists, such as the influential Marxist philosopher Henri Lefebvre, Danish artist Asger Jorn, and other prominent denizens of bohemian cafes that he frequented. Debord was particularly interested in Marx's ideas on alienation and commodity fetishism, which he explored in his most influential work, *The Society of the Spectacle*. While Debord briefly undertook formal studies at the University of Paris, Sorbonne, he did not complete a degree.

Debord was a contributing member of the avant-garde Lettrist International [LI] (1953–1957), and later became the central theoretician of the Situationist International [SI] (1957–1971). These groups sought to create new, revolutionary forms of social organization. As a powerful personality and prolific writer and theorist, Debord's work was decisive for both groups.

In addition to his formal and informal education in social and political philosophy, Debord was a self-taught artist and filmmaker. He adapted his theoretical treatise, *The Society of the Spectacle* (1967), into a film in 1973, a work that continues to inform and inspire critical media studies today. His artistic work was influenced by and critical of Dadaism and Surrealism. Debord shared the Dadaists' "negativity" and a general disdain for the values of "bourgeois society," which he characterized as being essentially "bankrupt" (McDonough, 2004, p. ix). Like the Dadaists, Debord saw art as an essential tool for exposing the foibles of the bourgeoisie. However, to the degree that Debord aspired to "go beyond the pure negativity" and to create "a new way of living," he adopted and developed the Surrealists' proto-experimental urban expeditions, "les dérives," to develop a constructive "psychogeography," defined as the "study of the specific effects of the geographical environment (whether consciously organized or not) on the emotions and behavior of individuals" ("Definitions" 2006, p. 52). From the Dadaists' anti-art tendencies – especially as manifested in collage – Debord and the Lettrists and Situationists developed the strategy of détournement, using art against itself, which became "the trademark" of these groups (Jappe, 2018, p. 59).

Debord's final years were marked by declining health, likely due to a lifetime of excessive drinking. He ended his life at age 62 in self-imposed exile in the small village of Champot in the Auvergne. On November 30, 1994, Debord shot himself through the heart (Merrifield, 2005, p. 8).

Introduction

Guy Debord's writings and creative contributions are renowned for their profound insight into visual culture and its effects on modern life; his trenchant analysis of the ways that images have the power to shape human experience, paired with his strategies for resisting their potentially destructive effects, anticipates much of the critical engagement of contemporary visual literacy. His oeuvre reflects the political and social unrest of the 1950s and 1960s that came to a head in the May Paris Uprising and general strikes of 1968, in which he played a central role (Jappe, 1999). Critical of consumerism and the commodification of culture, Debord sought to create a new, revolutionary form of social organization and art that would challenge the status quo.

Anticipating the work of later critical media studies, in *The Society of the Spectacle*, Debord argued that human relationships are now thoroughly mediated through images created by advertisement and other forms of mass media. These images have created false needs, leading to existential crises among individuals within capitalist societies (Debord, 2014, pp. 1–11). *The Society of the Spectacle* established Debord's reputation as one of the foremost theorists of anti-capitalist ideology; his subsequent adaptation of the work as a film further extended its reach and impact. The film uses a variety of techniques, integrating found footage, détournement, and montage, to explore the ways in which images are used to shape our understanding of the world. In doing so, it helps us to develop a critical eye for the images they encounter in their everyday lives and thus remains highly relevant for scholars and practitioners of visual literacy today.

Another critical text from Debord is *Comments on the Society of the Spectacle* (1988) which further elaborates upon the 1967 essay. Here, Debord describes how organizations like religious institutions or political parties increasingly relied on spectacle. Additionally, Debord explored how certain elements were used to propagate some ideologies or suppress others, providing researchers with great insight into theories concerning power dynamics between different social groups.

Debord's last major written work, a memoir of sorts, *Panegyric* (1989), was composed over several years during his later life and raises some important questions regarding class struggle, pleasure/waste, and immortality versus mortality – concepts that remain central points when looking at debates around modernity today. Taken as a whole, Debord's work constitutes an essential primer for those studying critical theory or anyone attempting to become critically aware consumers within an image-saturated world.

Debord's legacy continues undiminished since many contemporary discussions surrounding topics such as identity politics, artificial intelligence, globalization, etc., owe something to his prescient critique of the ways that images exercise an increasingly hegemonic power to shape and inform human existence – thus making their future study critical to researchers wishing to gain a comprehensive understanding of the issues facing the world in the twenty-first century. Debord's concepts of spectacle, détournement, and dérive are valuable touch points for expanding and deepening our understanding of the visual realm.

Spectacle, *Détournement, Dérive*

Before the advent of the all-pervasive TikTok and YouTube influencer video, Instagram, and Facebook feeds, Debord argued that images had already co-opted ordinary life. *The Society of the Spectacle* begins with the gloomy if eerily prescient diagnosis of the contemporary condition: "In societies where modern conditions prevail, life is presented as an immense accumulation of spectacles. Everything that was directly lived has receded into representation" (Debord, 2014, p. 2). The image has become the primary means through which individuals understand and experience the world around them.

The spectacle names the "vast accumulation" or network of images characteristic of capitalist societies. This network has become so pervasive that Debord believed that, for many, it had replaced reality and developed into "the focal point of all vision and all consciousness" (Debord, 2014, p. 2). Under the thrall of the spectacle, individual experience is subsumed, mediated, and filtered. The spectacle obscures and distorts "ordinary life". In this way, the spectacle must not be thought of merely as a representation of reality or as a "mere visual excess produced by mass-media technologies," but rather, the spectacle is "a social relation between people that is mediated by images" – "It is a worldview that has actually been materialized, that has become an objective reality" (Debord, 2014, p. 2). The spectacle influences not only the way we see the things of the world but also each other – an insight that sets the stage for the emergence of visual literacy as an essential field of study in the twentieth century and beyond.

Like the prisoners in Plato's cave, in spectacle society, Debord believed that individuals had been reduced to mere spectators, content to watch an endless series of shadows on a wall. Worse than that, they are no longer fully capable of discerning the real from its specularized doppelgänger. The spectacle subverts reality into representation, creating a "pseudo-world" that appears more authentic and genuine than reality (Debord, 2014, p. 2). The purse no longer primarily functions as a bag for holding items needed for the day, instead, a Birken Bag has become a ticket to a more prestigious friend set; wearing the wrong athletic footwear in the wrong place at the wrong time can result in an early demise. The spectacle does not passively reflect society's values but actively shapes and constrains them. In so doing, the spectacle creates a false sense of unity, affirmation, and community by producing new images and representations. As Debord observed:

> Understood in its totality, the spectacle is both the result and the project of the present mode of production. It is not a mere supplement or decoration added to the real world; it is the heart of this real society's unreality. In all its manifestations – news, propaganda, advertising, entertainment – the spectacle is the model of the prevailing way of life model. It is the omnipresent affirmation of the choices already made in the sphere of production and in the consumption implied by that production. In both form and content, the spectacle serves as the total justification of the conditions and goals of the existing system. The spectacle is also the constant presence of this justification since it monopolizes most of the time spent outside the modern production process. (Debord, 2014, p. 3)

The spectacle creates a world in which individual desires and needs are subordinated to those of the dominant order, in which authentic social relations are fragmented and alienated – the spectacle is nothing but "the visual reflection of the ruling economic order – goals are nothing, development is everything. The spectacle aims at nothing other than itself" (Debord, 2014, p. 5). In the aftermath of the "specularization" of the real, individuals are left at the mercy of its effect – left to "an autonomous movement of the non-living" (Debord, 2014, p. 4). The spectacle can subject human beings to itself because the economy has already subjugated them. "It is nothing other than the economy developing for itself. It is at once a faithful reflection of the production of things and a distorting objectification of the producers" (Debord, 2014, p. 4). The spectacle operates not unlike a zombie seeking its next feed. The spectacle proclaims: "nothing more than that which appears is good, that which is good appears" (Debord, 2014, p. 4).

As Debord anticipates, it is evident that visual imagery has a powerful impact on influencing public opinion or disseminating information (or disinformation) via social media platforms – a topic that has been dominating headlines worldwide during recent elections, ranging from Russian meddling in the Brexit vote and presidential election to internal political interference in Turkey, Venezuela, the Philippines, and over two dozen other countries. Debord's prescience is also evident in what he called 'the revolutionary transformation of images' – that is, the impact of images when discussing politics and current events is often undervalued. A number of problems have resulted from this, including alienation, passivity, and a loss of critical thinking abilities. In response to Debord's grim diagnosis, visual literacy, the systematic and critical study of how people interact and interpret images, offers some strategies for alleviating some of these problems – many of which we find already at work in Debord's thinking. In particular, his strategies of *dérive* and *détournment* are promising tools for negotiating an ever-changing "visual information" landscape, developing "visual discernment" and promoting "social justice through visual practice" as encouraged by the 2022 Association of College and Research Libraries (ACRL) *Framework for Visual Literacy in Higher Education* (ACRL, 2022, p. 5).

Détournement as Theoria

Although Debord did not publish *The Society of the Spectacle* until 1967, the looming specter of an invasive and all-pervasive new-image-driven social imaginary appears as early as 1953 in his work with the Lettrists. In the essay "Formulary for a New Urbanism," Ivan Chtcheglov gives voice to the concern:

A mental disease has swept the planet: banalization. Everyone is hypnotized by production and conveniences – sewage systems, elevators, bathrooms, washing machines.

This state of affairs, arising out of a struggle against poverty, has overshot its original goal – the liberation of humanity from material cares – and become an omnipresent obsessive image. (Chtcheglov, 1953, p. 8)

Indeed, references to what Debord would later name "the spectacle," that "omnipresent obsessive image," can be found throughout the writings of the Lettrists and Situationists – likely a testament to the force of Debord's influence on both groups. Concomitant with the gradual development of the critique of the spectacle is the call for effective countermeasures against the incursion of the image upon everyday life. Among the proposed strategies for resistance, the appeal for *détournement* – what today we might call "culture-jamming" – remains the best-known and most influential (Lasn, 1999; Sandlin & Milam, 2010).

In the 1956 essay, "A User's Guide to *Détournement*," co-written with Gil J. Wolman, Debord, and Wolman propose *détournement* as a form of "extremist innovation" and intervention into the "literary and artistic heritage of humanity," which they believed had devolved into mere apologetics and propaganda in support of the ruling class and economic order (Debord & Wolman, 1956, pp. 14–21). As they define it here, a *détournement* names the act of reusing or re-repurposing mass-produced or artistic elements to create new work – especially to expose and subvert the original meaning and context of the original elements:

> Any elements, no matter where they are taken from, can be used to make new combinations … The mutual interference of two worlds of feeling, or the juxtaposition of two independent expressions, supersedes the original elements and produces a synthetic organization of greater efficacy. Anything can be used.

> It goes without saying that one is not limited to correcting a work or to integrating diverse fragments of out-of-date works into a new one; one can also alter the meaning of those fragments in any appropriate way, leaving the imbeciles to their slavish reference to "citations." (Debord & Wolman, 1956, p. 15)

Perhaps to better distinguish *détournement* from the fine arts practice of collage, which likewise involves bringing together disparate elements to create new work, the author(s) of the later, "*Détournement* as Negation and Prelude" (1959) stipulates two "fundamental laws" of a successful *détournement*: "the loss of importance of each detourned autonomous element" and the "organization of another meaningful ensemble that confers on each element its new scope and effect" (Anonymous, 1959, p. 67). Also critical to the meaning of *déournement* is its critical function in exposing the failure and foibles of the past:

> *Détournement* is thus first of all a negation of the value of the previous organization of expression. It arises and grows stronger in the historical period of the decomposition of artistic expression. However, simultaneously, the attempts to reuse the "detournable bloc" as material for other ensembles express the search for a vaster construction, a new genre of creation at a higher level. (Anonymous, 1959, p. 67)

For Debord and his fellow Situationists, *détournement* was a subversive tactic meant to challenge the status quo and foster individuals' spontaneity and creativity – a kind of playful subversion, negation, or *Aufhebung*, of the dominant mode of production. As such, it may be usefully considered as a form of collage, but with a decidedly political or critical function. However, it was an approach to the status quo that was not without its pitfalls and perils, as the members effectively created art to challenge art.

The altered paintings of the Danish artist Asger Jorn are cited as successful *détournements,* as is Debord's and Jorn's collaborative book, *Mémoires* – a book made famous for its heavy-grade sandpaper cover, designed to inflict damage to any other book or surface it came into contact with – as well as Debord's "detourned documentary" film *On the Passage of a Few Persons through a Rather Brief Unity of Time* (Anonymous, 1959, p. 67). The range of works offered in the essay by way of example underscores the point that what is essential to the *détournement* is not necessarily about the materials used but rather the way the materials are turned against themselves to create a new meaning and context. Not surprisingly then, in 1967, the Situationists announced further opportunities for *détournement*, with René Viénet calling for "experimentation in the *détournement* of photo-romances and porno-graphic photos," "the promotion of guerilla tactics in the mass media," "the development of situationist comics," and the continued production of Situationist films (Viénet, 1967, pp. 274–275). More recently, James Trier has expanded the situationists' inventory of *détournements* to include their work with maps and space, graffiti, and galleries and museums (Trier, 2019, np).

Despite the decidedly anti-art sentiments that underlie Debord's and the Situationists' turn to the strategy of *détournement*, the fact that so much of the group's activity involved some form of artistic process (painting, film, etc.) further illustrates their ongoing concern that images have assumed too much power to shape and influence culture and society. Debord and the Situationists' approach to *détournement* emphasizes the power of imagery to shape and influence culture, and it encourages critical visual literacy, that is, an analysis of images that focus on the ways that images come to dominate our lives and shape our understanding of the world. Critical visual literacy is therefore about more than just under-standing and interpreting visual messages or the formal properties of images, but always concerned with the social relation that they reveal. In contrast to more traditional approaches to visual literacy, critical visual literacy is not simply about learning how to 'read' images. It is also about learning how to 'write' images – how to use images to create new stories and meanings. It is about using images to transform the world.

The Situationists understood that images can be used to create new meanings and contexts, and they sought to use these tools to bring about revolutionary change. By turning images against themselves, they aimed to spark a critical dialog about the power of visual culture to effect social and political transformation. The Situationist's call for *détournement* ultimately involves a deconstruction of the spectacle by exposing and understanding how images work to manipulate and control us – and as importantly, by playfully, if irrelevantly creating new images that challenge the status quo. The essays of the period reflect the group's awareness that their creative work, too, was subject to the totalizing effect of the spectacle and at risk of being co-opted and used on the back of playing cards or printed on umbrellas for sale at the museum shop:

> This combination of parody and seriousness reflects the contradictions of an era in which we find ourselves confronted with both the urgent necessity and the near impossibility of initiating and carrying out a totally innovative collective action – an era in which the most serious ventures are masked in the ambiguous interplay between art and its necessary negation, and in which the essential voyages of discovery have been undertaken by such astonishingly incapable people. (Anonymous, 1959, p. 68)

Détournement as Praxis

The idea that images have the power to transform – even supersede – everyday life has become even more relevant with the rise of digital media platforms over the past few decades. Debord's strategy of *détournement* offers both a form of creative expression and an act of critique, allowing practitioners to explore and subvert the messages in images to make a statement about society or the world. As Debord's work suggests, *détournement* is not merely a rearrangement of elements but rather an active transformation into something different from their original forms. Detourned material can be used to comment on political issues, cultural stereotypes, consumerism, and much more. It is a practice that allows for creativity by reworking pre-existing works meaningfully through juxtaposition or parody, and the effects can range from humorous to powerful depending on how it is used. Unlike mere appropriation, which simply takes an existing image and uses it without alteration, *détournement* actively transforms the image into something new, thus creating a social or political commentary or critique of the dominant social or political order. For example, the Dadaists used *détournement* by appropriating everyday objects to create absurdist works of art that challenged the norms of the time. Similarly, contemporary artists like Banksy have used *détournement* to create street art that critiques consumer culture and capitalism. Other artists have used *détournement* to challenge oppressive political systems, such as Ai Weiwei's *Fairytale* installation, which was a direct challenge to the Chinese government. Ultimately, *détournement* provides an alternative form of discourse that offers insight into both the artist's intentions and our cultural context. It is, therefore, somewhat surprising that this strategy is not employed more frequently in our curricula.

As Trier remarks in his essay *"Détournement* as a Qualitative Method" (2019), there is a curious absence of scholarly attention to Debord's and the Situationists' work in the field of education, let alone in the subfield of curricular development (Trier, 2019, n.p.). This is a missed opportunity for educators and practitioners of visual literacy more generally. While it is understandable that Debord's radical politics may be unsuited to every educational context, the basic structure of using images against themselves to create something new can be productive for exploring a wide range of subject matters and adaptable to a wide range of ages and abilities.

Collage is an obvious and inexpensive exercise that can be used to engage with Debord's work critically. While not every collage constitutes a *détournement*, to the extent that collage involves bringing together disparate elements to create new work, it lends itself well to introducing students to this strategy. I routinely use collage to demonstrate Debordian *détournement* in the context of my introductory level course in the humanities: HON 1010 "Ideas and Society." As the course title suggests, HON 1010 introduces first-year students to a range of ideas that have proved consequential to the development of contemporary society. I introduce Debord's work toward the end of the semester after students have had the opportunity to consider a range of philosophies and political theories. First, I ask students to skim through Debord's notoriously difficult *The Society of the Spectacle* and each is assigned one passage they must paraphrase. This initial exercise ensures that students understand and can communicate one idea clearly and concisely in writing. After students have completed their paraphrases, they are asked to translate the idea into an image using the medium of collage. For this exercise, I supply the materials, which consist of a blend of vintage images from old *Sunset* magazines from the 1950s and 1960s and contemporary lifestyle magazines like *Good Housekeeping, Vogue, Cosmopolitan,* and the like. Before students begin to illustrate their passages, I briefly introduce them to Debord's strategy of *détournement,* provide them with some examples of detourned work, past and present, then ask them to use one image from the contemporary magazine and one from the vintage work to create a detourned image that speaks to their assigned passage.

The results of this exercise have been largely successful. Not only do students enjoy a class period dedicated to cutting and pasting, but they also emerge with a better understanding of the text as they engage in the process of translating it – first in writing, to simplify and clarify it in the form of a paraphrase, and then in images to form a collage. Most importantly, students are exposed – many for the first time to the field and practice of visual literacy as the exercise requires them to engage with the artifacts of visual material culture and requires close and critical observation of the images they use and a sense of the social, political and historical contexts in which they are embedded. Finally, by recombining existing material, in this case, vintage and contemporary magazines, students can explore the potential of their creativity and form their unique interpretations of Debord's iconic text. As such, students can experience the meaning of "liberated creativity" firsthand and thus can better articulate its difference: alienation, totalitarian control, and spectacular passive consumption.

Dérive and Psychogeography as Theoria

As early as 1953, *dérive* – "a mode of experimental behavior linked to the conditions of urban society: a technique of rapid passage through varied ambiances" ("Definitions", 2006, p. 52), appears as a central strategy of the Lettrists' attempt to formulate and practice a "new urbanism." According to fellow Lettrist Chtcheglov, this new relationship to the city required the reclamation and "rejuvenation" of old archetypes, frigid architecture, abstraction, and the "pure plasticity" of modern cities (Chtcheglov, 1953, p. 2). From the outset, as David Pinder observed, the call for dérive, like the strategy of *détournement*, was as much a rebellion against the "modernizing and rationalizing" antiseptics of modernist architectural forms and city planning as it was a critique of capitalism and industrialism (Pinder, 2005, p. 153).

For the Lettrists, especially the young Debord, this reclamation process required more than creating new forms; it also demanded new attitudes of interaction with the city. In his essay, "Formulary for a New Urbanism," Chtcheglov identifies the cultivation of play and the "construction of situations" as being critical to this transformation (Chtcheglov, 1953, p. 4). "We know that the more a place is set apart for free play," Chtcheglov writes, "the more it influences people's behavior and the greater is its force of attraction" (Chtcheglov, 1953, p. 8). Some of the "situations" to improve the city of Paris the Lettrists playfully propose: "Street lamps should all be equipped with switches so that people can adjust the lighting as they wish," religious buildings should be "left standing but stripped of all religious content" and "children should be allowed to play in them," and "museums should be abolished and their masterpieces distributed to bars" (Lettrist International, 1955, p. 14).

These playful, if hyperbolic and irrelevant, proposals underscore Debord's and the Lettrists' focus on reclaiming individuals' free response from the totalizing effects of a preoccupation with efficiency, utility, privatization, and profit they believed defined the modern city. The *dérive* requires the cultivation of a particular disposition as much as a form of knowledge, noting, "the qualitatively or quantitatively different influences of diverse urban decors cannot be determined solely on the basis of a historical period or architectural style, much less on the basis of housing conditions" but rather, must be informed "in close relations with the sensations they provoke" (Debord, 1955, p. 10). From the beginning, *dérive* is proposed as a disposition – an experimental attitude – as a practice, technique, methodology, or concept.

As its name suggests, *dérive* or "drifting" is the art of wandering through different urban spaces without a predetermined destination or goal. By intentionally wandering through a city, Debord thought one could better observe and learn from the environment in a way that is impossible when following a predetermined path. Debord further differentiated the *dérive* from the stroll or walk, stating that *dérive* involves a "playful, constructive behavior" as well as a concentrated dis-engagement with habitual routine and societal expectation (Debord, 1958, p. 62) writing:

> In a *dérive,* one or more persons during a certain period drop their relations, their work and leisure activities, and all their usual motives for movement and action and let themselves be drawn by the attractions of the train and the encounters they find there. Chance is a less important factor in this activity than one might think: from a *dérive* point of view, cities have psychogeographical contours, with constant currents, fixed points, and vortexes that strongly discourage entry into or exit from certain zones. (Debord, 1958, p. 62)

These experimental forays through the city were to provide the data for a new interdisciplinary field, psychogeography, that focuses on the relationship between humans and their environment "through the study of the precise laws and specific effects of the geographical environment, whether consciously organized or not, on the emotions and behavior of individuals" (Debord, 1955, p.8).

As defined and practiced by the Lettrists and later the Situationists, psychogeography involves surveying and studying various factors such as geographic, historical, cultural, architectural, political, economic, and social structures to understand how these can influence our cognitive and affective experience of places. For example, a psychogeographer might explore how buildings or public transport systems are designed to create different emotional responses in those who use them. The aim is to understand human-environment interaction better so that we can design urban environments that foster a greater sense of belonging and freedom for their inhabitants and mitigate the effects of cultural fragmentation in capitalist society (Lefebvre, 1997, p. 80).

As part of his psychogeographical practice, Debord created *The Naked City,* a map constructed of 19 cut-out sections of a conventional map of Paris (Figure 3.1). These sections are linked by red arrows, documenting his "drifting" through the roads of Paris. The map's subtitle, "illustration of the hypothesis of psychogeographical turntables," reveals that Debord's map has less to do with a faithful representation of the actual spatial relationships of roads, buildings, and monuments – and more to do with the attempt to convey the forces, feelings, and atmosphere that attract and repel his attention as he moves through the city. As Tom McDonough observes:

> Each segment has a different "unity of atmosphere." The arrows describe "the spontaneous turns of the direction taken by a subject moving through these surroundings in disregard of the useful connections that ordinarily govern his conduct." Linking various "unities of atmosphere" and dictating the path taken by the given subject, these turns correspond to the action of the [railway] turntable, which links various segments of track and dictates the orientation of the locomotive. The implications of analogizing the subject to a locomotive are, of course, founded on a certain ambiguity: although self-propelled, the locomotive's path is determined within strict boundaries, just as for the situationists, the subject's freedom of movement is restricted by the instrumentalized image of the city propagated under the reign of capital. (McDonough, 2004, p. 243)

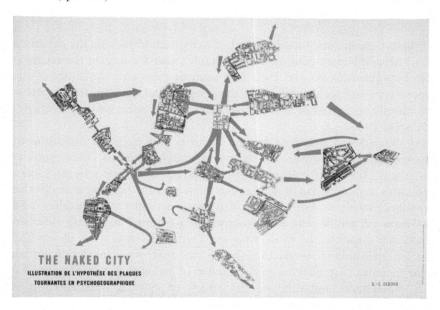

FIGURE 3.1   Guy Debord, *The Naked City*, illustration de l'hypothèse des plaques tournantes en psychogéographique (1957), lithography and ink on paper. Collection Frac Centre-Val de Loise.

The Naked City reveals unexpected connections between places and ideas that traditional cartographers ignored or overlooked due to their focus on physical objects instead of the psychological or affective effects of abstract concepts such as hidden ideology. As Pinder observes, Debord's maps "disrupt cartographic discipline and order; their broken and fragmented appearance refuse the coherence imposed by the spectacle. They challenge urban meanings and the representational regimes employing *détournement*" (Pinder, 2005, p. 153). Debord's map, *The Naked City* attempts to document the push and pull of the habitual and largely unconscious force of attraction that guides how humans interact and move throughout the city. Reflecting on the ways that psychogeographical maps can be used to document *dérive*, Debord writes:

> The production of psychogeographical maps, or even the introduction of alterations such as more or less arbitrarily transposing maps of two different regions, can contribute to clarifying certain wanderings that express not subordination to randomness but total insubordination to habitual influences (influences generally categorized as tourism, that popular drug as repugnant as sports or buying on credit. (Debord, 1955, p. 11)

With these "renovated cartographies," Debord sought to make visible what had previously been hidden or taken for granted within the modern industrialized city. In this way, *dérive*, psychogeography, and Debord's Situationist map serve to contest – and reimagine – the reign of the spectacle itself. Debord's *dérive*, psychogeography, and renovated cartographies can be seen as critical pedagogical tools for visual literacy. His maps and experimental *dérives* are intended to question the hegemony of the spectacle and reveal the underlying power structures in the modern city.

Dérive and Psychogeography as Praxis

Debord's interest in *dérive*, psychogeography, maps, and map-making to document and critique existing power dynamics in our cities and beyond provides a fruitful resource for educators and researchers interested in deepening the integration of visual literacy principles in their work.

The most obvious opportunity to use these Debordian concepts is in the context of teaching or researching social spaces. Along with dedicated courses on psychogeography, since the 1990s, many elementary, high school, and college educators have adopted place-based pedagogies. This multidisciplinary, experiential approach emphasizes learning in and about local environments, communities, and cultures with increasing attention to social justice and promoting equity and inclusion (Grunewald & Smith, 2014; Sobel, 2017).

In the context of my teaching in the Jesup Scott Honors College course at the University of Toledo, HON 2010: Multicultural Toledo, I have begun to incorporate Debordian strategies in multiple ways to foster a sense of belonging, orient first-year students to campus, emphasize the importance of attentive, critical, contemplative, and multilayered looking for qualitative research, cultivate a curiosity about and appreciation for the communities that surround the campus, and to develop the ability to read social and economic relationships in the structures and arrangements of the built environment.

In the context of my teaching HON 2010: Multicultural Toledo, I send students out of the classroom in small teams (typically in teams of three to four) to explore campus for 20–30 minutes. Students are asked to look for signs that the campus was designed to promote and support student learning (as they currently define it) and to note any missed opportunities or instances where the campus design impedes student learning. Upon returning to the classroom, students are asked to share their findings and to reflect on their sense of belonging (or alienation) in light of this research. The exercise proves beneficial in many ways. For example, (1) students have the opportunity to build relationships with their classmates through a small-stakes assignment; (2) students have the opportunity to familiarize themselves with the campus in a new way, perhaps seeing the campus anew as they interact with their peers to complete a task that forces them to think about their surroundings in a directed way; (3) students have the opportunity to share a range of feelings they may be experiencing as first-year students, and be reassured that they typically are not alone in feeling the way they do. Of course, many of these learning outcomes can be achieved using any number of assignments; what makes this assignment particularly impactful is that it gets students thinking early about the ways their identity as students is actively shaped and reinforced by the material culture (i.e. the architecture, geography, public art, flora and fauna, and general infrastructure) of the university. As I describe below, when paired with opportunities to integrate their own photography, artwork, or choice of images, this exercise encourages students to develop visual literacy skills as they analyze their environment to understand how it influences their sense of identity and belonging.

To deepen and expand upon this Debordian exercise, the following class period, having read and discussed Debord's short essay, "Theory of the Dérive" (1958), students are sent out individually to explore campus, this time to record their specific reactions to the spaces – the Debordian play of forces – to gather data and create a psychogeographical map of their cognitive and affective experience. Along with learning to apply an abstract theoretical text to their research, students also have the opportunity to reflect more deeply on the complexities of the campus, develop their sense of belonging, and begin to learn how to translate experience and data into a compelling visual form.

This mapping exercise is designed to provide students with additional tools to engage in more complex and nuanced work of reading the economic and social subtexts embedded in Toledo's surrounding communities. Using the City as Text pedagogy, developed through the National Collegiate Honors Council (NCHC), for the remainder of the semester, student teams are tasked with researching the history of a Toledo neighborhood and presenting their findings to the public at the end of the semester. While the NCHC curriculum does not explicitly promote or employ Debordian and psychogeographical principles, it does require students to engage in a series of "walkabouts," as well as iterative, deep-reflection on the students' cognitive and affective reactions to what they see in their exploration of these urban spaces. While Debordian psychogeography and the NCHC City as Text pedagogy are primarily focused on urban spaces, the practices of *dérive*, psychogeography, and "renovated cartography" are easily adaptable to the exploration of other built environments, including small towns, rural spaces, or indoor spaces.

The practice of *dérive* and psychogeography thus can be used to gain insight into how people view, understand, and interpret the world around them. It helps us understand how visual images communicate meaning in an urban context and can help broaden our understanding of visual literacy beyond text-based analysis. Students can use found visual images to capture the nuances of their environment, such as the architecture, the colors, the textures, and the natural elements. By way of example, I provide vintage *Sunset* magazines from the late 1960s (the same era of Debord's most prolific writing) to my students to use as collage elements in their maps. I encourage students to take photographs of the places they encounter to gain a deeper understanding of the ways that people interact with each other and make use of their environment. The architectural details of our older residential neighborhoods, for example, are particularly attractive to students, allowing them to draw critical inferences about the socioeconomic development of the area by documenting the changes they see from block to block. In combination with other artifacts, such as redlining maps, this visual evidence can explain why there can be such profound material differences even within a short radius.

Both *dérive* and psychogeography thus provide practical conceptual frameworks for practitioners of visual literacy, as they encourage creative thinking and allow us to experience our environment without preconceived notions or expectations. Through this practice, we can observe how visuals impact our understanding of the world and appreciate their power more deeply. Additionally, *dérive* and psychogeography help us examine our relationship to these visuals by allowing us to control where we go and what we see rather than being controlled by someone else's agenda or narrative. Finally, this practice opens up opportunities for creative engagement with different kinds of visuals, which can help broaden one's perspective on visual literacy and cultivate new ways of engaging with this field.

Conclusion: Debord for Ordinary Life

A conspiracy is a secret plan a group makes to achieve a shared goal, often for their gain. By looking at the way images may be used to draw viewers into believing things that might not necessarily be factual, visual literacy is a critical practice that can help us diagnose and strategically intervene in what Debord took to be the conspiracy of images against ordinary life. By this definition, Guy Debord is a conspiratorial thinker par excellence. His seminal work, *The Society of the Spectacle*, defined a modern age in which images and media have become ever-pervasive. His concept of 'spectacularization' argues that these images create an imaginary world where people become distracted from reality by focusing on what is presented to them by mass media. He effectively argued that this was a conspiracy against everyday life.

Debord believed that this phenomenon made it difficult for individuals to escape the influence of mass media. Through *détournement* and *dérive* – in films, books, paintings, and essays – Debord challenged those in power who use media for their benefit at the expense of others. Debord's creative and theoretical work conspired against the dominant social order by critiquing the way images and media were used to manipulate people for the benefit of those in power. His work highlighted the ways that individuals were distracted from reality by images, and how this manipulation conspired against everyday life. Debord's critiques are still relevant today as we grapple with issues such as disinformation campaigns, fake news, and political manipulation – all phenomena linked to his exploration of spectacle culture.

To the extent that we remain concerned with the encroachment of images in our ordinary lives, Guy Debord's work is an integral part of visual literacy. The field of visual literacy examines how images can be used consciously and unconsciously to guide – or manipulate – the viewer's understanding of reality. Visual literacy is essential in helping us better understand the power of imagery when deciphering truth from fiction, and is thus naturally aligned with Debord's conspiracy against the dominant visual order. Visual literacy allows us to identify potentially misleading information before it becomes widely accepted and believed, before a conspiracy can take hold. As such, visual literacy is well-positioned to continue the work that Debord and the Situationists initiated in the 1950s and 1960s to advance a critical approach to our image-saturated world. Rather than passively accepting our state, Debord encourages us to be more aware and conscious of these illusions, to take back control over our lives, and to make decisions based on thoughtful analysis rather than mass-marketed visuals. His pioneering theories continue to shape debates about visual culture today, making him an essential figure in understanding how images impact our thinking and actions.

Acknowledgements

I am grateful to the Collection Frac Centre-Val de Loire for granting permission to reproduce François Lauginie's photograph of Guy Debord's "Naked Lunch".

References

ACRL. (2022, April 6). *Companion document to the ACRL framework for information literacy for higher education: The framework for visual literacy.* American Library Association. https://www.ala.org/acrl/sites/ala.org.acrl/files/content/standards/Framework_Companion_Visual_Literacy.pdf

Anonymous. (2006 [1959]). Détournement as negation and prelude. In (Ed.), *Situationist international anthology* (pp. 1–8). Berkeley, CA: Bureau of Public Secrets.Knabb

Chtcheglov, I. (1953). Formulary for a new urbanism. In Knabb (Ed.), *Situationist international anthology* (pp. 1–8). Berkeley, CA: Bureau of Public Secrets.

Debord, G. (2001). *Considerations on the assassination of Gérard Lebovici.* TamTam Books.

Debord, G. (2006 [1955]). Introduction to a critique of urban geography. In Knabb (Ed.), *Situationist international anthology* (pp. 8–12). Berkeley, CA: Bureau of Public Secrets.

Debord, G. (2006 [1958]). Theory of the dérive. In Knabb (Ed.), *Situationist international anthology* (pp. 62–66). Berkeley, CA: Bureau of Public Secrets.

Debord, G. (2014 [1967]). *The society of the spectacle* (K. Knabb, Trans.). Berkeley, CA: Bureau of Public Secrets.

Debord, G., & Wolman, G. J. (2006 [1956]). A user's guide to *détournement*. In Knabb (Ed.), *Situationist international anthology* (pp. 14–23). Berkeley, CA: Bureau of Public Secrets.

"Definitions." (2006 [1958]). In Knabb (Ed.), *Situationist international anthology* (pp. 51–52). Berkeley, CA: Bureau of Public Secrets.

Gruenewald, D. A., & Smith, G. A. (Eds.). (2014). *Place-based education in the global age: Local diversity.* New York, NY: Routledge.

Jappe, A. (2018). *Guy Debord.* Oakland, CA: PM Press.

Knabb, K. (Ed.). (2006). *Situationist international anthology.* Berkeley, CA: Bureau of Public Secrets.

Lasn, K. (1999). *Culture Jam: How to reverse America's suicidal consumer binge – and why we must.* New York, NY: Harper Collins.

Lebebvre, H., & Ross, K. (1997). Lefebvre on the situationists: An interview. *October, 79,* 69–83.

Lettrist International. (2006 [1955]). Proposals for rationally improving the city of Paris. In Knabb (Ed.), *Situationist international anthology* (pp. 14–23). Bureau of Public Secrets.

McDonough, T. (Ed.). (2004). *Guy Debord and the situationist international: Texts and documents.* MIT Press.

Merrifield, A. (2005). *Guy Debord (critical lives).* London: Reaktion Books.

Pindar, D. (2005). *Visions of the city: Utopianism, power, and politics in twentieth-century urbanism.* Routledge.

Sandlin, J., & Milam, J. (2010). Culture jamming as critical public pedagogy. In J. Sandlin, B. Schultz, & J. Burrdick (Eds.), *Handbook of public pedagogy.* Routledge. 10.4324/9780203863688.ch2

Sobel, D. (2017). *Place-based education: Connecting classrooms and communities* (2nd ed.). Orion Society.

Trier, J. (2019). *Détournement as qualitative method.* Oxford Research Encyclopedia of Education. 10.1093/acrefore/9780190264093.013.349

Viénet, R. (1967). The situationists and the new forms of action against politics and art. In Knabb (Ed.), *Situationist international anthology* (pp. 273–277).

4

FONTCUBERTA AND POST-PHOTOGRAPHY

Unveiling the Border between Fiction and Reality

Ricardo Lopez-Leon

Universidad Autónoma de Aguascalientes

Biographical Sketch

Joan Fontcuberta, born in Barcelona, Spain in 1955, is an acclaimed conceptual artist and visual thinker whose life has been intertwined with photography since before his birth. In an interview for Spanish television, he spoke warmly of photography and its impact on his existence: "I owe my very being to photography" (La 2, 2021). He recounted how his parents met through a photograph that Joan's father sent to his mother while fulfilling military service obligations. As the training was tedious and dull, young men would exchange mail addresses of girls they knew and send letters, including their own photographs. The picture sent by Joan's father found its way into the hands of his future wife; thus began their correspondence until they finally met in person. Their love story culminated in marriage, and children – among them Joan himself – all thanks to photography.

As a young boy, Fontcuberta used to read war graphic novels until he began thinking they were too fictional for him. Instead, he began looking at books and newspapers, cutting photographs of generals, tanks, and other weaponry he found interesting. He started building scrapbooks of all his collected materials and making notes. He recalls these albums as his first encounter with photography, although this was mainly a collector's practice more than an image-producing one.

During the last years of high school, an art history teacher installed a photo lab in which students could experiment with developing and printing images. Fontcuberta's obsession with photography was born. He recalls thinking, "I want to do this for a living. I want to practice this type of

DOI: 10.4324/9781032651781-5

illusionism" (La 2, 2021). At the same time, Joan had easy access to the backstage of photographic advertising practices. His father owned an advertising agency where he often spent hours marveling at all the tricks, editing, and staging used to make images more appealing.

His interest continued during his college years when he took a part-time job in advertising while majoring in informational science. For him, journalism and advertising were "schools of deceit," an education through which he learned how to be a good liar or "lie well" (La 2, 2021) in his own words. Although he once hoped to become a photojournalist and dedicate his professional practice to that interest, he soon became disenchanted with the idea. An accident with chemicals when he was younger permanently damaged his left hand. The impossibility of using his left hand slowed down his work, a disadvantage that the faster pace of advertising and journalism photography could not forgive. A slow-paced practice drove him to approach photography differently and more conceptually.

The 1980s was a very prolific period for the photographic medium, with the creation of biennials and other events that emerged from the Rencontres d'Arles, which served as a basis for promoting Spanish and foreign photography. In the middle of that decade, the first public photography centers emerged in Spain, which combined their historical research activities with the exhibition and dissemination of contemporary photography. Photography magazines emerged in Spain as catalysts of photographic ideas and practices in this context. Thus, Fontcuberta and other colleagues founded in 1981 *PhotoVision*, a magazine that offered an alternative to the conventional model of photography in Spain, delving into the meaning and destiny of photography and the photographic process (Reina Sofía, n.d.).

Since then, Fontcuberta has been a photography teacher, theorist, critic, visual artist, jurist, curator, writer, researcher, and historian. He received the David Octavius Hill medal in 1988 and was named Chevalier of l'Ordre des Arts et des Lettres by the French Ministry of Culture in 1994. He also received the National Photography Award in Spain in 1998 and in 2011 the National Award of Culture for Visual Arts for his determinant role in contemporary photographic culture through his several activities. In 2013, he received the International Award from the Hasselblad Foundation.

Introduction: Synapsis of the Visual Thinker and the Artist

Fontcuberta represents the binomial par excellence between artist and thinker. Sometimes artists emerge who show their way of thinking through their artistic doings; other times, artists construct an eloquent verbal discourse through which they show their way of thinking, although their art is perhaps less clear evidence of it. To separate the visual thinker from the artist, in Fontcuberta's case, is impossible because he reflects through his art and has also written numerous texts between articles and books about deep reflections on visual images and photography.

Fontcuberta: The Visual Conspirator

From the beginning of his career, Fontcuberta was obsessed with plausibility. He declares that photography was doomed since it was born as "technology in the service of truth" (1997, p. 166). However, he states, even though the word derives from the prefix 'fos,' which means light, it would be more precise to spell it as 'fàos' which would take us closer to 'faein' and 'fainein.' These terms could be translated as 'appear' and not as 'shine' or 'glare' originating words such as phantom, fantasy, or phenomena. This lexicography would refer to semantic fields of illusions or apparitions. In that sense, Fontcuberta conspired against the essence of photography, proposing a new meaning: "the writing of appearances" (1997, p. 166).

Fontcuberta (2011) himself recognizes that mistrust in images is not a new topic. He recalls that very long ago, in early 1900, Edward Steichen (1903) insisted that photographs were forgeries from beginning to end and that trying to achieve impersonal and unmanipulated photographs was impossible. Nonetheless, photography's history is framed in a dialog between the will to take us close to the real and the difficulties in achieving it. For a long time, it was understood as a way for nature to represent itself. Consequently, photography practices would result in perceiving access to the truth. In that regard, for Fontcuberta, photography belongs to the ontology field more than the aesthetic field.

He recalls the obsession with the truth of modern thinking that drove different artists to declare that photography's function does not linger in offering aesthetic pleasure but in delivering visual truth. This school of thought also assumed that science's direct observation of nature was "the only access to reliable knowledge of the physical world" (1997, p. 148). Fontcuberta claims that photography was born as the climax of imitation practices that aimed to represent nature. However, photography should be able to aspire to portray beauty and not only truth (1997, p. 27).

Fortunately, the end of modernity's thinking would mean the end of the truth. For Fontcuberta, "the old debate between truth and false has been replaced by another between lying well or lying badly" (1997, p. 15). Still, "every photograph is a fiction presented as truth" (1997, p. 15). Therefore, we should focus on how the photographer uses it and with what intentions. When we squeeze the camera trigger, we press a spring that activates a series of ideological automatisms. Photography should not be measured by technicalities of light, optics, mechanisms, and others but by cultural and ideological values (Bravo, 2022).

In that sense, the camera commits treason, misleading us by presenting a picture as a reflection of the real when it is not. This visual betrayal is portrayed in one of the essential written works of Fontcuberta, *El beso de Judas*, or, *Judas' Kiss*. The title refers to a biblical passage in Christianism in which Judas, a disciple of Jesus, betrays him by selling him to the Roman Empire for 30 silver coins. In this work, Fontcuberta expresses his ideas about the camera's capability to produce images that seem real but that are filtered by ideology and intention, regardless of whether the photographer is aware of it. He also reviews the work of several artists that engage in false realism, presenting images that were intentionally transformed to challenge or play with truth-similarity and plausibility. For instance, he shows images that were transformed due to political issues, eliminating annoying characters from the image. What is important to highlight is that this idea is not exclusive to the artistic realm but also to social, political, and commercial practices such as advertising. In more recent years, an ongoing discussion emerged about the archetype of beauty that advertising campaigns promoted by showing photoshopped women, enhancing certain attributes, and hiding others. However, even when recent campaigns reject the use of filters and Photoshop for their advertising, they are claiming a return to the truth through the camera, falling, once again, into the myth of photography as a truth bearer.

"Today we must embrace ambiguity, everything is false and true at the same time. We need to rethink the social function of the image-producing technologies and redefine the notion of the real" (1997, p. 175). For this reason, it would be more appropriate to embrace plausibility or truth-similarity instead of truth and realism instead of reality. Realism is achievable through the camera, but not reality. Realism allows the manipulation of images, and realism acknowledges the photographer's framing, even when the final product is a journalistic or documentary picture.

Photography is a reality-production device. Photography had to get closer to fiction to show its artistic nature, translating facts into blows of imagination. Today, however, reality merges with fiction, and photography can close a cycle: giving back illusion to symbolism which are the pots where the interpretation of our experience cooks; this is the production of reality (1997, p. 185). It is more evident than ever that the computer is an extension of photographic practices and that we can no longer notice "digital interventions executed with scalpel and seamless" (p. 161), even though Fontcuberta declared it more than two decades ago in 1997. Moreover, with the emergence of artificial intelligence (AI), realism has a broader scope, and new variables have to be considered, such as copyright.

In *Judas' Kiss*, Fontcuberta presents 'Countervision' (1997, p. 184), a concept that originally represented a common project between Vilém Flusser, Andreas Müller-Pohle, and Joan Fontcuberta, intended to reflect on the study of photography "not about reality and its representation but about the way we see [...] relate, [and give meaning] to things and the role the camera plays in all this" (Soto & Guldin, 2012, p. 14). However, Fontcuberta's later reflection on countervision can be seen as his preliminary approach to post-photography. Countervision refers to the intentional disruption of visual routines or thinking patterns.

The author argues that countervision must subvert photography's conventional notion of reality, thereby challenging viewers to expand their understanding and interpretation beyond what is readily apparent in an image. This approach fosters academic growth in visual literacy by encouraging critical analysis and creative exploration of alternative perspectives. In the context of post-photography, countervision marks a significant shift in how images are created, consumed, and understood. Rather than accepting photography as a representation of objective reality, countervision suggests that images are constructed depictions that can be manipulated and interpreted in multiple ways. Therefore, countervision has emerged as the foundation for post-photography's rejection of traditional photographic practices in favor of alternative methods that prioritize experimentation and subjectivity. By embracing countervision and post-photography within visual literacy, artists can challenge established norms and push the boundaries of what is possible within the medium. Furthermore, countervision promotes a deeper understanding of societal and cultural issues by allowing alternative interpretations of the photographic image. Countervision furthers the scope of visual literacy, becoming a central tenet of post-photography as a means to subvert traditional photographic practices and encourage new forms of creative expression that challenge our perception of reality.

Fontcuberta: The Visual Artist

Joan Fontcuberta considers himself more of an artist than a theorist He himself declares that he does not speak from the perspective of the researcher or the theorist: "I am a creator. I call myself a curious artist and curiosity drives me to reflect on the subjects that interest me" (Fontcuberta & Alonso, 2020, p. 250). The work of Fontcuberta as a photographer of realism is extensive. Although, we can not cover every aspect of his work in this chapter, it is worth mentioning one of his first works, *Herbarium*, since this work set the tone for the years to come.

Fontcuberta admired the work of Karl Blossfeldt, an early twentieth-century German photographer that used to portray close-ups of nature and living things. His photographs zoomed plants in a way that outlines and textures were visible. Half a century after Blossfeldt's work, the nature he portrayed was degraded, deteriorated, and polluted. This deterioration motivated Fontcuberta to perform a visual critique of unsustainable practices in the 1970s. By manipulating garbage and industrial waste found in the outer limits of Barcelona and within the perimeter of Barcelona's factories, he produced *Herbarium* (Figure 4.1), a series of nature-like photographs composed of trash. First, Fontcuberta built leaves, roots, and stems using remains of wire, screws, and packaging, among other wasted materials. Then, the artist took photographs of these artificial plants imitating Blossfeldt's visual style. The result is that, as an audience, we almost cannot tell if the image in front of us is a photograph of a natural or fake plant.

FIGURE 4.1 Braohypoda frustrata, 1984. Artwork by Fontcuberta, part of the Herbarium exhibition.

In Fontcuberta's work, such as *Herbarium*, the process becomes as important as the final result, which allows us to bring to the discussion the concept of "photographic act" proposed by the French image theorist Phillippe Dubois (1983), through which he calls to observe the image as evidence of an event. The photographic image represents the action of the photographer and all those participating in it. The photographic act can be understood as an index and not as an icon, which from the semiotics of Charles S. Peirce (1974) means that the image should not be seen by its similarity to a real referent but rather as the trace of an action or event. Also, the image indicates the photographer's standpoint and intentions, and the photographic act does not end with the camera's click but with the contemplation of the image and the audience's response.

Since photography is a footprint, mark, or trace of light, Dubois also reflects on the obsession with the mimetic capabilities of photography and its theory. From his perspective, photography history should consider instead the ways of capturing light, photographs made by contact, taken long before the camera existed. In this regard, photography was born as a luminous trace, as an index, before any idea of mimicry or similarity was even considered. Therefore, Dubois highlights looking for photography's essential characteristic in its genesis and not its outcome (Dubois, 1983), which also considers the inscription of the subject as the receiver of the image, Roland Barthes' punctum (Barthes, 1980).

Fontcuberta's Herbarium allows us to see the photographic act, meaning the photographer's process since the fabrication of the fake plants, his intentions, and our participation as an audience. The artist mimics the style in pictures of nature, intending to mislead us into perceiving them as such. Our involvement allows those images to exist in the borders of the real. *Herbarium* is the work that gave birth, in his own words, to an "Encyclopedia-of-Fake" that has characterized his work since then.

In addition to *Herbarium*, Fontcuberta's body of work comprises over 20 photographic projects. The primary concepts of several of these projects can be traced. For instance, in *Fauna*, Fontcuberta depicted unexisting, fake, animals, including winged monkeys and foxes with chicken paws. The Barcelona Education Institute conducted a survey and found out that 27% of the audience thought those animals really existed. *Spudnik*, a 1997 work, is a parody, "an action of information intoxication that serves to call attention to the dangers of credulity". In it, the artist uses and transforms numerous historical documents to tell the supposed story of Ivan Istochnikov, a Russian cosmonaut lost in space. The artist has also discovered the existence of mermaid fossils, orthodox monasteries that teach how to perform miracles, and created geographical landscapes among other "places that are simultaneously real and fictional" (Keller, 2011,

p. 130). Joan also developed meta-images: *Googlegrams* (2005) are mosaic-pictures "constructed through a freeware photomosaic program connected online to the Google search engine" (Fontcuberta, 2005). In one of his latest works, *Prosopagnosia* (2019), Fontcuberta plays with facial recognition algorithms to produce faces. For the artist, the pictorial learning of artificial intelligence evokes "the very memory of art, from minimalism to expressionism, from surrealism to Bacon. But more than art history, this project interpellates the ontology of the image, [as] we witness the institutionalization of photographs without referent" (Fontcuberta, 1997) (Figure 4.2).

FIGURE 4.2 Ivan Istochnikov, 1997. The official portrait of the fictional cosmonaut, part of the Spudnik series.

Post-photography: Into a New Visual Realm

Fontcuberta reflects deeply on post-photography in his work *The Fury of Images* (2016). Among other characteristics, post-photography represents a shift from traditional film-based photography to digital image-making practices. It is hard to identify the exact moment in which Fontcuberta coined the term, but since 2010, the author has reflected upon the evolution of photography in his work *The Pandora Camera: Photography after Photography*. In this work, Fontcuberta refers to a seminar he coordinated in 2006 at the International University of Andalucia, Spain, entitled "The sing of the swan: Towards a visual culture of post-photography" which referred to an agonizing state of photography parallel to a technological revolution (Europa Press, 2006). It is necessary to identify that Fontcuberta had been envisioning post-photography since 2006, and how technology had contributed to new practices and the democratization of photography. In that sense, the author had envisioned post-photography long before Robert Shore's (2014) work, *Post-Photography: The Artist with a Camera*, that according to Carrigan (2015) misdeeds in "tacking 'post' onto [the] word [as] one of those art world tricks that's routinely wielded to great rhetorical effect, but has little denotative meaning" (Carrigan, 2015).

With the advent of digital technology, the field of photography has undergone a major transformation in recent decades. This transformation has given rise to a new era of photography known as post-photography, which, as said, represents a shift from traditional film-based photography to digital image-making which involves the use of software and algorithms in the editing process. This shift has blurred the boundaries between photography as a medium for capturing reality and other forms of visual art that involve digital manipulation. Furthermore, post-photography has challenged the concept of photography as a sole representation of objective truth and reality by enabling the manipulation and alteration of images. "If photography has been tautologically linked to truth and memory, post-photography fractures today those links" (Fontcuberta, 2016, p. 15).

According to Fontcuberta, the term "post" in post-photography refers to abandonment. In that sense, post-photography is not defined by what it is but by what it is not. This abandonment represents looking back in a nostalgic way, but evades what is yet to come. Fontcuberta declares that by the late 1990s, when the term post-photography appeared, scholars centered its definition on the new digital attributes of pictures. Fontcuberta himself thought that the digital realm meant the death of photography, erasing the discourse of photography as contact with a photosensitive surface. Photographs as traces of light seemed to capture traces of the real, and with the born of digital photography, that sense of realism faded (Fontcuberta,

2010). Post-photography refers to "the age of the inorganic image: a composite of littered information – collected, ordered, layered, buried, stored and discarded" (Moreiras, 2017, p. 56).

Technologically Driven Transformations

Additionally, "technology transformed the way we perceive the world" (Fontcuberta, 2016, p. 22). Fontcuberta refers to Technological Darwinism (2010) as a metaphor to describe the evolution of photographic technologies and their impact on our understanding of the world and the truth. By referring to Darwin's natural selection and survival of the fittest, the author allows us to reflect that photography has evolved similarly through the 'natural' selection of tools and techniques that have adapted better to society's needs. In that sense, he suggests that Technological Darwinism promoted a democratization of photography, allowing more people to access that technology and create images easily and efficiently. However, he also insists that the same democratization has led to a greater manipulation of images, eroding, even more, the borders of photography between reality and fiction. The death of photography suggests a radical change in how pictures are created, distributed, and consumed, which can also alter the way we understand reality. Digital photography has transformed how we experiment and understand the visual world. "We are immersed in a different visual order, and this new order appears framed by three factors: the immaterialness and transmittability of images; their availability and profusion; and their contri-bution to the encyclopedization of knowledge and communication" (Fontcuberta, 2016, p. 9). Immateriality refers to the fact that photography now has no relationship with photosensitive chemical processes, such as photographic film or paper, a fact that also promotes a seamless transmission across different platforms that have changed the way we access and interact with them, to which could be added the easiness with which they can be replicated. The availability of images is evident since it is easy to access photographs from any part of the world and they have become an essential component of modern communication. Finally, images can enhance under-standing and learning of complex concepts, particularly in disciplines such as science or history where visual representations are often used to illustrate abstract ideas.

Still, Fontcuberta declares that the post-photographic era consolidated with the turn of the millennium within a second digital revolution, in which the Internet, social media, and mobile phones became protagonists. In this era, people can extensively create, share, and modify images, which are activities that have banalized photography. Camera users now also aspire to quantity, a value in which more is better. The omnipresence of cameras, screens, and images keeps growing until the excess becomes an explosion. For Fontcuberta, this overwhelming and infinite stream of images also highlights those missing images, those that have never existed or that are not available anymore, banned, censored, and forgotten (2016, p. 26). At the same time that there existed an endless flow of visual representations, there also occurred instances where certain images underwent destruction. This phenomenon raises questions about the significance and permanence of visuals in human societies and culture. Further academic exploration into this subject matter can provide valuable insights into the role of imagery in shaping our collective understanding of reality.

Post-photography as a New Challenge for Visual Literacy

"The world is a great theater. A divorce between reality and representation is no longer visible" (Fontcuberta, 1997, p. 178). Press conferences, political conventions, and sports competitions are today complex events that stage several actions for cameras. Umberto Eco (1999) described how the cameras in a soccer game broadcast a completely different event from the one in the stadium since other resources were used, such as close-ups, slow motion, repetitions, and comments that are typical of the language of that medium. As a result, the game on television was no longer the same as the one watched by the fans in the stadium.

The camera has become a device that transforms reality. Therefore, post-photography brings out a new realm for visual literacy. With its emergence, there has been a significant shift in the way we consume and interpret visual images and how these visual images transform our perception of reality. Prior to the digital age, photography was often seen as a medium that captured objective reality. However, with post-photography, digital manipulation of images has evolved into an art form on its own. As a result, visual literacy has become essential for individuals to navigate and understand the physical and virtual world around them, how these worlds are represented, as well as to communicate effectively in today's society.

Fontcuberta's work also emphasizes the ethical aspects that correspond to the production and interpretation of images. Undoubtedly, the process of visual literacy must include sensitization and awareness of what is involved in taking a camera and producing an image. At the moment of clicking the shutter, the visual artist must take responsibility for the degree of realism that is imprinted on the image, and the interpretations that it generates. It should also be a component of visual literacy to address the responsibilities implicit in taking software to edit images, using visual filters on mobile devices, or using artificial intelligence to develop images. Fontcuberta's work, interpreted from the perspective of visual literacy, is a call to look behind the scenes in the processes of creation and interpretation of images.

Fontcuberta provides a post-photography manifesto (2016, p. 39) that will aid in understanding this new realm and its relation to visual literacy.

The Post-photographic Decalogue

1 *On the artist's role: it is no longer about producing "work" but about prescribing feelings.* Therefore, visual literacy should aid in observing the ways the artist seeks to provoke emotions, which ones, and in which audiences.

2 *On the artist's performance: the artist fusions with the curator, the collector, the teacher, the historian, the theorist …* In all these facets there is authorship, which hides in the artistic result like a chameleon or is diluted. Visual literacy should aid in identifying all the agents that have an influence on each piece of art.

3 *On the artist's responsibility: an ecology of the visual is emerging that will penalize saturation and encourage recycling.* Visual literacy could help in measuring image saturation and cultural impact.

4 *On the images function: circling the image prevails over the content of the image.* Visual literacy should focus on tracking and analyzing the replicability of images.

5 *On the philosophy of art: originality discourses delegitimize, and appropriation practices become normalized.* Interpreting appropriation and conveying meaning through image recycling should fall within the scope of visual literacy.

6 *On the subjects' dialectics: the author camouflages or is in the cloud. Formulation of alternative models of authorship, co-authorship, collaborative creation, interactivity, strategic anonymity, and orphan works.* With AI as a creative tool, visual literacy should research emerging processes of interpreting and creating images.

7 *On the social's dialectics: overcoming the tensions between the public and the private. The intimacy becomes a relic.* Visual literacy could aid in highlighting our role and responsibility as audience.

8 *On art's horizon: more ludic aspects come into play to the detriment of anhedonia (the solemn + the boring), in which hegemonic art tends to find refuge.* The ludic aspects of images and their creation process could be considered as part of visual literacy perspectives.

9 *On art's experience: creation practices that accustom us to dispossession will be favored: sharing is better than possessing.* Understanding creative processes should gain protagonism for understanding images.

10 *On the politics of art: do not give in to glamor or market to engage in agitating consciences.* Visual literacy could aid visual artists in identifying their social responsibility.

We are facing a new paradigm that unfolds between the borders of reality and fiction. We must now approach images with a skeptical lens. Visual literacy then becomes a doubt, a question. Visual literacy will also imply taking an attitude of questioning what we look at. If we were to take up the three questions proposed in Visual Thinking Strategies: what's going on in this picture? what do you see that makes you say that? and what more can you find? (Yenawine, 1999); we should consider adding some more questions. For example: what is fiction in this image? how does this image simulate reality? We could also consider some other questions about the authorship of the images and the tools used to generate them.

Understanding Photography: A Legacy beyond Conspiracies

Photography played a vital role in the visual conspiracy, it was "born as part of a driven visual culture to which it contributed in imposing and strengthening it" (Fontcuberta, 1997, p. 147). The camera, hence, became a device that aids in organizing and giving meaning to our existence. The images and the devices with which we generate images modify our relationship with space, memory, and identity (Fontcuberta, 2016, p. 169). Images no longer represent, but construct a new reality. In recent works, Fontcuberta introduces post-memory as part of post-photography (Fontcuberta & Alonso Riveiro, 2020), taking this idea from Hirsch (2015) stating that photography can show us new ways of relating with the past through the transformation of images that had registered facts, and we can reappropriate them through creative interventions to produce new empathic bonds with the past. Likewise, post-memory indicates that nowadays, photography has finally freed itself from its condition as a record. Photography as a memory device is no longer important since images can be immediately discarded after generating them, releasing them from the burden of the historical record. This new ontology layer opens exploration routes for art and commercial purposes. Also, besides reconfiguring a past reality, the camera has become a device that modifies a present reality. By referring to Deleuze and Guattari's (1987) work, Coats (2014) describes how the camera has become a nomadic weapon, as a device that "recomposes reality through creative forces, rather than a tool that reconstitutes a predetermined set of conditions" (2014, p. 5).

Moreover, the visual conspiracy has led to the viralization of image-generation practices. Anyone can have within reach a device to generate images, even those with no knowledge of visual communication. "Anyone, today, even those within the category of the incompetent, can take decent pictures: the image is no longer a minority power" (Fontcuberta, 2016, p. 113). This availability produces an infinite stream of images. "The characteristics of the post-photographic era are the massive production of images and their availability and circulation on the internet" (2016, p. 151). This is what Renobell (2005) recognizes as a new form of visual thinking that came to call hypervisuality, which "has as a characteristic sign the multiplicity of the visual (transmitters, media, receivers, authors and channels)" (2005, p. 5). In other words, hypervisuality offers the possibility of experiencing the same event from multiple channels, transmitters, visual formats, and time, among others. Hypervisuality has led us as a society to a "state of hypnosis and visual catharsis" (2005, p. 5). On the one hand, the amount of images perceived daily through different media is overwhelming, and at the same time, on the other hand, there is a liberating feeling in actively participating in the generation of images.

Romeo (2010) adds a new layer to consider. While discussing Ritchin's work, she claims that hyper-photography offers an evolving forum in which a viewer can comment at the exact time an image is recorded, also revealing the exact geographical coordinates of the event. Hypervisuality and hyper-photography unveil the kaleidoscopic relationships we have constructed as a society with images in the post-photographic era. We are, at the same time, transmitters and audiences of the same events, providing a wide range of perspectives, increasing our participation, evolving from passive interpreters of images to active participants, commenting, critiquing, and even providing our own creations. Fontcuberta's post-photography invites us to think about our actions regarding images and our experience within digital life (2016, p. 33).

As we can see, the camera has become a tool for interacting with the world, as a device for extending the human experience. To this day, it is "one of the principal devices for experiencing something, for giving an appearance of participation" (Sontag, 1973, p. 10). We live now in a world in which it is common to encounter photographs of cameras. In a concert or a sports event, a picture with hundreds of cameras pointing in the same direction to capture the exact same thing has become a symbol of our time, revindicating intensity, not originality. The photographer resigns taking pictures to instead act as collector (Fontcuberta, 2016, p. 186).

Our society has become dependent on images for the construction and transmission of meanings, provoking new forms of appropriation and signification. "The post-photographic practices aspire to a creational gesture that does not focus on fabricating images, but on knowing how to assign meaning to those that already exist, awakening them from their somnolence" (2016, p. 128). As such, post-photography has become an essential tool for artistic expression and visual communication in contemporary culture. The emergence of post-photography has also played a significant role in shaping the art and commercial industries. In the art world, post-photography has opened up new avenues for creativity and experimentation. Contemporary photography has become more accessible and offers a wide range of possibilities, creating new modes of artistic expression. For business, post-photography has offered new ways to develop branding and identity, as well as communicating with audiences. Additionally, post-photography has brought about new debates and discussions regarding the authenticity of images and the role of digital manipulation in shaping our perception of reality.

Photography, as a technology, has never stopped evolving since its invention. By shrinking down or scaling up, it has become a part of everyday life, the most prolific industries, and scientific research. It has found a way to establish a symbiosis with the technologies that gave birth to the digital era, nourishing and strengthening itself from them. In this context, Fontcuberta's thinking is still expanding the debate. Today, it is not enough to envisage the border between reality and fiction of an image, but a new frontier is approaching in which it will be very difficult to discern whether an image was human-generated or developed by artificial intelligence, breaching into a new realm; the "algorithmic image breaks away from any secure relationship between the image and the world" (Alves & Oliveira, 2016, p. 74). Truth-similarity will not only refer to visually imitating reality but also mimicking the photographic practices in all its meaning: framing, posing, scenarios, and topics. The photographic act will involve an algorithm; it is becoming a contradiction in itself. The process of generating images can be immaterial but meaningful, anonymous but collaborative, representing scenarios, objects, and people that do not exist. Computers and digital devices are "engulfing cameras and representation is no longer a product of imagination but of calculation" (Fontcuberta, 2019). An image has become an index of a society's obsession with visual depiction.

Joan Fontcuberta's pioneering thinking and groundbreaking work were pivotal in breaking free from the conventional understanding of photography. He provoked a paradigm shift spiking new perspectives and pushing boundaries that led to an innovative approach toward envisioning, comprehending, and generating images that continue to influence contemporary practices. Throughout his career, Fontcuberta consistently developed critical discourses around the medium, its credibility, and its societal implications. Fontcuberta became a transformative figure in the photography field due to his disruptive approach toward the medium. Furthermore, his ideas regarding photography and its relationship to truth invite us to reexamine the ethics involved in visual representation and its interpretation. It is impossible to overstate the impact that Fontcuberta's contributions have had on the understanding of photography, spiking new inquiries and challenges for visual literacy, and the awareness of the limitless potential of image-producing practices.

References

Alves, A., & Oliveira, D. E. (2016). Post-photography, or are we past photography? In A. Moutinho, A. Vicente, H. Ferreira, J. Gomes, & J. Primo (Eds.), *Post-screen: Intermittence+Interference* (pp. 68–75). Edições Universitárias Lusófonas.

Barthes, R. (1980). *La cámara lucida. Notas sobre fotografía.* Paidós.

Bravo, G. (2022). Joan Fontcuberta. Profesor de Fotografía. https://fotogasteiz.com/blog/fotografos/joan-fontcuberta-vida-obra-biografia/

Carrigan, M. (2015, January 15). *An out-of-focus look at post-photography.* Hyperallergic. https://hyperallergic.com/174956/an-out-of-focus-look-at-post-photography/

Coats, C. (2014). Thinking through the photographic encounter: Engaging with the camera as nomadic weapon. *International Journal of Education & the Arts, 15*(9), 1–22.

Deleuze, G., & Guattari, F. (1987). *A thousand plateaus: Capitalism and schizophrenia.* University of Minneapolis Press.

Dubois, P. (1983). *El acto fotográfico. De la representación a la recepción.* Paidós.

Eco, U. (1999). La transparencia perdida. *La estrategia de la ilusión* (pp. 84–92). Lumen.

Europa Press. (2006, September 19). *La Fotografía "Agoniza" y da paso a otro concepto de imagen que genera "Escepticismo," Según Fontcuberta.* europapress.es. https://www.europapress.es/sociedad/educacion-00468/noticia-fotografia-agoniza-da-paso-otro-concepto-imagen-genera-escepticismo-fontcuberta-20060919131332.html

Fontcuberta, J. (1997). *El beso de Judas.* Gustavo Gili.

Fontcuberta, J. (2005). *Googlegrams.* angelsbarcelona.com. http://angelsbarcelona.com/en/artists/joan-fontcuberta/projects/googlegrams/108

Fontcuberta, J. (2010). *La Cámara de Pandora. La fotografía después de la fotografía.* Gustavo Gili.

Fontcuberta, J. (2011). *Indiferencias fotográficas y ética de la imagen periodística.* Gustavo Gili.

Fontcuberta, J. (2016). *La furia de las imágenes.* Galaxia Gutenberg.

Fontcuberta, J. (2019). *Prosopagnosia.* angelsbarcelona.com. http://angelsbarcelona.com/en/artists/joan-fontcuberta/projects/prosopagnosia/1044

Fontcuberta, J., & Alonso Riveiro, M. (2020). Imágenes desquiciadas. Una conversación sobre (post)fotografía, tiempo y memoria con Joan Fontcuberta. *Discursos Fotográficos, 16*(29), 249–273.

Hirsch, M. (2015). *La generación de la posmemoria.* Carpe Noctem.

Keller, P. (2011). Joan Fontcuberta's landscapes: Remapping photography and the technological image. *Journal of Spanish Cultural Studies, 12*(2), 129–153.

La 2. (2021, June 2). *Joan Fontcuberta - Detrás del Instante [Video].* YouTube. https://www.youtube.com/watch?v=ac8ovdn1kFA&ab_channel=La2

Moreiras, C. (2017). Joan Fontcuberta: Post-photography and the spectral image of saturation. *Journal of Spanish Cultural Studies*, *18*(1), 57–77.

Peirce, C. (1974). *La ciencia de la semiótica*. Buenos aires.

Reina Sofia, M. N. C. de A. (n.d.). *PhotoVision*. Museo Nacional Centro de Arte Reina Sofia. https://www.museoreinasofia.es/coleccion/sala/sala-00110

Renobell, V. (2005). Redalyc. Hipervisualidad. La imagen fotográfica en la sociedad del conocimento y de la comunicación digital. *Revista Sobre La Sociedad Del Conocimiento*, *1*, 1–12. www.uoc.edu/uocpapers

Romeo, F. (2010, May 5). After photography by Fred Ritchin. *Bomb Magazine*. https://bombmagazine.org/articles/after-photography-by-fred-ritchin/

Shore, R. (2014). *Post-photography: The artist with a camera*. Lawrence King Publishing.

Sontag, S. (1973). *On photography*. Dell.

Soto, A., & Guldin, R. (2012, May 1). To document something which does not exist. Vilém Flusser and Joan Fontcuberta: A collaboration. *Flusser Studies*, *13*. https://www.flusserstudies.net/archive

Steichen, E. (1903). Ye, Fakers. *Camerawork*, *1*, 48–49.

Yenawine, P. (1999). *Theory into practice: The visual thinking strategies*. Paper presented at the conference, "Aesthetic and Art Education: A Transdisciplinary Approach," sponsored by the Caluste Gulbenkian Foundation, Lisbon, Portugal.

5

LITERACY FOUNDATIONS IN JUNE KING MCFEE'S ART EDUCATION PHILOSOPHY

Margaretha Häggström

University of Gothenburg

Biographical Sketch

June King McFee (1917–2008) was born in 1917 in Seattle, Washington. She grew up in a time when women were expected to act 'ladylike'. This was something she found unfair and difficult, even discriminating. She was reprimanded at school when she wanted to play baseball with the boys. This incident created strong frustration and hostility to society. At age twelve, she decided to become an artist, with both pressure and applause from her mother who was pushing her to 'be something,' McFee wrote (1975). When she began to study art in Chicago, she was fortunate to have Alexander Archipenko as her teacher, who had great respect for women and their intellect. He was significant to her, and instilled confidence and encouragement in her. Nevertheless, it turned out to be difficult to overcome prejudice as a working woman and she encountered resistance just because of her gender. Repeatedly, she experienced differential treatment between men and women, and the perception of a so-called glass ceiling, that is, an unacknowledged barrier to advancement in a profession, due to the organizational culture at the college in relation to gender. Eventually, in 1965, she was recruited to the University of Oregon. She agreed to come if she could initiate and start a doctoral program. The president of the University, Arthur Flemming, who, according to McFee (1975), was a man who was ahead of his time because he wanted more women on the faculty, agreed to her request. This art doctoral program was based on a fairly radical new thinking and was innovative, as it included for example folk art, popular art, and class-centered perspectives. She brought

DOI: 10.4324/9781032651781-6

in perspectives from outside of art education, such as educational psychology, sociology, philosophy, and curriculum. She advocated for an anthropological-based art history. The program increased female accessibility and cultural pluralism. McFee developed the university-based community art studies institute, and she started the doctoral program in art education. Her recurring experiences of gender discrimination formed her social commitment and principles, from which she created her educational standpoints. She developed a critical, yet embracing, perspective on visual art pedagogy. McFee's mission was to reach all students, regardless of their background and gender.

McFee was productive and published several articles, chapters, and books. She wrote about multicultural approaches to art and teaching, environmental design and how psychology can help explain the way we see, understand, and know art and the world in general. When discussing cultural diversity and visual culture, she employed a feminist social theory perspective. She emphasized integrity, impact, and improvisation as essential qualities of art and art making (McFee, 1966). June King McFee passed away on January 14, 2008.

The June King McFee Award, established by National Art Education Association Women's Caucus in 1973, is given annually to honor an individual who has made distinguished contributions to the profession of art education, and one who has brought distinction to the field through an exceptional and continuous record of achievement in scholarly writing, research, professional leadership, teaching, or community service.

Introduction

Art is one of man's basic means of communication – sharing the essence of experience from man to man and from generation to generation. (McFee, 1998, p. 101)

Both viewing and creating art can be understood as entering a communicative exchange between the artist, the viewer, and the artwork. This communication is guided by the same rules that govern human verbal conversation, which involves a communicator, a context or field situation, an interpreter, and content or "a body of signs or symbols utilized for significant meanings between communicator and interpreter with varying degrees of commonality" (Bernberg, 1953, p. 23). Human communication arises in a situation in which the communicator and interpreter are "thrown together" into an interdependent relationship through the signs, or semiotic resources (prod)used (Halliday, 1978). Communicative behavior is a way to order one's experiences into meaningful patterns through a structuring process (Bernberg, 1953). This process depends on the order existing in the external world, and on the functional needs of the individual. Meaningful experiences form the basic process in a communicative situation. Sometimes, this is more evident in artworks, such as paintings, than in verbal conversations. However, the artwork itself cannot add comments to the cooperative principle of the conversation with the viewer. "Art as a major communication system is often neglected or not recognized in education courses," McFee (1999, p. 37) claims, and continues "for art to be recognized as a basic in education in this visual information age, it must be recognized for what it is and what it is doing." McFee devoted her work to doing just that.

McFee's Theoretical Foundations

McFee adopted a complex and multifaceted theoretical foundation. And indeed, humans, art, and learning are all complex phenomena that cannot be described or justified in a simple way, especially as they are intertwined in art education. She contends that art communication changes one's experiences in a qualitative way (Keifer-Boyd et al., 2016). Her viewpoint is rooted in both sociocultural and phenomenological perspectives, in addition to social psychological views, even though she did not formulate her thoughts as such.

First, I wish to dwell on McFee's connection to anthropology. In 1963, Elliot Eisner reviewed McFee's book *Preparation for Art* (1961), and he was happy to report that McFee constructs "a network of ideas about the teaching of art by building on relevant research findings from various behavioral sciences" (p. 227). In that book, McFee draws on a wide range of research findings from anthropology, psychology, as well as sociology, when presenting her perception-delineation theory. This theory, or framework, describes and emphasizes the diversity of intertwined and synergistic conditions that affect children's artwork. The first aspect is the psychosocial readiness of the child or student, the second is the specific context in which the child or student learns, the third, the student's perceptual ability, and the fourth, the ability to organize and communicate aesthetic content. The framework offers a toolbox for understanding some of the factors that influence the child and student when working in art. McFee does not provide a definition of art in this book, but refers to Melville Herskovits, who explains that art is any aesthetic expression that requires knowledge and skills in some form of aesthetic activity (McFee, 1961). Herskovits, who was an anthropologist, incorporated the concept of culture. At that time, culture replaced race as an explanation for human behavioral differences, which meant that cultural influences, not race, were the main determining factors of human behavior and thinking (Gershenhorn, 2017). This new perspective also repudiated cultural hierarchies.

As I understand the influences of these theories regarding art and art making, images engender images; cultural affiliations are shown in artworks and will simultaneously create and disseminate influences from a certain culture. However, as is shown in Figure 5.1, artists communicate by resonating visually with other artworks. Figure 5.1, *Sociocultural and Phenomenological preparation*, includes inspirations from Indigenous artwork, fashion from 1920s, when McFee was young, and several metaphors of various kinds, to link the image to history, human roots, and time.

FIGURE 5.1 Sociocultural and Phenomenological preparation, 2023, gouache painting by Margaretha Häggström.

McFee was noticeably inspired by Herkovits, and in her book from 1961, *Preparation for Art*, she concentrates more on the animate relationship between the four factors, mentioned earlier, that influence human actions and communication through visual arts. In 1977, McFee co-authored the book *Art, Culture, and Environment: A Catalyst for Teaching*, together with Rogena M. Degge. Their standpoint is that art, as communication, should be taught to all students, by all teachers, which implies that all teachers should use art as a pedagogical tool, just as they use reading and writing as a communicative medium in any school subject (McFee & Degge, 1977). The main theme in their book is to prepare students with different cultural backgrounds to cope in society without devaluing their own cultural background. Art is here viewed as a communication system and a catalyst for general education, rather than for art education in specific. In his review of this book, Kenneth D. Jenkins (1978) stresses that the book's most important contribution to the general educator is the authors' understanding of the relationship between art, culture, and society. In this view, art plays a wider role in people's lives, which is evident in for example people's beliefs and rituals. The anthropological approach to art focuses on the social processes involved. This might explain why McFee does not define art itself but concentrates on the relations between art and life. Ever since McFee's encounters with what she probably perceived as a cultural clash, in terms of gender expectations and class differences, she had a great interest in how to overcome social and cultural differences. Art provides a democratic way of shaping, expressing, and sharing human values, rather than sharing artifacts from a specific social group. Art, as a human communicative behavior, also helps shape the manner through which we understand ourselves and the world around us.

Both Eisner (1963) and Jenkins (1978) highlight some shortcomings they identify in McFee's writings; the lack of defining art is the mutual denominator. Art is treated as if there is a general consensus about art's distinct meaning, they claim. If we want to explain artistic behavior, from an anthropological perspective or not, we need a definition of art (Svasek, 2007). However, the acceptance of art as a human cultural phenomenon, has long been a problem in the anthropology of art (Layton, 1981/1991). Many anthropologists stress that the Western categories of, for example, painting, sculpture, drama, or lyrical poetry, comprehended as autonomous artistic activities, do not exist, or occur in significantly different forms, in most non-Western contexts. Hence, there is no agreement on a cross-cultural definition of art in anthropology (Morphy & Perkins, 2006).

It is clear that McFee's main attention is directed toward the social processes involved in making artworks, not the aesthetic objects as mere objects. She argues that "Because art and culture are so intertwined, it is difficult to teach about one without the other. Art communicates culture and culture contributes to what is created as art" (McFee, 1999, p. 37). She seeks to understand the manifold of interactions between social behavior and communication, based on the assumption that every social cultural pattern and performance involves communication, implicit through for example body languages, glances, and postures, or explicit through for example verbal conversation, dancing, music-making, and more. Accordingly, art as communication is an intersubjective act. I will now proceed to McFee's compound theoretical foundation, starting with what I regard as a phenomenological viewpoint and the concept of intersubjectivity.

Intersubjective Epistemology from a Phenomenological Viewpoint

Phenomenological perspectives suggest that human experience is not private, secreted, or incomprehensible but something that shines through our bodily, linguistic, and emotional expressions (Mascolo & Kallio, 2020; Merleau-Ponty, 1964). Human ability for intersubjective involvement develops substantially as an individual's language capacity enhancement. Social skills arise from intersubjective processes between people, and from intersubjective corroboration (Mascolo & Kallio, 2020; Merleau-Ponty, 1964). In line with Mascolo and Kallio (2020), I interpret intersubjectivity as the basis for the development of language, and accordingly for the development of art. Art, as any form of expression, is a system for creating, representing, and communicating thoughts, opinions, emotions, attitudes, and beliefs that have social origins in cultural history. The world is intersubjective, we share it with each other and the more-than-human world (Häggström, 2019). This means also that we carry the past, while addressing ourselves to the future, yet making our decisions in the present. This threefold constitution is comprised of who and how we were, are and will become. Through art, humans create shared representations of our existence and make it intelligible to ourselves and to others.

To McFee, art and culture are entangled. She advocates that the structure of culture is:

> Dependent on the multiple forms of the arts; how people dress for status and role, how they enhance and decorate objects for themselves and for barter, how they design their habitations, organize communities, enhance their sense of reality and worship, and celebrate shared events. (McFee, 1999, p. 35)

Thus, art is a communicator of information about the design and meaning of its culture. Often, art underpin changes in a culture, and simultaneously has the power to resist changes to maintain culture, McFee claims.

McFee understood arts learning as comprising structural, performative, bodily, and existential dimensions, and as intersubjective meaning-making. What she truly wanted was to bring about fusions of horizons (Gadamer, 1989, p. 306). McFee wrote:

> We must increase communication across perspectives and revitalize education as a central force in all our complex society. Then, art can be taught as a major communication system of education – a cohesive force for mutual understanding in a multi-cultural society. (1998, p. x)

This is not only about listening to, or taking part of someone's experiences, culture, and life. This is about learning and growing. The individual always brings her or his horizon of understanding, including a set of preconceived notions, assumptions, and prejudices, into dialogue with for example an artwork. Ideally, these pre-understandings are engaged, challenged, and expanded. It is first when we understand one another that we can connect to each other's experiences, or horizons, and a fusion of horizons may occur (Gadamer, 1989). This intersubjectivity and relation between people's cognitive perspectives are illustrated in Figure 5.2, *Human intersubjective abilities.* During this process, we can discover our capacity horizon, and push the limits of what we thought was conceivable (Berndtsson, 2001). In turn, we may reach a horizon of action, which indicates a move toward enlarged knowledge and competence. Each of us can continuously discover new capacity horizons, reach new action horizons, and gain increased understanding and competence. This is a precondition for lifelong learning (Berndtsson, 2001).

FIGURE 5.2 Human intersubjective abilities, 2023, gouache painting by Margaretha Häggström.

Embodied Lived Experiences and Ethical Reflections

Here, I would like to emphasize the importance of embodied lived experience for building relationships, for mutual understandings, and for ethical considerations. Ethical phenomenology pinpoints three crucial concepts, which I recognize in McFee's writings: Otherness, responsibility, and ethical reflections (Levinas, 1979). The substantial reflection occurs in the meeting with the Other, or in face-to-face encounters and interactions. Through these encounters a sense of responsibility can be evoked. This entails ethical decisions to accept the Other for its Otherness. Bridges can be built through empathy and open acceptance. McFee has such an approach. She talks about art education as multifaceted cultural communication and notes art teaching requires "highly developed understandings of individual and cultural diversity" (1998, p. 21). Intersubjectivity is crucial here, and it goes beyond direct meetings between people. From birth, humans are surrounded by an intersubjective world, full of sense making activities, including meaningful symbols, language systems, tools, works of art, and more. We build a store of experience from all sediments of tradition – inherited and learned. In reciprocal acts of giving and processing meaning to both yourself and others, intersubjective social life is constructed (Schütz, 1945). Social participation is thus a prerequisite for understanding the world one shares in each place and time, through the presence of others, and what they leave behind. This is interpreted in Figure 5.3, *Embodied lived experiences*, which is a paraphrase of Paul Gauguin's painting *Three Tahitians* (1899). The three women symbolize women's different appearances and roles historically with a contemporary view.

FIGURE 5.3 Embodied lived experiences, 2023, gouache painting by Margaretha Häggström.

Participatory Epistemologies

Here, following Schütz, I will use intersubjectivity as an interactional process to understand McFee's underlying epistemologies; that is, to consider intersubjectivity as experiences in the "in-betweenness" of a subject and an object. What is happening in this intermediate space? Here lies a participatory reality that cannot be divided into subject and object, as if they were self-sufficient entities, since they are always intertwined and affecting each other. The in-betweenness melts together experience and reality, mind and matter, body and soul. Art and other human expressions emerge from experiences in this intermediate space, as do play and dreams. This place could also be phrased as "sub-universe" or "finite province of meaning" (Schütz, 1945), which represent specific accents of reality.

Participatory epistemologies, as a knowledge theory, state that meaning is endorsed through the participation of the human mind with the world. It attempts to bridge the subject–object distinction, by explaining that meaning is not only found outside the human mind in an objective world, nor is it only constructed by the subjective mind. Participatory understanding occurs in co-creating events, through relations in for example a community, a collective identity, or a place. Through McFee's work, in which she repeatedly claims that art is communication, a participatory point of departure is clear. Shared experiences and meanings of culture emerge through participation in active environments. To McFee (1999) interaction between cultures is a force for change. Participation should here be regarded as embodied interactions, incorporated in a social as well as material realm, where a "we-relationship" is created. According to McFee (1999), learning occurs as changes through such social participation.

Social Psychology Factors

McFee's reasoning elucidates her interest in human behavior, and the fact that an individual's behavior does not happen in a vacuum. The environment, other humans, and organisms affect one's behavior and personality. Human act is in certain ways, depending on the surroundings, the society, the assembly, and the situation. We make social adjustments to ensure that we fit into a group, to confirm social values and norms, and when we feel that we should react to an incident. Social dynamics occur anywhere people gather and form groups. For example, in classrooms students (and others) constantly try to adjust and behave according to norms of different groups. That can sometimes be a hard task, as each individual is quite unique. McFee knew about social pressure and demanding norms. In my reading of her texts, her reaction, as an art teacher, to the pressures of a demanding social environment, was for students to be (1) open and proud of their background, (2) curious to know and welcoming others, (3) appreciating others for their Otherness. In this spirit, when we meet a person that we do not yet know, a person that we might find different in a way, even annoying, each of us could try to look at the other person through the eyes of the people who love her or him. McFee wanted to minimize the distance between a 'you' and a 'me,' and art was one way of doing that; to be an 'us' yet thriving on the otherness (McFee, 1975, 1998). That is to both close and reopen the gap, and to work with both the known and the unknown, and to allow oneself to find the familiar within a stranger.

Sociocultural Factors

In line with the already mentioned epistemologies and factors, McFee's work is based on sociocultural learning theories, which assert that learning is a social process in which development occurs through interactions with people (Vygotsky, 1978). Lev Vygotsky, who developed this theory, suggests that the child (or student) enhances knowledge and various abilities in interactions with a person, who possesses more knowledge or skill than the child. Zone of proximal development (ZPD) explains the ability of an individual to extend beyond her or his inherent ability through interaction with "more knowledgeable others". Again, this may explain how images engender images, and that art does not emerge out of the blue. This is shown in Figure 5.4, *Visual Culture Art Education*, in which a Paul Cézanne inspired still life is placed on a table, and paintings depicting this still life with inspiration from Aboriginal art, Wassily Kandinsky, and Hilma af Klint.

Learning, as a cultural phenomenon, implies that teaching must embrace different pedagogical methods. Teachers and peers influence individual learning, as do cultural beliefs and attitudes. Vygotsky asserted that children, through playing and imagining, will be able to expand their conceptual abilities and understandings of the world. Learning is mediated by cultural tools, such as language and the arts. Tools and signs contain all things and all sign systems in a person's background and particular culture that can give sense to an experience. Art, drama, music, and dance are all different forms of language that can be used for mediating knowledge development. To sum up McFee's non-traditional approach to art education, it is relevant to link her teaching and learning methods to Visual Culture Art Education (Buhl, 2005). Visual culture in art education concentrates on critical thinking skills, on encouraging students to reflect on the connotations and ideals expressed in their everyday visual world. McFee (1999) stressed that art teachers ought to face the evolving use of the visual arts in mass media, and their use of visual languages, to meet and resist

FIGURE 5.4 Visual Culture Art Education, 2023, gouache painting by Margaretha Häggström.

the influence of mass media on our culture. Visual Culture Art Education aims at decoding and deconstructing visual symbols in any work of art.

Visual Literacy as Sociocultural Interactions

So far, this exposé has covered the pedagogical and didactic questions of how to teach and learn this specific item and why it is important to do so. Just as essential, according to visual literacy, is the question of what. What are the learning objectives here, that is, what should students know or be able to do that they couldn't do before a lesson or a course? And what does "the language of art mean"?

The broad definition of visual literacy is "the ability to read, write and create visual images" (Harrison, n.d.). Before being able to use, create and engage with visual expressions, as well as analyze, interpret, and scrutinize visual messages, students need to learn about visual basics. If we regard art as a language, what are the grammar and syntax of visual media?

I have previously used a re-designed version of Freebody & Luke's (1990, 1999) Four Resources Model to describe visual literacy (Häggström, 2019, 2020). The purpose with this redesign was to mark a shift from the linguistic to the pictorial. Following their four resources, visual literacy incorporates four abilities, enhanced through four social practices: visual code-breaking, visual meaning-making, visual use, and visual analysis. Underlining social practices foregrounds how visual literacy is interrelated with and influenced by cultural contexts, including social power relations, which is in line with McFee's educational philosophy. Becoming visually literate requires certain abilities, like other types of literacies. Here, the four resources will be presented and developed in relation to McFee's pedagogical approach, as I comprehend it.

1 *Visual code breaking* involves processes of noticing and discovering the elements and structure of visual images, such as shape, color, light and shadow, and composition, as well as recognizing visual grammar and expressions students have access to in their lives. Visual code breaking is a prerequisite for a person's ability to create meaning from visual expressions, and to be able to create, use and critically examine images. Following McFee, gender, class and cultural background ought to be taken into account when aiming at visual code breaking. This implies that one's context, such as upbringing environment, family traditions etc., play an essential role in how an individual perceives and uses visual expressions. McFee stresses the teachers' competence and ability to recognize each student's psychosocial readiness and perceptual ability, to be aware of the specific context. Diversity and social interactions are therefore important in art class, for developing students' understandings of diversities as such, and the importance of genuine plurality, according to McFee. Visual code breaking is never about finding the 'right' interpretations, but rather to illuminate the variations of decodings, and discuss the sources of the variations. Sociocultural traditions shape how humans think and therefore how they decode visual communication.

2 *Visual meaning making* involves processes of communication and interactions in practices, in which visual language is central. This includes reflecting on, and understanding the context of various narratives, drawing on a wide range of media, and to ask authentic questions in relation to one's own and other's lived experiences (Häggström & Schmidt, 2021). Visual meaning making is based on one's personal experience of encountering images, which in turn is based on sociocultural contexts. In accordance with McFee, images from different cultures must be represented. It is a matter of democracy. Interactive performances within the art class allow for the possibility of sharing students' variety of experiences and perspectives as an intersubjective act. Intersubjectivity is crucial here at a relational level, and in establishing mutual understandings, as well as in recognizing the circumstances of

others. Differing beliefs among students who subscribe to different thought communities may thus be visualized and discussed. Also, it is significant to remind students that human experiences and expressions are always collective in one way or another. Visual communication exists as shared representations, and do not emerge from nothing. Often, they represent fusions of horizons and create intersubjective meaning-making. However, as cultural backgrounds differ, individual representations may be perceived as unique and harder to understand. Here, the art teacher can offer exciting meetings with 'the Other' and to minimize the distance between various 'you and me,' and to create a new 'we.'

3 *Visual use* involves processes of developing knowledge regarding what to do with one's meaning making knowledge. This includes using and creating images through processes that include all one's social and cultural resources, and with critical awareness, relying on one's ability to judge various sources' reliability. Visual use empowers a person's creation of visual communication and relies on sociocultural pictorial features (Häggström, 2019). To McFee, each student should be encouraged to show and use their specific and personal visual traditions and cultural heritage. The teacher should draw students' attention to how to organize and communicate visual content. Through creating visual expressions of different kinds, and being able to experiment, imagine and try out new ways of expressions, students can expand their understanding of others and of the world. Using each other's knowledge and backgrounds through co-creating events, will enhance the participatory understandings and new collective identities.

4 *Visual analysis* involves the process of developing critical perspectives on visual media in relation to society, social sustainability, and social justice. This is a crucial aspect in McFee's reasoning. This primarily involves close analysis of various sources to ask relevant questions, that is to being critically aware of social justice in relation to visual language, power, and identity (Häggström & Schmidt, 2021). Such analysis has great potential to increase students' awareness of sexist, racist, and postcolonial structures, which was a theme that McFee continuously worked on and struggled with. Visual analysis deepens the understanding of each visual components' construction, functions, and impact on the viewer. It can expose underlying messages, intentions, and ideologies, and is based on the ability to use image language (Häggström, 2020). Adopting a Visual Culture Art Education, is in line with McFee's intentions and achievements, as it intends to develop students' critical thinking skills.

Visual literacy is not about an isolated phenomenon, or a single process, but how different processes are connected. McFee is clear in explaining that all the choices you make have their origins in the culture and social context you belong to. This applies to color choice, shapes you use, and the composition of the image. Nothing happens by chance; thus, visual expressions are multidimensional socio-cultural constructs that require literacy abilities, based on the four resources. Even when you analyze other people's images, you carry the imagery of your culture with you as a filter. McFee emphasizes the importance of being aware of this. And as Freedman (2003) put it, "art educators must constantly be aware that they are representing a representation, interpreting an interpretation" (p. 5).

The pedagogical implications of McFee's art educational beliefs regarding visual literacy direct teachers to rethink their pedagogical approach. The didactic questions need to address the consequences of the participatory, social, and interactional perspectives. How can classroom practice encourage interactions? What kind of interactions are needed and practicable? Who shall interact and with whom and with what? And who is to decide these actions? McFee was known for asking more questions rather than giving answers, as a way of raising awareness, provoking new thoughts and actions. For further reading on McFee's pedagogical foundations, the book *Art, Culture, and Environment: A Catalyst for Teaching* (McFee & Degge, 1977) is recommended.

McFee's Legacy to Art Education

McFee was ahead of her time, and her work remains relevant today. She had both an anthropological and a psychological background and she melded the two. She knew that solving social problems through education needed to be a huge part of art education's mission. McFee's theoretical foundation reflects her upbringing, her experiences of exclusion and the contemporary times in which she worked. She did not fear complexity, instead, she used it to explain the basis of the art teacher's mission, and as an explanatory model for what art can be and what art can do. Through her articles, she concentrated on the task of art, "The big question for the art educator, it would seem is: how can art experience and symbolic communication contribute to a sense of identity and social participation?" (McFee, 1966, p. 132).

Art can transform influences from the external world, and all the things that happen to an individual. Art is described as an essential tool in empathy. McFee argues for weaving the arts into the main classroom curricula, as well as teaching specific artistic skills and abilities. As this chapter suggests, it means to integrate the four abilities included in the Four Resources Model (Freebody & Luke, 1990; Häggström, 2020). For example, to teach students about color, shape, layout, perspective, and various techniques that are essential in visual presentations, and simultaneously, use art to develop creative problem-solving skills, social skills, critical thinking skills and how to be more cautious about how we observe the surrounding world. McFee dedicated her work and life to promote and explain the importance of art education in a school's curriculum. She argued that entire societies gain from an investment in the arts, through for example higher levels of civic engagement and social tolerance. Especially, she engaged in promoting arts to fight inequalities tied to gender, ethnicity, family income, and whether a school is located in a city, suburb or rural area. Integrating art and creative expression with other fields and school subjects was indeed McFee's pedagogical strategy. McFee's work is still important for several reasons. She "re-envision the field of art education in a way that does not reduce or confine it to the institutions and practices of schooling" (Lackey, 2003). McFee acknowledges educational art practices across in-formal and formal settings and supports research outside school contexts.

McFee's most important contribution to the field of visual literacy is her holistic point of departure, based not only on interdisciplinary approaches, but on a relational caring pedagogical approach (Adams, 2018; Aspelin, 2018). Relational pedagogy is a comprehensive pedagogy, in which civic direction, knowledge development, and care for the pupils creates an intertwined unity (Aspelin, 2018). Communication processes and interactions are central to relational pedagogy. Professor Paul Bolin, a former graduate student to McFee, who often visited McFee in her office, tells "whenever I would enter her office, she made me think that nothing in the world was of greater import than carrying on our conversation at that moment in time" (Bolin, 2004, p. 5). He was given her full attention, and she was one of the best listeners he had ever met. Thus, visual literacy cannot, should not, be based on a techno-centric approach, focusing only on the grammar and syntax of visual language. Instead, and in line with McFee's reasoning, visual literacy should aim at enhancing students' ability to reflect upon their values, attitudes, and social behaviors, in order to offer opportunities for integrating new awareness and embrace new insights from multiple perspectives. Visual language includes "design in clothing, household goods, cities, buildings, television, movies, magazines, books, and advertising" (McFee & Degge, 1977, p. 6). McFee believed in people and their capability to create a harmonious future of diversity. That is a message of hope that seems more important than ever. Art education has the power to influence communities in such a direction.

The world has strong examples of cultural differences from extreme efforts to preserve and enforce cultural norms compared to more multicultural national societies which strive to maintain basic human rights and yet allow for cultural diversity that does not infringe on these basic rights. (McFee, 1999, p. 35)

A Note on the Chapter's Images

The chapter's images are made by the author, Margaretha Häggström, as interpretations of McFee's theoretical multifaceted foundations. The images serve as small nods to historical art-works illustrating humanity's anchoring in the past, the present, and the future, as well as cultural links and intersubjective existence. This demonstrates how visual literacy fosters an understanding of visual culture.

References

Adams, K. L. (2018). *Relational pedagogy in higher education* [Dissertation]. University of Oklahoma, Department of Instructional Leadership and Academic Curriculum. https://hdl.handle.net/11244/299945

Aspelin, J. (2018). *Lärares relationskompetens. Vad är det? Hur kan den utvecklas?* [Teachers' relation competence. What is it? How can it develop?] Liber.

Bernberg, R. E. (1953). Prestige suggestion in art as communication. *The Journal of Social Psychology, 38*, 23–30.

Berndtsson, I. (2001). *Förskjutna horisonter. Livsförändring och lärande i samband med synnedsättning eller blindhet.* [Shifting horizons. Life changes and learning in relation to visual impairment or blindness.] Doctoral thesis. University of Gothenburg.

Bolin, P. (2004). The impact of June King McFee and Vincent Lanier on my life and beyond. *CultureWork, 9*(23), 2–7.

Buhl, M. (2005). Visual culture as a strategic approach to art production in education. *International Journal of Education through Art, 1*(2), 103–114.

Eisner, E. W. (1963). Reviewed work(s): Preparation for art by June King McFee. *The Elementary School Journal, 63*(4), 227–230.

Freebody, P., & Luke, A. (1990). Literacies programs: Debates and demands in cultural context. *Prospect, 5*, 7–16.

Freebody, P., & Luke, A. (1999). *Further notes on the four resources model.* Reading International Reading Association. www.readingonline.org

Freedman, K. (2003). *Teaching visual culture: Curriculum, aesthetics and the social life of art.* Teachers College Press & Reston.

Gadamer, G. (1989). *Truth and method.* Crossroad.

Gershenhorn, J. (2017). Africa and the Americas: Life and work of Melville Herskovits, *Bérose - Encyclopédie internationale des histoires de l'anthropologie, 1092*, 1–5.

Häggström, M. (2019). Visual genealogy of portraits, self-portraits, and selfies: Same phenomenon, different phase of history. In D. M. Baylen (Ed.), *Dreams and inspirations: The book of selected readings 2018* (pp. 66–83). International Visual Literacy Association.

Häggström, M. (2020). Embodied connective aesthetics: A collaborative art project guided by mirroring. In D. M. Baylen (Ed.), *Crossing boundaries and disciplines: The book of selected readings 2019* (pp. 82–96). International Visual Literacy Association.

Häggström, M., & Schmidt, C. (2021). Futures literacy – to belong, participate and act! An educational perspective. *Futures*, *132*, 1–11. 10.1016/j.futures.2021. 102813

Halliday, M. A. K. (1978). *Language as social semiotic: The social interpretation of language and meaning*. University Park Press.

Harrison, K. (n.d.). What is visual literacy? https://visualliteracytoday.org/what-is-visual-literacy/

Jenkins, K. D. (1978). Review of art, culture, and environment: A catalyst for teaching. *Journal of Teacher Education*, *29*(3). 10.1177/00224871780290031

Keifer-Boyd, K., Bailey, I., Blandy, D., Congdon, K. G., Degge, R., & Staples, J. (2016). Looking back, looking forward. *Visual Arts Research*, *42*(2), 73–85.

Lackey, L. M. (2003). Theorizing a network called art education: Re-envisioning and extending the field. *Studies in Art Education*, *44*(2), 101–116.

Layton, R. (1981/1991). *The anthropology of art*. Cambridge University Press.

Levinas, E. (1979). *Totality and infinity*. Springer.

Mascolo, M. F., & Kallio, E. (2020). The phenomenology of between: An intersubjective epistemology for psychological science. *Journal of Constructivist Psychology*, *33*(1), 1–28. 10.1080/10720537.2019.1635924

McFee, J. K. (1961). *Preparation for art*. Wadsworth Publishing.

McFee, J. K. (1966). Society, art and education. In E. Mattil (Ed.), *A seminar in art education for research and curriculum development* (pp. 122–140). Pennsylvania State University.

McFee, J. K. (1975). Society and identity: A personal perspective. *Art Education*, *28*(7), 5–8.

McFee, J. K. (1998). *Cultural diversity and the structure of art education*. The National Art Education Association.

McFee, J. K. (1999). A position essay on art and culture in emerging art education. *Journal of Cultural Research in Art Education*, *17*(1), 35–38. 10.2458/jcrae.5061

McFee, J. K., & Degge, R. M. (1977). *Art, culture and environment*. Kendall/Hunt.

Merleau-Ponty, M. (1964). *The primacy of perception*. Northwestern University Press.

Morphy, H., & Perkins, M. (2006). Introduction. In *The anthropology of art: A reader*. Blackwell Publishing.

Schütz, A. (1945). On multiple realities. *Philosophy and Phenomenological Research*, *5*(4), 533–576.

Svasek, M. S. (2007). *The anthropology art and cultural production*. Pluto Press.

Vygotsky, L. S. (1978). *Mind in society: The development of higher psychological processes*. Harvard University Press.

6

VISUAL LITERACY DEVELOPMENT THROUGH PICTUREBOOKS

The Contributions of John Warren Stewig

Geri A. Chesner

National Louis University

Biographical Sketch

John W. Stewig is an acclaimed author and educational scholar whose work centers on helping young people deliberately develop visual literacy skills through picturebooks. Stewig, an expert in language arts, children's literature, and the arts, attended the University of Wisconsin, Madison, where he received his BA in elementary education, MS, and his PhD in 1967. At the time, as an undergraduate working as an elementary education major, he was required to complete two art history courses, where he delightedly built up his experience and interest in teaching the arts. He reminisces fondly, stating it was a "looser time" as there was not a strong emphasis on testing, which allowed him to engage students extensively in the arts. Stewig served much of his career in higher education at the University of Wisconsin-Milwaukee as a professor of language arts and later at Carthage College as the founding director of the Center for Children's Literature. During that time and beyond, he educated and guided countless preservice teachers, graduate students, educators, and children in understanding the innate value of integrating drama, art, and literature into the curriculum.

To expose teachers to various design and art styles, Stewig was the founder of a well-received course at the university titled *Books and Pictures for the Young Child* which he held at the Milwaukee Art Museum. His students gained knowledge in and viewed picturebook illustration and design elements and visited galleries to view art that could have been antecedents to the illustrations. For example, his students compared the picturebook art

DOI: 10.4324/9781032651781-7

of Ludwig Bemelmans, author, and illustrator of the well-loved Madeline books, to that of artist Raoul Dufy, a French painter whose style includes similar aspects of line, color, and composition as that of Bemelmans (J. W. Stewig, personal communication, March 12, 2023). Much of Stewig's work with students and teachers he used for research purposes.

Not only dedicated to working with teachers, Stewig found great value in listening to and guiding children with whom he shared picturebooks. He facilitated field trips with area schools as teachers brought their students to the art museum. He supported young students' learning about picturebook art and design and how to view art while at the same time modeling for their teachers how to move into asking critical questions about the illustrations as a means of fostering visual literacy.

As an academic, Stewig actively engaged in and shared his research with numerous national and international organizations throughout his career that helped form the basis of his visual literacy theoretical guiding framework, including the International Visual Literacy Association, International Reading Association (as a member of the children's book award committee), American Library Association, Association for Childhood Education International, National Council of Teachers of English (serving as president and member of the standing committee on censorship). His active leadership and scholarly connections with experts in children's literature and professional relationships with numerous authors and illustrators greatly impacted his research and writing. It also benefitted educators as he invited esteemed authors and illustrators to the university and local conferences as a way to make them more accessible to children and teachers.

A distinct honor in children's literature, Stewig served first as a member and later as the chair in 1997 of the esteemed, long-standing Caldecott Award Selection Committee, established in 1938. Subsumed within the American Library Association, the Association of Library Services to Children convenes a committee made up of 14 members and one chair whose charge it is "to select from the books published the preceding year … the most distinguished American picture book for children" (Association for Library Services to Children, 2023, para 1). This award requires the committee to view the picturebooks as whole, multimodal objects where the emphasis is primarily the illustration; however, the other components of a book, the written text, and the overall design can be considered as well. In addition to being a picturebook scholar, Stewig authored several picturebooks; among them, his *Princess Florecita and the Iron Shoes: A Spanish Fairy Tale* received an Aesop Honor designation from the American Folklore Society.

Introduction

Do you have a favorite book from childhood? You most certainly remember the characters and probably the situations in which they found themselves, likely (and ultimately) finding their way successfully through those challenges. Maybe you connected powerfully with a character whose circumstances were similar to yours or whose characteristics mirrored your own. It may be a book where the setting and situation were unfamiliar but exciting and new, drawing you in like an adventure. You might remember where you were when you encountered those books. Maybe you were a young child and a loved one read the book to you several times, sharing the story and spending time pouring over the details in the illustrations and sharing a loving environment. Picturebooks are powerful and can make lasting impressions on us for many reasons. John W. Stewig's work endeavored to move children, teachers, and others beyond solely enjoying the story and describing the illustrations as "cute" or "colorful" but to see the inherent information and power in the visual elements.

Books in the United States published for children began including illustrations in the late eighteenth century. Over time, their deliberate design included visuals to engage, inform, and entertain young readers through more than just the text. Visuals, especially illustrations, serve as support for comprehending or deciphering the narrative, as well as pushing readers' imaginations further. Within the last five decades, picturebooks have become intelligently and skillfully designed and often complex multimodal art forms, supporting literacy and visual literacy development in young children.

The visual aspects of picturebooks have been investigated, critiqued, and lauded for decades in the United States; however, around the 1970s, illustration gained strong support within the academic world as being as important as the narrative. The result was the insurgence of various definitions of picturebooks. However, a commonly accepted definition of a picturebook is a 32-page book that contains words and illustrations in a complete design. It is

> an item of manufacture and a commercial product; a social, cultural, historic document; and foremost, an experience for a reader. As an art form, it hinges on the interdependence of pictures and words, on the simultaneous display of two facing pages, and on the drama of the turning page. (Bader, 1976, p. 1)

Although various definitions were highly debated, all hinged upon the assertion that the images were more than mere decoration and were also extolled as objects of art (Cianciolo, 1970; Evans, 1998; Marantz & Marantz, 1988; Sipe, 1998).

The Impact of Stewig's Work on the Field

In reviewing the life, work, and impact of John W. Stewig, it is helpful to follow the path he took in developing as a visual literacy proponent and scholar. Stewig began his career as an elementary teacher, dedicated to working with young children and their teachers, engaging them in reader response (Rosenblatt, 1978), and studying picturebooks to enhance children's literacy, understanding, and appreciation. His background and interest are grounded in the arts. Many of his published scholarly works center on teaching children about visual messages and learning about and responding to them through well-designed picturebooks. He felt it was imperative to work within classroom spaces with children to learn directly from them as they engaged in visual development, followed by reflecting and writing about their interactions and findings in his research. Stewig provided evidence that visual literacy can be developed and supported by teaching about and sharing visual texts with children, especially picturebooks. Stewig is among the most notable in bringing attention to the academic world that book illustration and design are essential teaching and learning tools in a highly visualized world that will only continue to demand having the skills to view, develop, and critique what we see.

Stewig published his extolled book *Looking at Picture Books* (1995), a thorough compilation that provides readers with a "conscious awareness of picture books ... with a possible outcome of becoming more discerning consumers of picture books" (p. xv) and to "gain an understanding themselves and share picture books more meaningfully with children so they can become more skilled observers" (p. xvi). Written in an accessible manner for all who may be interested in depth deep learning about the visual components of children's picturebooks, the content includes chapters on pictorial elements in art and illustration, including composition (the organization of illustration that conveys a message), common media utilized in picturebook illustration, book design elements, the influence of art movements on illustration, and appendices that include annotated bibliographies of books about art and artists, genres of literature commonly found in picturebook format and exemplary picturebooks. Another significant component is that Stewig includes sidenotes on almost every page, which provide strategies that include extensive further research and connections to other picturebooks. Some book reviewers lamented that there are only 12 colored plates in a separate section (Jellema, 1995). Stewig quickly points out that many do not understand the considerable expense of utilizing color prints within a book (J. W. Stewig, personal communication, March 12, 2023). However, this critique can be taken lightly, as most pages throughout the 269-page book include black-and-white reproductions of picture book illustration that exemplify the content shared.

Looking at Picturebooks was important when it was first published because it was one of the first that clearly and concisely delineated how art and design elements are intentionally designed and utilized within books for children and was written for educators and other interested adults. This influential publication continues to be a learning tool for teachers and researchers who use and study picturebooks today. Since 1995, it has been and still is in the Caldecott Committee handbook as one of the recommended books for members to read to further their knowledge of how illustration works in picturebooks to depict a complete art object. This longevity and accolade speak to the impact of Stewig's work in teaching about visual literacy and the foundation of art and visual semiotic development using children's picturebooks.

Stewig began publishing scholarly work related to children's literature and its facility for teaching literacy (verbal, written, movement, and visual), in the early 1970s. He wrote books such as *Spontaneous Drama: A Language Art* (1973), *Exploring Language with Children* (1974), and *Read to Write: Using Literature as a Springboard to Writing* (1975b). His edited monograph, *Using Literature in the Elementary Classroom* (Stewig & Sebesta, 1978), included a chapter he wrote, "Book Illustration: Key to Visual and Verbal Literacy," in which he shared a strategy for encouraging children to interact with illustrations by developing three skills: describe what you see, compare two different objects, and learn to determine and compare value through using a variety of materials such as variants of the same story and poetry to do so. This strategy formed the framework that guided his work in helping others teach and embrace visual literacy in educational contexts.

His first book for children, *Sending Messages* (1978), which includes photography by Richard D. Bradley, might be considered his first published work emphasizing visual literacy; however, this terminology was not specifically indicated. The content encourages young readers to think about how messages and ideas can be sent verbally, visually, and through movement and action. The theoretical underpinnings of this book's theme find their connection in semiotics, the study of signs and symbols (Kress & van Leeuwen, 1996), and Stewig demonstrates his desire to assist young readers in understanding the myriad ways humans can communicate messages through visual means.

The 1970s was a time when racism and sexism in materials for children were being examined, and Stewig engaged in "critical" visual literacy with picturebooks long before the term was conceived. Critical visual literacy analyzes the "socio-political consequences of semiotic choice in visual texts, and on reading against rather than reading with the visual text" (Newfield, 2011, p. 1). Stewig's interest in stereotypes in picturebook illustration is evident in his research, where he critically analyzed the illustrations in 154 picturebooks to determine the occurrence of sexism as portrayed in women's roles, sharing the results in *Girls Grow Up to Be Mommies: A Study of Sexism in Children's Literature* (Stewig & Higgs, 1973). He completed a follow-up study, resulting in *Sexism in Picturebooks: What Progress?* (Stewig & Knipfel, 1975) in which he found some, but little positive change was evident, with males still being cast as the main characters in most of the analyzed books. MacCann and Richard (1973) were researchers who also explored problems they found in picturebooks, including stereotypes in illustration and graphic elements.

Theoretical Underpinnings and Stewig's Contributions

To understand the association between picture books and visual literacy development, a definition must be shared. Twenty-first-century schools' definition was adapted from John Debes' (1969a) early definition and states that being visually literate is "the ability to interpret, recognize, appreciate and understand the information presented through visible actions, objects, and symbols, natural or man-made" (Finley, 2014, para 2). Like others, Stewig (1986) grounded his research and work on Debes' fundamental definition. Fransecky and Debes (1972) estimate that the focus on visual literacy development in education for young people began around 1966. The interest and research began to accelerate after the first National Conference on Visual Literacy in Rochester, New York, in 1969, where papers and presentations focused on topics across disciplines and many emphasized implications for education from elementary to college level, including teacher education.

During these early years, there were two significant areas focused on using images and visuals with young people. First were educators and researchers who espoused the use of visuals and media (such as television) as learning tools through photography and audiovisual instruction (Debes, 1969b). Stewig (1988) agreed with this understanding and engaged in research of this type as he investigated fifth-grade students' preference to film to help teachers avoid choosing them for classroom use based only on content but to capitalize too, on student interest to help make learning more effective. Other research of the time emphasized using visuals in disciplines and content areas, such as social studies (Elwell & Hess, 1979), to develop media literacy (Debes, 1969b), to support remedial readers (Barley, 1969), for English as second language learners and newcomers

(Fransecky, 1969), and for reading instruction and developing comprehension skills (Kossack & Bader, 1980). Research was being published in audiovisual and literacy-related journals such as the *English Language Arts* journal, *Reading Teacher*, and those published by the National Council of Teachers of English. This area of study at the time emphasized educationally related components of utilizing visuals from early childhood to high school within the curriculum.

Throughout his life, Stewig engaged in utilizing and sharing his artistic talents, as well as appreciating and teaching about them. In his personal life, he served as the organist in his church and dabbled in painting. His art education background led to his interest in research with young people engaged in aesthetic experiences with art in picturebooks and claims, "what goes on in the art world affects what goes on in picture book art" (1995, p. xvii). Another area that provided a historical framework for using picturebooks for teaching visual literacy skills comes from scholars identifying books as art and aesthetic objects (Sipe, 2002). Primarily in art and art education, they emphasized encouraging young people in aesthetics and looking closely at and appreciating art and illustration. Stewig engaged in research of this type, completing a study to determine young students' preference in pictures related to art and design elements of color, shape, proportion, detail, and space (1975a). Later, he continued his emphasis on art and visual literacy development in a year-long study in two first-grade classrooms exploring students' oral response to visuals to determine how visual strategies taught impacted the response of first-grade students in an urban and a suburban school (Stewig, 1994). In this study, Stewig taught weekly lessons in both schools using picturebook illustrations, reproductions of artist's paintings, and film emphasizing content on visual elements, artists, illustrators, and awards such as the Caldecott Medal. He modeled how to respond to the visuals and engaged the students in writing and group discussions. Key findings from his study showed that children (especially children in urban schools) who are engaged in responding to art produce large amounts of language and high levels of participation. Stewig suggests that using art, including picturebook illustration and other artworks, teaching about them, and emphasizing rich discussion, are productive means for integrating art, especially in schools where cuts to arts curricula continue to occur.

Historically, the wave of research and ideas directly impacting children's visual literacy was not always explicitly stated or identified as such. One possible reason is that visual literacy is a growing and diverse area of study in a wide range of education-related disciplines, including language, library science, art, and psychology (Serafini, 2017). Another reason may include the rise of multiliteracy frameworks within literacy scholarship overall.

Today not only is the academic focus on general literacy, but also the many forms that humans develop proficiency in, including digital and media literacy, audio literacy, and spatial literacy, to name a few. Skills of communicating, creating, and analyzing are needed to engage functionally in these multiliteracies, which is also true of visual literacy.

Important to note as well, visual literacy had not traditionally been explicitly taught in most teacher preparation programs at its genesis. Today, however, general literacy education is viewed as multimodal and all-encompassing, including verbal and visual components that learners need to develop. As evidence of this, the National Council of Teachers of English/International Reading Association's joint current standards for English language arts include standards that point to various literacies using and creating visuals (NCTE/IRA, 1996). However, more work is needed to help teachers and others see the importance of visual literacy development in education.

Visual Literacy and Picturebooks

Stewig can be credited as one of the scholars who examined the value of the marriage of text and image and its impact on children's development of visual literacy skills. However, it is beneficial to know a bit of the history of visual literacy and its connection to reading-viewing picturebooks, including other prolific scholars, along with Stewig, who moved this idea forward. Ken and Sylvia Marantz's book *The Art of Children's Picture Books: A Selective Reference Guide* (1988) emphasized that the picturebook is primarily a visual object and helped to establish ways of looking at them. Nodelman's (1988) book, *Words About Pictures: The Narrative Art of Children's Picturebooks*, is a seminal work that draws on literary, semiotics, art history, and aesthetic research, and he credits visual literacy scholar Rudolf Arnheim's impact on his ideas. A highlight of picturebook study and visual literacy would not be complete without emphasizing the extensive work of Lawrence W. Sipe, whose prolific research on children's picturebook response to the narrative and visual and design elements began in the late 1990s. Stewig and Sipe, both educators first, emphasize the visual-verbal reading of picturebooks urging teachers to explore both sign systems with their students to "encourage this diversity of interpretation (to) facilitate their students' abilities to integrate visual and verbal information" (Sipe, 2008, p. 232).

Bringing Visual Literacy to Educators

As a teacher educator and academic scholar, one of Stewig's goals was to help adults and teachers integrate visuals into the curriculum and utilize them for comprehension, analysis, and appreciation. One way he did this was through teaching resource kits he created for teachers to utilize in literacy and art curriculums (1987, 1991). Each illustrator kit includes four posters depicting images from the illustrator's work (Ezra Jack Keats, Nonny Hogrogian, Marcia Brown, Trina Schart Hyman, and others) and includes an introduction defining visual literacy ("the ability to really look with perception") to assist teachers to work with children to "embark on an adventure to enhanced seeing" (p. 4). This adventure is realized as he includes suggested activities for using the illustrators' work to nudge children's visual literacy growth and involve them in making art, along with information about the illustrator and comments from critics about the art and design of the books portrayed. There are beneficial features in each kit that include information for teachers related to the books' genres, illustration techniques (i.e. crosshatching, color, composition, typeface), and recommended experiences for children before, during, and after the study of each print. His dedication to supporting teachers in learning about visual literacy is especially exemplified by the kits and his accomplishment discussed earlier, the Books and Pictures for the Young Child University course he designed and taught in the Milwaukee Art Museum, emphasizing art and illustration in picturebooks for teachers and using them with their students. His dedication to spreading the importance of visual literacy as a part of learning for educators is exemplified through these professional accomplishments.

Stewig's Writing for Children

Stewig believes in teaching about visuals and literature with teachers and adults, but first and foremost, he is passionate about sharing quality picturebooks with children. His passion for folk literature and alphabet books led him to retell and write 13 books, publishing, to name a few: *The Fisherman and His Wife* (1988) and *Stone Soup* (1991), both illustrated by Margaret Tomes; *Clever Gretchen* (2000), illustrated by Patricia Wittmann; *The Animals Watched: An Alphabet Book* (2007), illustrated by Rosanne Litzinger and semi-autobiographical, *Making Plum Jam* (2002), illustrated by Kevin O'Malley. Stewig's *Princess Florecita and the Iron Shoes: A Spanish Fairytale* (1995), illustrated by K. Wendy Popp, was awarded an Aesop honor designation from the American Folklore Society, an organization that supports and encourages the study of folklore and advocates for the continued study and teaching of folklore. In Stewig's beloved fairytale retelling of *El rey durmiente en su lecho* (The Sleeping King in His Bed), the strong and determined female heroine makes a long journey in iron shoes that will wear out when she finds the prince she is to save, and, of course, live happily ever after. This retelling has similar elements to Sleeping Beauty and Snow White; however, it is the prince who is in an enchanted sleep that Princess Florecita must awaken. It is a delightful, well-told tale that is in keeping with Stewig's dedication to emphasizing critical literacy.

Stewig espouses "Picturebooks have been an important part of my life" and are "containers for many visual delights" (Candlewick Press, 2013). He points out that viewers of picturebooks, and essentially all art, need to have a basic knowledge of the terminology of visuals and how they work (and how they work together with text), including how to read an image to be able to move beyond just the literal interpretation. He advocates that children can learn about illustration and book design and thus develop visual literacy not through didactic means but through guided looking and looking again. Teachers and librarians are responsible for exploring the art in picturebooks with them, allowing the discovery of new insights and "delights" in what Stewig recalls hearing defined as the "child's first art gallery". Although still not emphasized to the degree in which he wishes it was integrated into the curriculum today, Stewig is pleased with the growth in using picturebooks beyond merely as tools for learning to read and states, "If when I started, I would say, 'I am going to talk about picturebook endpapers (the pages before the story starts),' they would have said I am crazy!" (J. W. Stewig, personal communication, March 12, 2023).

Conclusion: Picturebooks as the First Step to Visual Literacy

Stewig's early contributions to visual literacy, especially as it relates to children's development of the ability to read and interpret the art and design inherent in picturebooks, continue to be valuable for children, their adults, and education today. His dedication to guiding teachers and young people to learn the language of the visual elements and design of picture-books helped to set the groundwork for others to expand their under-standings. As is the norm with children's book writers and illustrators, professors, and scholars, Stewig has shared his life's academic work for study by others. He donated his professional papers to Arizona State University at Tempe, curated and stored within the Child Drama Manuscript Collection with other playwrights, university professors, authors, managing designers, K-12 art specialists, puppeteers, arts advocates, and directors. A collection of written and illustrative materials related to 10 of the 13 picturebooks he published are at the Kerlan Collection of Children's Literature at the University of Minnesota.

Researchers and educators have used his work to inform their studies, as evidenced in McAdams' study done in 2015, furthering Stewig's investiga-tion of female characters depicted in children's literature. Adukia et al.

(2023) did as well in their working paper entitled, "What We Teach about Race and Gender: Representation in Images and Text of Children's Books," as they evaluated both gender and race in picturebooks. To determine Stewig's impact on the foundations of visual literacy development through the use of picturebooks, one only needs to do a scholarly Internet search to find studies that currently reference Stewig's work on picturebook design and illustration in specific children's books (Çelik, 2022), connecting art in museums with picturebook art (Lehman et al. 2021) and encouraging young children to view design elements such as picturebook case covers, endpaper, orientation, size, and font, (McNair, 2021) to name just a few. There is no way to know just how many Caldecott award-winning books since 1995 have been analyzed and ultimately chosen as winners based on the committee members' reading and using Stewig's *Looking at Picture Books*!

Within the last two decades, picturebook authors, illustrators, and designers' work has progressed with societal changes and more deliberately reflects socio-cultural underpinnings. Postmodern picturebooks, where the text and illustrations are not as supportive of one another as in the past, and multimodal texts, those that include a variety of modes for comprehension and appreciation, including graphic novels and digital texts (Serafini, 2011), require readers to use knowledge of how images work both with and independently of the narrative. In addition, for deep interpretation and understanding, reader-viewers must bring their schema about the world and how it works to the task of reading and viewing. Leading students to analyze visuals beyond illustration to make meaning, research on the design of books and their paratextual (Higonet, 1990) and peritextual elements (Pantaleo, 2022) has flourished, for example, investigating endpapers (Chesner, 2019; Duran & Bosch, 2011; Sipe & McGuire, 2006), page breaks (Sipe & Brightman, 2009) and other design elements.

Current research on picturebooks and visual literacy includes nurturing students to use critical visual literacy to interpret postmodern multimodal texts (Kim & Serrano, 2017; Papen, 2020). Critical content analysis and systemic-functional semiotics of picturebook illustration are extolled and modeled in writing by Short and Painter in *Critical Content Analysis of Visual Images in Books for Young People: Reading Images* (Johnson et al., 2019), with urgings to continue this mode of analysis and teach students to engage. These advanced ways of viewing call for a well-educated, well-rounded reader-viewer, and the seminal work done by Stewig and others in understanding the basics of how visual semiotics work in picturebooks are the frameworks that helped scaffold and build this field. Research on visual literacy and children's picturebooks continues to evolve amid the various literacies essential for success today.

Visual literacy development begins the moment we are born into the world and explore our surroundings and continues developing throughout our lives in more sophisticated ways as visuals and technology abound. Starting early, in natural and enjoyable ways, children develop the necessary skills to be visually literate through well-developed picturebooks designed for them. Stewig's career in furthering visual literacy demonstrates, "Picturebooks are highly sophisticated aesthetic objects, worthy of study and research by readers and viewers of all ages" (Sipe, 2012, p. 4). There is still much to investigate and learn about how picturebooks and all literacies, especially visual literacy, are connected. The research of John Warren Stewig and other esteemed children's literature and picturebook researchers are foundational works that have and will continue to guide future researchers and those interested in the marriage between visual literacy and children's development.

References

Adukia, A., Eble, A., Harrison, E., Runesha, H. B., & Szasz, T. (2023). *What we teach about race and gender: Representations in images and text of children's books.* NBER Working Paper 29123. National Bureau of Economic Research. http://www.nber.org/papers/w29123

Association for Library Services to Children. (2023). *Randolph Caldecott medal.* https://www.ala.org/alsc/awardsgrants/bookmedia/caldecott

Bader, B. (1976). *American picturebooks from Noah's ark to the beast within.* Macmillan Publishing Company.

Barley, S. D. (1969). *A visual literacy approach to developmental and remedial reading* (ED057583) ERIC.

Candlewick Press. (2013). *John Warren Stewig talks about the art of the picture book.* https://vimeo.com/71281160

Çelik, N. (2022). An analysis of the fable of Frederick by Leo Lionni with a semiotic perspective. *Turkophone, 9*(1), 18–31. 10.55246/turkophone.1035227

Chesner, G. (2019). Engaging with endpapers: A visual literacy experience upon opening a picturebook. In D. M. Baylen (Ed.), *Dreams and inspirations: The book of selected readings 2018* (pp. 13–31). Carrollton, GA: International Visual Literacy Association.

Cianciolo, P. (1970). *Literature for children: Illustrations in children's books.* Dubuque, IA: Wm. C. Brown Company.

Debes, J. L. (1969a). The loom of visual literacy: An overview. *Audiovisual Instruction, 14*(8), 25–27.

Debes, J. L. (1969b). Some hows and whys of visual literacy. *Educational Screen and Audiovisual Guide, 34*, 14–15.

Duran, T., & Bosch, E. (2011). Before and after the picturebook frame: A typology of endpapers. *New Review of Children's Literature and Librarianship, 17*(2), 122–143. DOI: 10.1080/13614541.2011.624927

Elwell, W. C. & Hess, M. (1979). Visual literacy and the social studies. *The Social Studies, 70*(1), 27–31.

Evans, D. (1998). Picture book, picture book, on the wall ... *Horn Book Magazine*, *74*(2), 258–262.

Finley, T. (2014, February 19). Common core in action: 10 visual literacy strategies. *Edutopia*. https://www.edutopia.org/blog/ccia-10-visual-literacy-strategies-todd-finley

Fransecky, R. B. (1969). Visual literacy and teaching the disadvantaged. *Audiovisual Instruction, 16*, 27–31.

Fransecky, R. B., & Debes, J. L. (1972). *Visual literacy: A way to learn—a way to teach.* Washington, DC: Association for Educational Communications and Technology.

Higonnet, M. R. (1990). The playground of the Peritext. *Children's Literature Association Quarterly, 15*(2), 47–49.

Jellema, M. E. (1995). Professional materials: Reading Horizons. *A Journal of Literacy and Language Arts, 36*(2). https://Scholarworks.wmich.edu/reading_horizons/vol36/iss2/7

Johnson, H., Mathis, J., & Short, K. (2019). *Critical content analysis of visual images in books for young people: Reading images.* Routledge.

Kim, H. Y., & Serrano, A. (2017). Enhancing critical visual literacy through illustrations in a picturebook. *WOW Stories, 5*(3), 13–27.

Kossack, S. W., & Bader, B. (1980, November 12–15). *Visual literacy: Foundation for comprehension.* [Paper presentation]. Southeastern Regional Conference of the International Reading Association, 6 h Annual Meeting, Norfolk, VA, United States.

Kress, G., & van Leeuwen, T. (1996). *Reading images: The grammar of visual design.* Routledge.

Lehman, M., Phillips, S. M., & Williams, R. (2021). Beyond visual literacy: Listening, speaking, reading and writing in the art museum. In L. A. Henry & N. A. Stahl (Eds.), *Literacy across the community: Research, praxis and trends.* Taylor and Francis.

MacCann, D., & Richard, O. (1973). *The child's first books: A critical study of pictures and texts.* H. W. Wilson Company.

Marantz, S., & Marantz, K. (1988). *The art of children's picture books: A selective reference guide.* Garland.

McAdams, J. (2015). *Portrayals and presence of adult female characters in children's picture books: A content analysis of bestsellers from the past five years.* 10.17615/06pv-6690

McNair, J. C. (2021). Surprise, surprise! Exploring dust jackets, case covers, and endpapers in picture books to support comprehension. *Reading Teacher, 74*(4), 363–373.

National Council of Teachers of English and International Reading Association. (1996). *Standards for the English language arts.* NCTE/IRA. https://ncte.org/resources/standards/ncte-ira-standards-for-the-english-language-arts/

Newfield, D. (2011). From visual literacy to critical visual literacy: An analysis of educational materials. *English Teaching: Practice and Critique, 10*(1), 81–94.

Nodelman, P. (1988). *Words about pictures: The narrative art of children's picturebooks.* The University of Georgia Press.

Pantaleo, S. (2022). An investigation of the functionality of peritextual elements in graphic novels. *Children's Literature in Education, 53*(4), 507–525.

Papen, U. (2020). Using picture books to develop critical visual literacy in primary schools: Challenges of a dialogic approach. *Literacy, 54*(1), 3–10.

Rosenblatt, L. (1978). *The reader, the text, the poem: The transactional theory of the literary work.* Southern Illinois University Press.

Serafini, F. (2011). Expanding perspectives for comprehending visual images in multimodal texts. *Journal of Adolescent and Adult Literacy*, *54*(5), 342–350.

Serafini, F. (2017, February 27). *Visual literacy*. In Oxford research encyclopedia of education. 10.1093/acrefore/9780190264093.013.19

Sipe, L. R. (1998). How picture books work: A semiotically framed theory of text-picture relationships. *Children's Literature in Education*, *29*(2), 97–108.

Sipe, L. R. (2002). Picturebooks as aesthetic objects. *Literacy Teaching and Learning*, *6*(1), 23–42.

Sipe, L. R. (2008). *Storytime: Young children's literary understanding in the classroom*. Teacher's College Press.

Sipe, L. R. (2012). Revisiting the relationships between text and pictures. *Children's Literature in Education*, *43*, 4–21.

Sipe, L. R., & Brightman, A. E. (2009). Young children's interpretations of page breaks in contemporary picture storybooks. *Journal of Literacy Research*, *41*(1), 68–103.

Sipe, L. R., & McGuire, C. E. (2006). Picturebook endpapers: Resources for literary and aesthetic interpretation. *Children's Literature in Education*, *37*(4), 291–304.

Stewig, J. (1978). *Sending messages*. Houghton Mifflin.

Stewig, J., & Higgs, M. (1973). Girls grow up to be mommies: A study of sexism in children's literature. *School Library Journal*, *19*(5), 44–49.

Stewig, J. W. (1973). *Spontaneous drama: A language art*. Merrill.

Stewig, J. W. (1974). *Exploring language with children*. Merrill.

Stewig, J. W. (1975a). Assessing visual elements preferred in pictures by young children. *Reading Improvement*, *12*(2), 94.

Stewig, J. W. (1975b). *Read to write: Using literature as a springboard to writing*. Hawthorn Books.

Stewig, J. W. (1986). *Visual and verbal literacy*. Paper presented at the National Council of Teachers of English annual meeting, San Antonio.

Stewig, J. W. (1987). *Reading pictures: Marcia Brown*. Child Graphics Press.

Stewig, J. W. (1988). Children's preferences in film. *Journal of Visual, Verbal Languaging*, *8*(1), 74–78.

Stewig, J. W. (1991). *Reading pictures: Trina Schart Hyman*. Child Graphics Press.

Stewig, J. W. (1994). First graders talk about paintings. *Journal of Educational Research*, *87*(5), 309–316.

Stewig, J. W. (1995). *Looking at picture books*. Wisconsin: Highsmith Press.

Stewig, J. W., & Knipfel, M. L. (1975). Sexism in picture books: What progress? *Elementary School Journal*, *76*(3), 151–155.

Stewig, J. W., & Sebesta, S. (1978). *Using literature in the elementary classroom*. National Council of Teachers of English.

7

ABIGAIL HOUSEN

Visual Thinking from Museums to the Classroom

Michele Colandene

George Mason University

Biographical Sketch

Abigail Housen's journey to understanding aesthetic development began as a child touring local art museums. Abigail's mother was an art historian and often brought Abigail to the museums where she worked. Abigail walked the halls as her mother presented to audiences at the museum, marveling at the artwork. She described the enjoyment she gained each time she encountered works of art. As a young child, Abigail Housen had opportunities to develop an understanding and appreciation of art. With her mother's guidance, she could create a nuanced account of the artwork she viewed. However, she noticed her experiences and art knowledge were unique when she attended college.

Abigail attended Wellesley College in Massachusetts, where she encountered art appreciation diversity among her peers. As an art patron herself, Abigail questioned why some naive art viewers grow into fine art connoisseurs while others remained unsophisticated in their understanding of art (Housen, 1999). She then began her career as a research and production assistant for WGBH Television in Boston. She worked on a research project for the Children's Television Workshop and Harvard University to understand the artistic elements of the programming that engaged viewers (Housen, 1983). Shortly after this experience, Abigail Housen began working with Harvard University as a doctoral student in education.

In her early research, Abigail Housen charted the physical movement of museum visitors in an Impressionist art gallery in the Boston Museum of Fine Arts. After charting the art patrons' movement throughout the

DOI: 10.4324/9781032651781-8

exhibition, she interviewed them about their experiences. The findings of this study indicated that path types differed based on education level, age, amount of overall time spent in the museum, their reflection time on the artwork, and time they engaged in reading labels or written placards. Subsequent studies identified not only a path type of the art viewers but a level of art viewing, which Abigail Housen called aesthetic levels of awareness and understanding (Housen, 1983). In her dissertation, she developed a manual for analyzing art patrons' experiences that identified their level of aesthetic knowledge. Using the framework from her dissertation, *Eye of the Beholder: Measuring Aesthetic Development*, she and her colleagues have collectively interviewed more than 6,000 art patrons uncovering their levels of aesthetic development. The research team asked the patrons basic questions, such as: 'what is going on in the painting?' and 'is there anything else you see?'. This allowed the art viewers to provide stream-of-consciousness thinking and reflect on their art-viewing thought processes. This process became the foundation of the Visual Thinking Strategies (VTS) project, a collaborative effort with colleague Philip Yenawine, and various art museums to provide visual thinking education to the public. Abigail Housen died in 2020, aged 75.

Introduction

Wandering through the corridors of a museum, Abigail Housen became fascinated by patrons' reactions as they viewed the artwork. She wondered why some art viewers seemed bored or complacent while others seemed exhilarated and energized by the works (Housen, 1999). As a cognitive psychologist, artist, and teacher, Housen wanted to understand the museum goers' experience, and more importantly, she wanted to know their thoughts about the art they viewed. This would be a challenging task. Aesthetic experiences involve more than simple viewing and thinking; they involve personal judgments combined with "sensations or thoughtful feelings" (Housen, 1983, p. 4). Exploration and identification of individual aesthetic experiences would require a unique measurement method, which became the driving force behind her research.

The researchers on Housen's team used two distinct methods for understanding the data they collected. They identified the reflections into "thought Domains," which identified broad statements regarding the art, and then "Categories," which were different distinctions within the domains (Housen, 1999, p. 7). The data obtained through these specific interviews supported her theory that visual thinking occurs in a five-stage developmental process from superficial art viewing to a sophisticated comprehension of artwork (Housen, 1999). Philip Yenawine, a long-time colleague described visual thinking as a way to make meaning from imagery (Yenawine, 1997).

Theoretical Background: Aesthetic Stages of Development

Housen and her team (1983, 1999, 2001–2002) interviewed museum patrons at the Museum of Modern Art (MoMA) in New York City while they viewed artworks created by Pablo Picasso, Henri Matisse, and various other modern artists. The stages of aesthetic development emerged through these thousands of interviews. Beginning viewers discussed artwork from their personal perspective, whereas more experienced viewers talked about the materials used to make the paintings and their overall messages communicated.

The stages begin with a novice understanding called Accountive, a simple listing of things seen in a piece of art. In the second stage, Constructive, a viewer can develop a framework to explain a work of art using information from placards and museum brochures. Om stage three, Classifying, viewers can classify the artwork into genres and understand artists' choices due to the time period and place it was created. In the last two stages, Interpretive and Re-Creative, viewers can view the work of art and develop new nuanced understandings with each new encounter.

To illustrate how these levels emerged, I provide examples of the possible comments associated with each stage using a computer-generated example of modern art (Figure 7.1). These examples are not direct quotations but theorized responses based on excerpts of data from Housen's research (1983, 1999, 2001–2002). Using computer-generated imagery allowed me to circumvent issues with artistic copyright while still providing the reader with visual support for understanding the stages of aesthetic development. While reading through the transcripts of Housen's dissertation and many publications, I synthesized patterns of responses museum patrons made while viewing different works of art. The patterns of responses and Housen's thick descriptions of their meaning supported my development of the possible responses to the computer-generated image. As stated earlier, Housen's initial research took place in the MoMA, and the participants in her studies viewed modern masterpieces by Picasso and Matisse. Many paintings art patrons viewed depicted human emotions created in a cubist style. Therefore, I prompted the computer program Dall-E Open Artificial Intelligence (AI) to create a cubist-style image containing human subjects and interactions.

FIGURE 7.1 Colandene, M. (2023). Figures in cubist style painting. Generated by Dall-E open AI.

Stage I, Accountive

People became storytellers in the first stage or level of aesthetic viewing, and the painting became the story. Observations provided basic observable details combined with their personal feelings and thoughts. Using Figure 7.1 to illustrate this point, art patrons at this level might say things such as, "I see both men and women in this painting … they might be a family" and "They don't have any expressions." The judgments made about the piece were based on what the viewer knows or feels. Housen states that some comments seem to "unfold like a drama" (Housen, 1999, p. 9). The key tenets of this stage rest on the viewer's observations, preferences, assumptions, and evaluations (Housen 1983, p. 146).

The details the viewers described at this level were all from a distinctly individualistic perspective and almost imaginative. In Housen's work, the viewer discusses specific aspects of the art object while leaving out others. Using the example in Figure 7.1, art viewers might point out that the "stained glass" style of the image used an abundance of blue-colored shapes yet ignored how the shapes created a narrative for the piece. Without any mental framework for understanding the artwork, viewers' personal accounts combined with imaginative explanations shape their understanding of the art.

Stage II, Constructive

Philip Yenawine, Abigail's long-time colleague, described this level of aesthetic development as factually driven. The viewer of the piece may now have some background knowledge of the artist's life and works, and they are eager to share these facts with others (P. Yenawine, personal communication, March 20, 2023). Unfortunately, at this stage, the facts understood by the viewer often have little to do with the actual painting in question. Much like in stage I, the viewers still approach understanding the art pieces from a personal perspective, driven by their observations and assumptions. However, the evaluation of the painting is judged by how well its physical appearance and medium reflect what is seen in the real world.

Viewers build a mental schema that supports the facts they have gained and aligns with their social, moral, and emotional perceptions of the world. This is especially evident in viewers trying to connect abstract art, including humans, to the physical world. One comment about Figure 7.1 might include, "The hair on the person in the middle is blue, and that is possible, but there are no facial features, no eyes, nose or mouth." This conflicting evidence propels the viewer to dig more deeply to understand the artist's choices. The viewer builds a framework for classifying and understanding the image, and in the process, they begin to see the craftsmanship and physical properties of the piece. "I like the texture," "It must have taken a long time to paint," and "It must be worth a lot of money" (Housen, 1983, p. 147).

Stage III, Classifying

In this stage of aesthetic development, the viewer becomes a diagnostician of the artwork and views the artwork as a puzzle that can be decoded and categorized. The viewer looks for clues within the image to uncover the underlying meaning. The viewer's goal is to uncover the messages beneath the surface of the painting and to correctly classify the piece into the historical periods and genre of painting style (Housen, 1983). For example, a viewer might approach Figure 7.1 by describing the use of form, line, and shape to illustrate the artist's intentional nod to the cubist painting style.

The classifying viewer can dig deeply between the layers of paint on the canvas to speculate on its intended meaning. They can discern the complex layers of meaning and believe all artwork can be rationally categorized (Housen, 1999, p. 6). In other words, classifying viewers understand the brush strokes were intentional on the part of the artist and his work was influenced by the history, politics, and socioeconomic climate in which he or she was living. All of these factors contribute to the classification of the pieces viewed, except the personal feelings and thoughts of the viewer.

Stage IV, Interpretive

At the interpretive stage, the viewer can take their classification knowledge from stage III and connect this to personal emotions and feelings. In stage III, Housen (1983) states that refrain from including personal feelings to categorize the piece. However, in the interpretive stage, art patrons revisit their personal feelings in connection to the classification. At this stage of aesthetic development, viewers understand that they can only classify and explain the artist's actions up to a point. They understand that not all information presented in the artwork can be explained; it simply must be enjoyed. They intertwine the meaning of the piece with their own emotions. Some comments at this level regarding Figure 7.1 might address the thickness of the lines surrounding the figures. For example, a viewer might say: "The images are all outlined in black lines, which is kind of dramatic."

Using knowledge and background of the piece, viewers use feelings and emotions to situate the symbolism of the artist's abstractions. They also know that these interpretations are subject to change with subsequent viewings. The interpretive viewer can classify the pieces he or she views, but they also know that art is created to elicit an experience for the viewer. Each time the interpretive viewer encounters a familiar piece of art, they reconnect with feelings and emotions. They use these personal emotions to remind themselves of the artist's use of color, symbolism, shape, and form. In short, artwork can only be understood through the personal and emotional connections the viewer experiences.

Stage V, Re-Creative

At this stage, the viewer is knowledgeable about the artist and his works but approaches the image like seeing an "old friend" for the first time in years. Familiarity and high regard are present, but new pathways are opened to see new transformations. Art viewers approach the paintings with a child-like wonder, opening up new possibilities and discoveries (Housen, 1999, p. 8).

In other words, I guess what I'm doing, in a way, is what I try to do when I look at paintings that I don't know about, which is to – you can't do it completely, but try to set aside your preconceptions and judgments and look at it as though you're seeing it for the first time. (Housen, 1983, p. 162)

The recreative viewer approaches the familiar artwork with a new set of eyes. They approach the pieces as if they have never seen them before. This allows the viewer to create new experiences with a familiar piece of art. In the process, they develop new insights about the image, developing new emotions and feelings. Housen writes, "I suppose viewing good artwork is like building a puzzle. They tell as much about the observer as about the painter" (1983, p. 162).

Art viewers understand not only the facts about the piece of art, but understand that art is subjective and interpretation rests entirely in the eyes of the beholder. Most importantly, personal connections with a piece of art can change over time. As we grow and engage in new social environments, we develop an alternative lens through which we see the world. The recreative viewer of art understands that this can change his connection with the artwork he or she views and redirect his thoughts and emotions.

Development of Visual Thinking Strategies

All of Abigail Housen's early research was focused on the art viewers' visual thinking as they interacted with artwork. However, this work would uncover surprising results. Most of the thousands of interviews her team collected and analyzed revealed a superficial and naive understanding of the artwork. That means that most art patrons were in the accountive or categorizing stage of aesthetic development. Additionally, Housen (2001–2002) found that art viewers did not necessarily move to a higher level of visual literacy with multiple viewings of artwork. Therefore, she and her colleagues developed an intervention that combined art viewing with discussion to support visual thinking transfer, called Visual Thinking Strategies (VTS). The development of VTS strategies began as a way to meet the novice art viewer at their level of aesthetic understanding and support their construction of new ideas with art. Housen's levels of aesthetic development provide a way to understand an individual's level of visual fluency, but this is not a static or fixed position. With VTS thinking strategies Housen and her research teams uncovered a way to enhance visual thinking and learning.

Visual Thinking Strategies (VTS)

Using a constructivist approach to learning, VTS is an instructor-led art discussion mainly directed by the participants' responses (Hailey et al., 2015). Housen (2001–2002) developed strategies through her research focused on critical thinking about art and all types of visual materials using three basic questions: what is happening in the picture?; what do you see that makes you say that?; what else can you find? (Duke & Housen, 1998; Housen, 1983, 1992, 2000, 2007). Although these three questions seem simplistic, they were developed over years of research and refinement to meet the viewer at their stage or level of aesthetic development. Growth and development that improves aesthetic thinking require regular and continued artwork exploration in collaborative spaces and personal reflection (P. Yenawine, personal communication, March 20, 2023). To reach educators in museums and public schools, Housen and Yenawine developed a non-profit organization called Visual Understanding in Education (VUE) to educate the public on and improve aesthetic development. This organization is still actively educating teachers worldwide under the name of VTS.org.

The open-ended questions listed above allow for discussion and visual thinking. When an art viewer thinks they have seen everything in a painting, the researcher/VTS teacher pushes them to look again more closely. It is important to note that these open-ended questions were intended for social or group interactions. Through discussion and multiple viewings of artwork, individuals constructively build a deeper understanding of the image in question and can move to a higher level of visual fluency.

As patrons engaged in group discussions about the art pieces they viewed, a kind of visual thinking and learning took place, which Housen (2002) called a "critical thinking studio" (p. 101). Critical thinking studio and social interaction with peers and experts promoted careful observation, evaluation, synthesis, justification, and speculation of the artwork being viewed. The opportunity to discuss what was seen and to learn in a social setting was instrumental in developing critical thinking skills concerning visuals of all kinds (Housen, 2002). The technique was soon seen as a possible way to facilitate critical thinking in the classroom, thus, helping students make deeper connections to content information where visuals were commonly used (Housen & Yenawine, 2001; Yenawine, 2013).

Connection of Housen's Aesthetic Levels of Development to Education

In a school setting, students develop skills and knowledge that can be applied and reused in other aspects of their life. For example, students who learn to calculate percentages in school can use this skill to figure out their

GPA or calculate how much money they might save on a 40% off sale. This skill of transferring knowledge will help students succeed in other subjects and life in general. The VTS framework develops critical thinking and helps students to transfer knowledge from one area to another (Housen, 2001–2002; Yenawine, 2013).

In the 1990s, VTS was researched in a longitudinal study that followed two cohorts of elementary students in Byron, Minnesota (Hailey et al., 2015). Housen's aesthetic stages of development protocol (1983) were used to understand the student's level of aesthetic understanding before receiving VTS education and then at the end of each school year to measure aesthetic developmental growth. A control group was also measured using Housen's protocol (1983) at the beginning of the study and yearly to measure gains in visual fluency unrelated to the intervention. Students participating in the study's experimental group received approximately 30 hours of VTS discussion with various images and art pieces. All of the students receiving VTS instruction increased their aesthetic development by at least one stage. That is, most of the students were at level one, or basic visual literacy entering the study: accountive aesthetic stage of development, and by the end of the study, all the students in the experimental group were found to be at the constructive aesthetic stage three, or emergent visual fluency of development or higher (Housen, 2002). In contrast, students in the control group did not make as many observations or inferences with visual evidence. Their basic level of visual literacy did not change much from the beginning of the study (Hailey et al., 2015).

As students are given opportunities to view visual representations critically, they learn to develop visual thinking from basic memorization of information they view to constructing visual knowledge. In a recent study, VTS strategies were taught to a group of second-grade students in a New Jersey public school (Scully, 2020). The year-long study found significant gains in students' abilities to write and reflect compared to the control group. Students, especially those for whom English was a second language, made considerable gains in inferences based on what was observed in the images they viewed (Scully, 2020).

Observation and inference-making are essential skills for students to develop as they learn to interpret various visual representations. Following practice and multiple discussions surrounding a specific visual, students may apply this knowledge to analyze visuals of all kinds. The skills of reading visual representations help students become informed citizens who can glean information from various media sources. As an example, many graphic images were used in press conferences during the global COVID pandemic in 2020. Graphs and charts were commonly used to explain worldwide conditions. Transference of knowledge from the science classroom and the ability to read and digest the information presented visually could ease anxiety and give readers a better grasp of the disease's progress.

Connecting VTS to Higher Order Thinking in Education

Visual thinking is at the core of visual literacy. Visual thinking is required in the process of becoming visually literate. Using the theoretical lens of Avgerinou and Pettersson (2020), and as illustrated in Fig. 7.2, *The Five Pillars of Visual Literacy*, visual literacy is obtained through the five interwoven pillars that include: (a) visual communication or the use of pictures and images to express ideas, (b) the design aspects of the image that produce a visual language, (c) using visual language to learn from and with visuals, (d) visual perception which helps the viewer obtain clarity from what they see and, (e) visual thinking which involves the internal visualization necessary for understanding complex aspects of the world (Avgerinou & Pettersson, 2020). Visual thinking is central to all the other parts of visual literacy because without the ability to think about the visual language and reflect upon perceptions the image makes, visual learning and further visual communication most likely will be affected (Avgerinou & Pettersson, 2020).

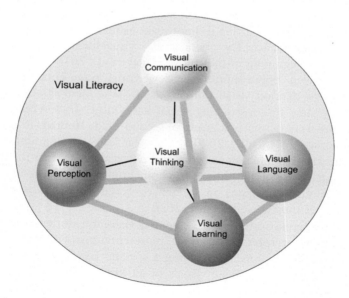

FIGURE 7.2   The five pillars of visual literacy, adapted from Avgerinou, M. D., & Pettersson, R. (2020). Visual literacy theory: moving forward. In S. Josephson, J. Kelly, & K. Smith (Eds.), *Handbook of Visual Communication* (pp. 433–464). Routledge.

Housen's Impact on Visual Thinking

One reason Housen sought to implement VTS in the classroom was its impact on students' visual thinking skills development. In education research, the ability to classify the domains of human learning has resulted in a revised classification of skills, beginning with the most straightforward functions and ending with the most complex (Wilson, 2016). This system, named for the primary author, is known as Bloom's taxonomy (Bloom, 1956). It has been used widely in education to support the development of critical thinking. Housen understood that visual thinking does not happen with increased exposure to visuals; it must be taught to be understood.

Abigail Housen's (1983) levels of aesthetic development can be aligned with Bloom's taxonomy (Figure 7.3). The *accountive stage* is related to the *remembering* stage of Bloom's taxonomy, where students do little more than recall precisely what was taught. The *constructive* stage can be associated with *comprehending and applying* Bloom's taxonomy when teachers or students can now do more than just understand a concept and begin to apply knowledge. The next stage of aesthetic development of *classifying* can be compared to Bloom's taxonomy level of *analysis,* where students can apply knowledge. The final two levels of visual fluency described by Housen (1983), *interpretative* and *re-creative,* can be related to the levels of Bloom's taxonomy called to *evaluate and create.* At this level of understanding, students apply, recreate, and reconstruct knowledge in

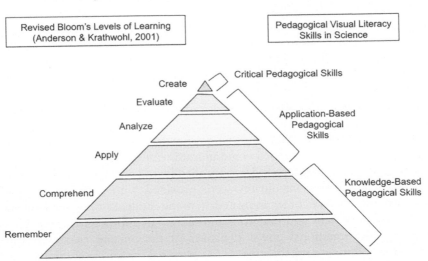

FIGURE 7.3 Visual proficiency alignment of Bloom's taxonomy and levels of aesthetic development. Adapted from Emanuel & Challons-Lipton (2014).

multiple scenarios and situations beyond its intended use (Emanuel & Challons-Lipton, 2014) (Figure 7.3).

As a visual thinker, Housen understood that students need opportunities to reflect critically on the images they encounter in the classroom. She also recognized that different types of visuals encountered require more or less cognitive effort to access the underlying content. Yenawine (1997) states that some images we encounter can be understood at "face value" (p. 845), while others require some unpacking to be fully understood.

Housen's Impact on Visual Literacy Learning

Housen's work, specifically the development of VTS strategies, has influenced many different disciplines in education, including adult learning in engineering, nursing, and medical school training. Most importantly, the process of VTS has empowered individuals with opportunities to make sense of the visual world around them, permitting them to wonder (Albert et al., 2022; Yenawine, 2013). Through the exploration and study of images, students in various fields are forced to slow down and critically look at visuals for information. This process also requires the viewer to reflect on what he or she sees to understand the meaning conveyed thoroughly.

In engineering education, researchers explored critical thinking and reflection regarding engineering design and its environmental impacts. Using VTS in an engineering setting allowed students to visually think, communicate and navigate ambiguous visual information essential in engineering fields (Campbell et al., 2020). Graduate students in engineering courses collaborated with students at the university school of art. Engineering students used critical discussion and reflective writing to examine and rethink their previous environmental projects. This process empirically identified an improvement in students' engineering design work to include accommodations for diverse communities (Campbell et al., 2020).

In nursing programs, Housen's work provided students with the critical observation skills necessary to communicate with patients effectively. The study followed 55 nursing students enrolled in an entry-level public health course. The nursing candidates were provided with VTS educational training and the outcomes indicated that the students developed better active listening skills and oral communication. In addition, learning VTS removed the traditional power dynamics of the nursing classroom and provided a more equitable space for personal visual meaning-making (Moorman et al., 2017).

Medical education programs used Housen's work to improve and develop visual literacy. The Museum of Fine Arts in Boston and the Harvard Medical

School partnered to research the impact of VTS on students in the dermatology residency program. Using a pre- and post-test design, students participated in four workshop sessions in the art gallery using VTS discussions and visual training exercises (Zimmermann et al., 2016). The pre- and post-test questions included art images and medical images used to assess the medical students' visual observational and communication skills. Medical students markedly improved the number of visual observations they made about patients after VTS training. Researchers reported being surprised to note that students' collaboration abilities in a group setting increased after the VTS intervention (Zimmermann et al., 2016).

The impact of Housen's work on visual learning places group interaction and meaning-making at its core. It includes a constructivist approach to learning in which individual group members make meaning through participation in group discussions. As group members reflectively discuss the group interactions, they build new ways of viewing and understanding the world. Socially constructive narratives are used in group discussions to promote a sense of wonder. The wonder motivates the viewer to look for new or different ways to understand the visual.

Importance of Housen's Legacy

Abigail Housen provided the world with a way to understand and improve aesthetic development and visual thinking. Understanding visual thinking is especially important in all areas of education, and visual thinking and learning are critical in a visually saturated society. Visuals we encounter are never viewed in isolation, and it is through societal input that we learn to understand meaning.

At the highest levels of Housen's aesthetic levels of development, individuals transfer what they understand visually to other areas of their life. For example, a nurse that is visually observant and reads health indicators through the visual appearance of her patients may be able to identify these same destress factors in others when walking to the park. Her ability to see distress signals in everyday situations could help save the life of someone she simply encounters on the street. Being visually observant is a skill that develops with visual support. In all areas of education, Housen has provided methods for developing visual literacy and improving discipline-specific transference. This, of course, requires time and routine interaction with art and images of all kinds. Most importantly, it requires collaborative meaning-making and reflection for visual thinking growth to happen.

In visual literacy research, further studies must focus on the nuanced skills needed to achieve visual fluency. Housen set the foundation for understanding levels of visual literacy. Research is needed to develop skill sets for each aesthetic level based on discipline outcomes.

Conclusion: Housen's Legacy to Visual Literacy

We live, work, and play in visually saturated societies that compel us to look but not look critically. Visual literacy requires individuals to make meaning of an image they see and reflect on the meaning. The constant bombardment of visual stimuli alone desensitizes individuals and causes a reduction in thinking time (Robson, 2017). Visual literacy cannot be achieved through TikTok reels, it requires regular thoughtful interaction with all kinds of visuals and reflective thought.

Abigail Housen understood that not all individuals naturally apply visual thinking when it comes to artwork and visual images; therefore, she dedicated her life's work to improving novice visual thinking. Her work developed into a protocol for understanding aesthetic levels of visual development. Her VTS contributions to empirical research provided us with a way to improve visual literacy. She actively sought to embrace the visual conspiracy by developing VTS instruction. In education, Housen's work propels students to think and reflect on what they see to construct meaning. Her work has proven results in the PK-12 environment and higher education disciplines. The process of careful looking can support learners in understanding not only the artwork but all visual objects of the world around them. Being a visual consumer in a visually saturated world requires a specific set of visual literacy skills. The work of Abigail Housen, Philip Yenawine, and their colleagues has provided a solid foundation for researchers and educators to build upon.

References

Albert, C. N., Mihai, M., & Mudure-Iacob, I. (2022). Visual thinking strategies – theory and applied areas of insertion. *Sustainability*, *14*(12), 7195. 10.3390/Su14127195.

Avgerinou, M. D., & Pettersson, R. (2020). Visual literacy theory: Moving forward. In S. Josephson, J. Kelly, & K. Smith (Eds.), *Handbook of visual communication* (pp. 433–464). Routledge. 10.4324/9780429491115-40.

Bloom, B. S. (1956). *Taxonomy of educational objectives, handbook: The cognitive domain*. David McKay.

Campbell, R., Reible, D., Taraban, R., Kim, J. H., & Na, C. (2020, June). Fostering reflective habits and skills in graduate engineering education via the arts and humanities. In *Proceedings of the 2020 American Society for Engineering Education (ASEE) Annual Conference*.

Duke, L., & Housen, A. (1998). Responding to Alper: Re-presenting the MoMA studies on visual literacy and aesthetic development. *Visual Arts Research*, *24*(1), 92–102.

Emanuel, R. C., & Challons-Lipton, S. (2014). Critical thinking, critical looking: Key characteristics of an educated person. In L. J. Shedletsky & J. S. Beaudry (Eds.), *Cases on teaching critical thinking through visual representation strategies* (pp. 335–353). IGI Global. 10.4018/978-1-4666-5816-5.ch013

Hailey, D., Miller, A., & Yenawine, P. (2015). Understanding visual literacy: The visual thinking strategies approach. In D. M. Baylen & A. D'Alba (Eds.),

Essentials of teaching and integrating visual and media literacy (pp. 49–73). Springer. 10.1007/978-3-319-05837-5_3

Housen, A. (1983). *The eye of the beholder: Measuring aesthetic development* (Publication No. 8320170) [Doctoral dissertation, Harvard University]. ProQuest Dissertations & Theses Global.

Housen, A. (1992). Validating a measure of aesthetic development for museums and schools. *ILVS Review: A Journal of Visitor Behavior, 2*(2), 1–19.

Housen, A. (1999, September 27–29). *The eye of the beholder: Research, theory, and practice* [Conference presentation]. Aesthetic and Art Education: A Transdisciplinary Approach, Lisbon, Portugal.

Housen, A. (2000). *Eye of the beholder: Research, theory and practice.* Visual Understanding in Education.

Housen, A. (2001–2002). Aesthetic thought: Assessment, growth, and transfer arts. *Learning Research Journal, 18*(1), 99–131.

Housen, A. (2002). Aesthetic thought, critical thinking and transfer. *Arts and Learning Journal, 18*(1), 99–132.

Housen, A. (2007). Art viewing and aesthetic development: Designing for the viewer. In P. Villeneuve (Ed.), *Periphery to center: Art museum education in the 21st century* (pp. 172–189). National Art Education Association.

Housen, A., & Yenawine, P. (2001). Visual thinking strategies: Understanding the basics. Retrieved from http://www.vtshome.org/system/resources/0000/0039/VTS_Understanding_the_basic.pdf.

Moorman, M., Hensel, D., Decker, K. A., & Busby, K. (2017). Learning outcomes with visual thinking strategies in nursing education. *Nurse Education Today, 51,* 127–129. 10.1016/j.nedt.2016.08.020

Robson, G. J. (2017). The threat of comprehensive overstimulation in modern societies. *Ethics and Information Technology, 19*(1), 69–80.

Scully, S. S. (2020). *Visual thinking skills and elementary students' writing* (Publication No. 28155053) [Doctoral dissertation, Drew University]. ProQuest Dissertations & Theses Global.

Wilson, L. O. (2016). "Anderson and Krathwohl–Bloom's taxonomy revised." Understanding the New Version of Bloom's Taxonomy. https://pdfslide.net/documents/anderson-and-krathwohl-blooms-taxonomy-revised-anderson-and-krathwohl-blooms.html

Yenawine, P. (1997). Thoughts on visual literacy. In J. Flood, S. B. Heath, & D. Lapp (Eds.), *Handbook of research on teaching literacy through the communicative and visual arts.* Routledge.

Yenawine, P. (2013). *Visual thinking strategies: Using art to deepen learning across school disciplines.* Harvard Education Press.

Zimmermann, C., Huang, J. T., & Buzney, E. A. (2016). Refining the eye: Dermatology and visual literacy. *Journal of Museum Education, 41*(2), 116–122. 10.1080/10598650.2016.1163189

8

UNLEASHING PERCEPTION

Exploring Michael Matyushin's Expanded Vision

Nikolai Selivanov

Non-profit organization 'Studio of Art Designing'

Biographical Sketch

Born in Nizhny Novgorod on the Volga in 1861, Michael Matyushin (1861–1934) was the illegitimate child of Irina Petrovna Matyushina, a serf, and Nikolai Alexandrovich Saburov, an accountant hailing from a theatrical family. At nine years old, he constructed his own violin and, at the age of ten, he began studying at the Nizhny Novgorod Conservatory. After completing his studies in the Moscow Conservatory in 1882, he joined the Court Orchestra in St. Petersburg as the first violinist.

Matyushin enrolled in the Drawing School of the Imperial Society for the Encouragement of Fine Arts and pursued his studies from 1894 to 1898. In 1900, Matyushin traveled to Paris to explore new trends in European art. He was captivated by Eduard Manet's *Breakfast on the Grass*, works by Claude Monet and Edgar Degas, but it was Giovanni Segantini's pointillism that left the greatest impression on him. Matyushin particularly identified with the unique effects of light achieved through "alternating colored cords" (Matyushin, 2011).

In the years 1903–1905, Matyushin continued his studies at the renowned studio of Jan Ciągliński, and from 1906 to 1908, enrolled in the studio of Elizaveta Nikolaevna Zvantseva, where he studied alongside artists-symbolists such as Mstislav Valerianovich Dobuzhinsky and Lev Samoilovich Bakst. In 1904, he married Elena Genrikhovna Guro, who was a poet, novelist, and artist. The couple actively sought new ideas and became involved in the circle of avant-garde artists and poets. Their house on Peschanaya Street in St. Petersburg became a gathering place for futurist poets and artists,

DOI: 10.4324/9781032651781-9

including David Davidovich and Vladimir Davidovich Burliuk, Vasily Vasilyevich Kamensky, and Velimir Khlebnikov. It was also where the first collection of futurist poetry, 'Sadok Sudei,' was published. Matyushin and Guro were the initiators of the St. Petersburg society of artists called the "Union of Youth" (1910–1914), which organized six exhibitions representing the diverse directions of the St. Petersburg avant-garde (five in St. Petersburg and one in Riga).

Elena Guro possessed a unique perception as a synesthete, and for Matyushin, as a musician engaged in visual art, encountering this phenomenon directly was particularly significant. He drew upon this experience in his concepts of visual perception, which shed light on the hidden possibilities of the human brain. The artistic philosophy that united Matyushin and Guro revolved around the idea of the unity of nature and humanity, the interconnectedness and spirituality of all living things – a pantheistic worldview. Matyushin and Guro embarked on developing an original theory called "new pantheism," which advocated a holistic perception of the world through sound, color, space, and movement. New Pantheism served as the theoretical foundation for Matyushin's central theory of Organic Culture, which he developed alongside Boris Ender, Guro's student, and Ender's sisters Ksenia and Maria. Elena Guro passed away in 1913.

Matyushin pursued a career as an art critic and theorist in 1914. He published a book by Albert Glaes and Jean Metzinger, who had formulated the theoretical foundations of the Cubist movement in their treatise *Cubism* (Gleizes & Metzinger, 1912). Cubism exerted the most significant influence on the young artists of the Russian Empire, who developed their own distinct direction in painting known as Cubo-Futurism. Matyushin then acts in the logic of an apologist for visual literacy, seeking to open up the methodology of a new visual language to all. This desire to radically change not only the language but also the very forms of communication in art eventually leads him to participate in the most symbolically significant Futurist project. In 1913, Matyushin composed the music for the opera "Victory over the Sun" intended to be part of a trilogy along with "Victory over War," and "Victory over Imperialism." From 1916 to 1918, Matyushin designed a new type of violin suitable for playing in the new system of doubled chromatism. After 1923, Matyushin no longer pursued music and music theory, devoting himself entirely to the visual arts. In developing his theory of visual perception, Matyushin used music theory, bringing musical concepts into the territory of visual culture. From the position of visual literacy, we can say that the language of Matyushin's theory has musical specificity.

In 1918, Kazimir Malevich invited Matyushin to the State Free Art Workshops as a teacher, where he established his first art educational structure, the 'Workshop of Spatial Realism'. In 1921, the studio closed, and 1923, his and his students' work were transferred to the State Institute of Artistic Culture (GINKhUK) in St. Petersburg. At this time, due to the need to organize his disparate reflections and developments for the purposes of pedagogical and research activities, Matyushin transforms ideas and hypotheses into his original theory and methodology, which today we can understand as his system of visual literacy.

From 1924 to 1926, Matyushin founded and led the Department of Organic Culture to study the possibilities of visual perception and the concept of Expanded Vision. The department's activities included developing research programs, conducting scientific experiments, analyzing the results, holding discussions, giving public lectures, and organizing exhibitions (in 1924, 1925, and 1926). It was a real scientific laboratory of visual culture; Matyushin's lab activities developed and utilized specific tools, including schematizations and infographics. The research results were published in the form of graphical tables. In 1927, a series of tables was specifically created for Malevich's trip to Europe, and these tables are now located at the Stedelijk Museum in Amsterdam.

From 1927 to 1933, he dedicated his efforts to the work on the *Colour Handbook* (Matyushin, 2007). Matyushin considered the *Colour Handbook* to be his life's work and was determined to publish it at any cost. In the 1960s, based on his concepts, a system of coloring buildings on Nevsky Prospect in St. Petersburg was developed. Experimental activities of Malevich and Matyushin continued for another three years at the State Institute of Art History and concluded in 1932–1933 within the walls of the State Russian Museum.

Michael Matyushin passed away on October 14, 1934, in Leningrad. It was only in 2006 that the Museum of St. Petersburg Avant-Garde was opened in the house on Pesochnaya Street where Matyushin and Guro resided. Another museum associated with Matyushin's name, the Museum of Organic Culture, was established in Kolomna. It houses a collection of works by Matyushin, his students, and followers.

Introduction: Theoretical Context of Expanded Vision

Matyushin saw the *Colour Handbook* as the embodied outcome of his research activities, in which he formulated his main ideas related to visual perception. But much more original hypotheses, experiments and creative research were connected with the idea of Expanded Vision, which unites Matyushin's artistic creativity, research, and pedagogical activity of many years.

Expanded Vision implies overcoming the automatism of perception, utilizing the physiological and psychological potential of the human for active visual perception. Active visual perception becomes the impetus for the creativity of the thought process based on the resources of memory and imagination. The theoretical context of Expanded Vision is grounded in various strands of evolutionary theory.

Matyushin was deeply acquainted with Henri Bergson's theory of creative evolution. At the core of Bergson's philosophy lies the cosmic biological process of life's creation, characterized by unceasing impulses that generate qualitatively new phenomena. Humanity serves as the conductor of these creative life impulses, and time represents not merely quantitative changes but qualitative transformations. Bergson illustrates his view of dynamic processes in life by discussing form. He states, "Form does not exist at all since form is something stationary; reality is movement. Reality is only the continuous change of form; form is the instantaneous image of some process" (Bergson, 1914, p. 269). Matyushin found inspiration in Bergson's idea of form as an image capturing a moment within the continuous process of matter's transformation, eventually turning it into his main conceptual metaphor, the crystal. The metaphor of the crystal as an instantaneous image of the continuously changing matter of life became a formative idea for Expanded Vision and influenced the content of Matyushin's research and pedagogical programs. To explore Matyushin's legacy from the perspective of visual literacy, it is necessary to keep this context in mind. "For Matyushin, all matter is filled with life, meaning movement, which can be observed through various visual techniques. Matyushin combined these visual methods and techniques into a single concept of Expanded Vision" (Tilberg, 2008, p. 283).

Another line of thought that influenced Expanded Vision's idea is related to a shift in the concept of world space, introducing a fourth dimension. Vision had to learn to perceive this fourth dimension. This idea was introduced to the world by the British mathematician and fiction writer Charles Howard Hinton. His book *The Fourth Dimension and the Era of New Thought* (Hinton, 1915) became a must-read for all avant-garde art representatives in Russia. Hinton argues that gaining an intuitive perception of higher space requires freeing ourselves from the notions of right and left, up and down, inherent in our position as observers in a three-dimensional world (De Witt, 2013). It is these ideas that help Matyushin to formulate the main goal of Expanded Vision in overcoming the automatism of visual perception. He proposes to overcome this automatism through the development of special creative skills of active perception, which also includes the development of intuition and imagination. Visual literacy in the context of this goal can be understood as a set of competencies for creative perception of the environment.

Johann Wolfgang von Goethe, in his *Theory of Colours*, tells us that when he studied plants, he would close his eyes, and clear images of flowers would appear before him, arranged in the form of rosettes or other regular shapes. It is possible that just as visual representation of an object can be induced by imagination, the sensation of touch can also be induced by imagination (Hinton, 1915). The instrumentality of fantasy and the expansion of perception through the development of imagination become crucial methods for Matyushin's work on Expanded Vision. Hinton's ideas of the fourth dimension are further interpreted by another influential author to Matyushin, Peter Ouspensky. Ouspensky understands the fourth dimension as the space of time, the unity of the lived past and the anticipated future, corresponding to the perceptually perceived present moment. This space can only be visually represented by human consciousness:

> Our thought is not bound by the conditions of sensory perception. It can rise above the plane on which we move; it can see far beyond the circle illuminated by our ordinary consciousness. Then our thought can see the past, the present, and the future lying on the same plane. (Ouspensky, 1916, p. 30)

Inner vision, visual perception with closed eyes becomes a part of practical experiments within the concept of Expanded Vision. "They sat with their backs to the river and painted it!" – is how a casual witness describes one of Michael Matyushin's classes on the Neva embankment in St. Petersburg with students (Tilberg, 2008). Or observing landscapes with closed eyes during Matyushin's field trips with students to nature in the vicinity of St. Petersburg. Matyushin includes the skill of inner vision in the Expanded Vision competence.

The third group of theories that directly influenced the development of the Expanded Vision hypothesis is related to synesthesia. Synesthesia is described as the merging of different perceptual channels, where stimulation of one sensory modality automatically evokes another. Matyushin utilized the properties of synesthesia as the foundation for organizing his research program on expanded vision, which involved the synchronous inclusion of various sensory channels. He was interested in the possibility of intensifying and modeling visual perception by incorporating additional associations evoked by all the senses, including touch. Synesthesia as a research subject and the observation of color dynamics in nature were introduced to Matyushin's work thanks to Elena Guro, a genuine synesthete who sought to make sense of her experience of perceiving nature. The collaboration between Guro and Matyushin synthesized an original theoretical framework that paved the way for the further implementation of the research program on Expanded Vision and the creation of the *Color Handbook*.

Michael Matyushin's concept of expanded vision was formed in the context of several influential ideas of the time, associated with radical changes in the perception of the surrounding world. The creative evolution of life, the moving matter of the world and the visual possibilities of its perception, the fourth dimension and inner vision, synesthesia and multi-modality of perception – these ideas Matyushin considered as the basis for the organization of practical activity. And this activity was organized by him in the form of a scientific laboratory, where the methodology of the new visual culture was being created.

Expanded Vision: Laboratory Organization and Practical Experiments

The anticipation of the discovery of supersensible possibilities of perception guided Matyushin and his colleagues to search for scientific, near-scientific and unscientific knowledge and ideas that might constitute an intellectual context for their avant-garde project. As a result, a unique theoretical platform was formed, in which knowledge from the psychophysiology of perception was combined with the latest research in optics, crystallography, theory of biological evolution, philosophy of knowledge, yoga, theosophy, history of visual art, music theory, and many other fields. Such a broad and omnivorous theoretical platform, which opposed the limitations of naïve positivism, made it possible to organize a scientific laboratory whose programs were aimed at exploring the possibilities of developing creative thinking as the basis for artistic generative activity. Systematicity for the organization of the laboratory activity was created by the context – critical analysis of the history of fine arts. Visual literacy allowed verifying ideas, selecting content, inventing experiments.

The commitment of the leaders of the avant-garde to radically change the social meaning of art through the creation of an academic context was embodied in the work of the State Institute of Artistic Culture (GINKhUK/ Petrograd-Leningrad, 1924–1926), which was part of the Museum of Artistic Culture, headed by Kazimir Malevich. "Museums must become scientific institutions creating a unified science of art," wrote Osip Brik, one of the theorists of the avant-garde (Pchelkin, 2019, p. 18). Malevich understands the research institute as a "modern form of art." And Matyushin calls GINKhUK "the first scientifically staged avant-garde" (Encyclopedia of the Russian Avant-Garde, 2017), positioning art as an artistic science that integrates research into the foundations of the evolution of life on the planet and the regularities of human perception of the surrounding space.

The concept of Expanded Vision is at the core of the research program that Michael Matyushin conducted at the Department of Organic Culture at GINKhUK. The structure of the Department of Organic Culture initially included three laboratories: vision, hearing, touch, and three offices – color-form, sound-rhythm, and surface-structure. Later there is a reorganization – two laboratories appear: a general laboratory of vision, hearing, touch, and a laboratory for the study of peripheral perception of color-form.

A document titled "Plan and Methods of Work of the Organic Culture Research Unit at the Museum of Art Culture" (see Table 8.1) has been preserved for posterity, and reveals the meaning and content of the Expanded Vision concept. The document, preserved in the Pushkin House Manuscripts Department of the Institute of Russian Literature of the Russian Academy of Sciences (IRLI RAS, St. Petersburg, f. 656, Matyushin), refers to the early 1920s, but does not have an exact date.

TABLE 8.1 Matyushin M. Plan and Methods of Work of the Organic Culture Research Unit at the Museum of Art Culture (Organica, 2000, p. 57)

Plan and Methods of Work of the Organic Culture Research Unit at the Museum of Art Culture
The task of the Organic Culture Research Department is to comprehend nature and the world as a unified organism through new methods in four directions: touch, hearing, sight, and thought. Its aim is to cultivate a new culture and a new perceptual organism within the artist. To achieve the integrity and completeness of spatial perception, the functional apparatus of the nervous system of touch, hearing, vision, and thinking must be vigorously developed. This determination guided the work of the research department in four areas, with the requirement of consolidating all knowledge in each endeavor.
I TOUCH represents the first stage of sensory understanding of space. The research method is based on various forms of tactile sensation in connection with visual sensations and impressions. The work in this area includes: A Studying the vital movements of growing materials such as roots, knots, bumps, etc., to identify the strongest manifestation of "liberated movement."   B Investigating various forms of tactile sensation in connection with vision while observing metal, stone, bone, and other crystalline formations to reveal primary volume and material dissonance.   C Conclusion: Construction of a new spatial volume.
II HEARING constitutes the second stage of space cognition. Different forms of sound sensations are explored in connection with visual sensations: A Exploring sound on the plane of noise and the line on the plane of light.   B Analyzing the simultaneous conduct of several voices.   C Cubist construction of volume.   D Investigating sound mass as the body of light, an approach to exploring a new volume.

(Continued)

TABLE 8.1 (Continued)

Plan and Methods of Work of the Organic Culture Research Unit at the Museum of Art Culture

III SIGHT represents the third stage of comprehending space. Different light impressions are investigated in connection with tactile and auditory elements, serving as the foundation for new pictorial work. This includes:
  A Contrasting curves and straight lines and forms.
  B Studying primary and complementary colors using models.
  C Analyzing dissonance in color material, sound, and touch.
  D Investigating color-volume through the observation of color-shape on special models with an extended angle of view, including sound timbres and tactile timbres (surface property) (coloration of sound), overtones.
  E Exploring the mutual influence of contrasting tones in Expanded Vision (influence of the background on the front model) and the contrast sensations of sight and touch (movement by touch, movement by sight).
  F Perception of a full 360-degree circle, integrating sound and touch throughout the circumference. Exploring the timbres of sound and the new harmony of consonance and dissonance.

IV The research involves an exploratory work of thought that encompasses and connects the whole array of impressions into a unified comprehension of the world. It explores the beginnings of organic life, the Earth, plants, animals, and humans, and lays the foundation of positive knowledge in areas such as geometry, technology, and the fundamentals of light and sound. The evolution of eye development in animals and humans, as well as the history of fine art in relation to the development and history of objects, rhythm of sound and image, are also considered.

This document is a key resource for understanding Michael Matyushin's theoretical ideas, particularly his concept of Expanded Vision. It is widely referenced by researchers. The concise style used to present this extensive and unconventional program necessitates additional commentary. The sequence of items in the Plan is not accidental; it is connected to the notion of directional evolution.

I. TOUCH. The first point addresses the sense of touch. Matyushin describes touch as the first sense that reveals objects to us through their manifestations. Touch, the primary vision, serves as the foundation for hearing, seeing, tasting, and smelling. It establishes itself in new brain centers, as if separating vision from the undifferentiated shell of the organism during the course of evolution. Matyushin states:

One part of the skin turned out to be in the most favorable conditions for evaluation of spatial sensations and magnitudes; it became the most sensitive to light, was hidden in a reliable protection of the bone box of the brain and consistently developed, transmitting and replacing the crude way of experiencing space with vision. (Matyushin, 2011)

In the section titled "Touch (A)," the proposal is to investigate organic objects that exhibit pronounced signs of growth. Rather than focusing on the nature of the objects' surfaces, Matyushin suggests attempting to represent them in terms of growth dynamics. The regularities of this dynamic process become the subject of observation and analysis. By the way, this is a very interesting creative task for building visual literacy in terms of developing spatial imagination competencies.

In "Touch (B)," when discussing tactile sensations "in connection with sight," Matyushin suggests forming an artistic model in the mind immediately. The properties of materiality are explored through contrast, described as "dissonance." Matyushin employs musical terminology, which adds depth to the task. Simultaneously, a unique task is introduced – "revealing the primary volume." What does this mean? What does "primordiality" refer to? One could assume that it pertains to representing different materials as abstract spatial models. Matyushin likely draws on his artistic experience, particularly the creation of one of his most significant images – crystal. This hypothesis is reasonable, as the mention of "other earthly crystalline formations" follows the reference to the primary volume (Organica, 2000).

II. HEARING. The second section of the Organic Culture Division's work plan relates to sound. Sound is the domain of Michael Matyushin's professional activity as a musician and composer. However, the conceptual core of the research program lies in the spatiality of sound – the construction of a sound environment that can be envisioned within one's own mind.

"Hearing (A)." How Matyushin envisions spatial sound can be discerned from the painting "Pictorial and Musical Construction" in George Kostaki's collection in Thessaloniki. Resembling a whirlwind, the composition consists of two layers: a lower layer with broadly painted dark-colored arrays and an upper layer of light dots in various sizes and colors, forming moving arrays. The dots serve as metaphors for rhythmic sound articulations within the overarching melodic flow.

In the subsequent item "Hearing (B), "Listening to Multiple Voices Conducted Simultaneously," Matyushin incorporates a history of spatial sound models into his program, including polyphonic, organ, and symphonic music. Matyushin developed an original course on the history of music in 1923, which encompassed the music and musical instruments of ancient civilizations, as well as the historical and cultural contexts in which musical phenomena emerged. These polyphonic spatial sound models are presented in a sequential and hierarchical manner.

In the following point of the plan, "Hearing (C)," Matyushin contrasts this hierarchy with the "cubistic" principle of synchronously organizing sound borrowed from painting.

In the final section, "Hearing (D)," Matyushin introduces three new concepts: "sound mass," "light body," and "new volume." The question arises as to how one can perceive a "sound mass" and a "light body" in order to "investigate" a new volume. Matyushin actually provides an answer to this question, which defines the primary objective of the Organic Culture Department's work – the concept of Expanded Vision. This concept is elaborated upon in the third section of the Division's work plan.

III. SIGHT. At the outset of this section, Matyushin defines the research goal as correlating "light impressions" with tactile and auditory sensations to establish the foundation for new pictorial work. It implies that the resulting pictorial works will represent the outcomes of specifically conducted internal perceptual synthesis. Matyushin then outlines the practical "studies" aimed at achieving this synthesis.

Point "Sight (A)" deals with curves, straight lines, and forms, focusing on the differences and unity between organic and inorganic forms and their constructive basis. It represents a visible concept of Organic Culture, demonstrating the primary feature of organic forms – curvature, which contrasts with the geometric nature of crystals and artificially created objects.

The next point "Sight (B)" in the program is an exploration of models involving primary and complementary colors. The perception of complementary colors requires practical skills, referred to by Matyushin as Expanded Vision. The key technological aspect of this point in the program is the research on models, which will serve as the primary method employed by the Organic Culture Department. Here, "models" refer to cards displaying different color combinations.

Moving on, point "Sight (C)" centers entirely on artistic innovation in the process of creating dissonance. Any dissonance activates perception and imagination, eliciting emotional responses, associations, and metaphors. Dissonance, not only characteristic of hearing but also of sight and touch, is a compositional technique in music based on pronounced differences.

The subsequent sections of the Work Plan of the Department of Organic Culture are dedicated to developing this idea further. Paragraph "Sight (D)" delves into the more subtle aspects of perception, encompassing color, sound, and tactile "timbres" and "overtones." It is noteworthy that Matyushin employs musical terminology to encompass the entire complex of perception, enabling him to address visual, auditory, and tactile senses concurrently.

In point "Sight (D)," the program emphasizes the study of subjective perceptions. It suggests investigating color not only on a plane but also in space. The objective is to observe the dynamics of perception of colored spatial objects, referred to as "color-volume through observation of color-form." Matyushin introduces the concept of color-form in this context. "No less interesting results were obtained from experiments on color-form. It was discovered that color possesses formative properties" (Matyushin, 2011, p. 287). Among the special models utilized at GINKhUK were three-dimensional figures, including a red sphere, a yellow ellipsoid, and a green tetrahedron. The study of "color-volume" incorporated dynamic conditions through movement during the experiments.

The following point "Sight (E)" focuses on researching the mutual influence of contrasting tones in expanded vision, specifically the impact of the background on the foreground model. To incorporate the background into the perception process, it is necessary to relax the eye muscles, enabling the viewing of the entire visual field without focusing on the foreground. Matyushin defines this technique of perceiving the entire visual field simultaneously as "expanded vision." It is important to note the subtle semantic difference between the two closely related concepts Matyushin employs, which becomes evident in the context of the described experiments. Matyushin uses the term "dilated viewing" to describe the method of looking by relaxing the visual muscles, attempting to combine forward and lateral vision to encompass the entire available visual field. However, when Matyushin engages in general theoretical reasoning, "expanded vision" refers to the synthesis of the entire complex of perceptions within a creative thought process. In this segment of the program, Matyushin proposes investigating contrasting sensations of sight and touch not in a static state but in motion. The specific organization of these experiments remains unknown. However, it can be assumed that the contrasting colors of the object and the background maintained their intensity and sustained chromaticity during extended viewing. Through these experiments, Matyushin demonstrates the possibility of extending the time interval of visual perception activity through dilated viewing, achieved by mastering the relaxation of eye muscles and maintaining a "volitional" approach to controlling the entire visual field.

The final point of the program "Sight (F)" is dedicated to the central idea of Matyushin's Expanded Vision, which involves perceiving a complete circle in 360 degrees. This highly original concept, often leaving first-time encounters in a semantic dilemma, became one of the program manifestos of the avant-garde. A practical method for altering one's perception and, consequently, transforming oneself was discovered. This artistic and scientific path toward creating a new superman repre-sented a utopian goal for Matyushin and all members of the Department of Organic Culture at GINKhUK, who were captivated by this brilliant and holistic idea.

Today, analyzing this program in the context of contemporary problems of visual literacy, the ecological content of Matyushin's ideas, which considered the subject's perception in its organic relationship with the environment, becomes evident. It is not by chance that Matyushin understood his own subjective perception as a part of the general research program.

Michael Matyushin's Own Experience Using Expanded Vision

Matyushin describes many of his own experiences using Expanded Vision. Over several years, he gradually developed the concept of perceiving and encompassing the space surrounding him in a single visual image. This idea was rooted in his deep emotional experiences of open natural spaces. These vivid impressions, which Matyushin consistently focused on, instilled in him a sense of the all-encompassing unity of nature, beyond the reach of ordinary perception. This awe-inspiring and anticipatory quest for the discovery of supersensible, universal knowledge fueled Michael Matyushin's creative will, artistic imagination, and systematic research endeavors. In fact, Matyushin developed and described a competence for creative perception of the surrounding space, synthesizing visual perceptual experience and spatial imagination. Is this competence part of visual literacy? I think it is. Moreover, this competence can be propaedeutic and basic for the formation of other competences of visual literacy, providing creative activity in the sphere of visual culture.

> When you witness a blazing fiery sunset and immediately turn around to see a deep purple-blue cold, you will comprehend and feel their mutual influence on your central perceptual faculties. You will know and sense that they both simultaneously and inseparably affect you. (Matyushin, 2011, p. 119)

The most important aspect of these experiments is time, its duration – the rapidity of the change of visual impressions allows the "large-format image" to be held in short-term memory. Hence, Matyushin frequently employs words like "quickly" or "instantly" to describe his experiments and experiences. Equally significant is his continuous reference to a "volitional image," indicating a conscious effort to retain the image within the realm of present perception. Two surviving schemes by Matyushin elucidate the extraordinary concept of achieving a 360-degree coverage of the visual field.

A scheme titled *The Reality of the Four Sides* (Figure 8.1), illustrates a concept similar to the previously described experiments on expanding visual perception. In this scheme, the visual impressions of the front and rear views are combined through the rapid change of viewpoints, referred to as an "instantaneous turn." The speed enables both views to be retained in memory, while spatial imagination "stitches" them together into a unified panorama, creating a distinct memory pattern.

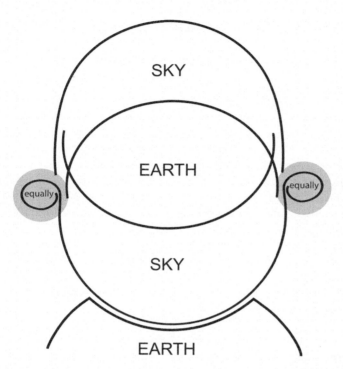

FIGURE 8.1 Selivanov, N. Graphic interpretation of Matyushin's drawing "The Reality of Four Sides." The Reality of Four Sides. Paper, pencil drawing. Manuscripts Department of the Institute of Russian Literature of the Russian Academy of Sciences, St. Petersburg. F. 656, Matyushin, album 40, sheet 44.

In this diagram, arched and concave shapes representing sky/ground/ sky/ground alternate vertically. This sequence offers another way to visually encompass space, with the gaze moving from bottom to top and then the head and body turning back. It represents a rotation of the gaze around the horizontal axis rather than the vertical one. One can experience a similar impression, for example, while swinging on a swing and tilting the head backward. Although it is challenging to depict the continuous connection between the celestial dome, the ground, and the two mirrored horizons in a linear scheme, Matyushin employs an expressive device to indicate this. He twists the ends of the arc symbolizing the celestial vault. These twisted ends may evoke associations with a skipping rope, which, when rotated, describes a full 360-degree sphere. The inscription in the center of the diagram, clearly signifies the perception of a complete spherical space.

Another scheme, signed by Matyushin as the *Scheme of Visual Abilities* (Figure 8.2), depicts the functional anatomy of Expanded Vision. The diagram has a radial structure, with Matyushin placing the center of visual perception in the middle of the brain ("1" in the diagram). Various sensory organs direct information flows to this central point, including the eyes as organs of optical perception. Matyushin's expanded vision considers the eye as only one component of the visual apparatus, operating in conjunction with the ears and skin within a system of "peripheral perception" centrally controlled by the brain (Tilberg, 2008). This perspective on the multi-component nature of visual perception emerged from the romantic idea of artistic synthesis and the phenomenon of synesthesia, in which Matyushin was directly involved.

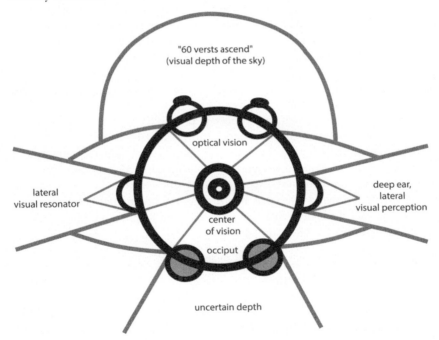

FIGURE 8.2 Selivanov, N. Graphic interpretation of Matyushin's drawing "The Scheme of Visual Capabilities" Matyushin, M. (1924). The Scheme of Visual Capabilities. Paper, pencil drawing. Manuscripts Department of the Institute of Russian Literature of the Russian Academy of Sciences, St. Petersburg. F. 656, Matyushin, album 40, sheet 14.

In the diagram, Matyushin delineates the visually perceived space in front of a person as an arc ("2" in the diagram). This limited space of natural vision, defined by angles and depth, contrasts with the concept of "indefinite depth" or infinity ("3" in the diagram), accessible through occipital perception. However, Matyushin's most intriguing graphic constructions emerge on the sides, where he combines lateral vision, occipital perception centers, and hearing ("4" on the diagram). These remarkable structures, with ears at their center, are defined by Matyushin as "resonators of lateral vision".

Both of these schemes serve a projective rather than an analytical purpose. They create a framework for contemplating the possibilities of perception, which are directly influenced by the development of intellect and creative imagination. For Matyushin, the development of visual perception reflects the increasing complexity of intellect throughout its evolutionary process. He unequivocally links the ability to perceive space and color with the development of higher mental functions of the brain.

Matyushin substantiates his concept of organism development from a central point that becomes the center. He believed that this law of organic life growth corresponds to the human organism's inclination to visually perceive the whole, the spherical space around itself. Moreover, this sphere is filled with color, sound, and material entities that human perception can simultaneously apprehend.

In these schemes, visual perception is portrayed as a multicomponent cognitive phenomenon that possesses the potential for self-development while concurrently fostering the entire thinking system. Through his studies of dilated vision, Matyushin sought to establish the interdependence between intellectual development and direct contact with the external world, with the environment, known as "Spatial Realism" – a fundamental concept in his theory. "Spatial Realism" remains concealed from ordinary vision, requiring considerable effort to sense and perceive.

> Matyushin created a training program aimed at opening communication channels between the various sense centers in the human brain and thus developing a new type of perception. This program was supposed to increase a person's awareness of those processes that occur automatically in the body. It was supposed that the training, or cultivation of the body and senses, would lead man to a new path – to a new consciousness that could be modified and eventually completely transformed so that he could see reality as it really is: a new Spatial Realism. (Tilberg, 2008, p. 217)

Essentially, all these exercises can be understood as creative experiments with vision, in which optical perception is complemented by spatial imagination. By active perception, Matyushin meant a volitional effort that evokes a perceptual impulse that stimulates the process of creative imagination.

These two schemes can be seen as an illustration of Matyushin's ideas about the evolutionary perspectives of visual perception. Matyushin's experiments have transformed our understanding of visual perception, enabling the establishment of general patterns and identification of subjective factors that influence the images perceived by human cognition. They have also allowed for the formulation of assumptions regarding the potential development of visual perception. The concept of Expanded Vision is rich with unexpected and fruitful ideas that can be further explored by other researchers and creators. Three ideas within Matyushin's project particularly stand out:

1 The experiments conducted by Matyushin assumed simultaneous activation of several perceptual channels along with visual perception, which influenced the formation of visual images synthesized by spatial imagination. Vision was considered not as an isolated optical system functioning independently, but as a basis of perceptual synthesis. These experiments by Matyushin, in particular, create a new understanding of the visual system, which is important for the formation of modern concepts of visual literacy. This understanding can be expressed in graphical schemes representing visual perception as a cognitive process based on perceptual multimodality and including spatial imagination as an integral part of the unified system that forms a visual image in consciousness.

2 The experiments employed pronounced contrast in the perceived stimuli, exploring the dissonance of sensations. The investigation of impressionistic dissonance resides within the realm of aesthetics, as it delves into the creative construction of impressions. Such practical experiments open up the possibility of perceiving artistic reality and can be the basis for aesthetic associations. For visual literacy, such experiments can be immersive tools that incorporate the cognitive motivation of mastering artistic heritage.

3 The temporal dimension, specifically the effects of duration and short duration, held particular significance in the observations of the visual perception process. The utilization of short-term memory in the development of skills for creatively constructing visual images was also examined. The duration of observation determines what information the human mind can adapt, how complex the perceptual process will be, whether imagination is included in the perceptual process, or whether only short-term visual memory is used. For the purposes of visual literacy, understanding this pattern opens up the possibility of building skills in visual arts

perception, developing visual memory and associative thinking, or, for example, building skills in visual shorthand – sketchnoting.

Overall, these ideas shed light on the multifaceted nature of visual perception and emphasize the role of perceptual synthesis, aesthetic dissonance, and temporal factors in this process. They provide valuable opportunities for further research and development of visual literacy theory and practice.

The most important consequence of these experiments is the assumption of the dominant role of vision in perceptual synthesis. Vision synthesizes what we can imagine and comprehend, store, and reproduce with the help of memory in a visually perceived form – an image. But with each reproduction, the image is built anew from the resources that memory has at its disposal. We can remember what a flower that surprised us looks like, but, remembering it every time, we will imagine it differently. The richer the visual memory, the more vivid and complex the imagined image. Visual literacy develops visual memory, thereby complicating imaginative thinking. That is, visual literacy can be understood as an intellectual environment that shapes the perceptual capabilities of visual perception.

Matyushin's most creatively intriguing experiments involved perceptual dissonances. Experiments with aesthetics and artistic expression were used to investigate creative thinking. The integration of aesthetic and perceptual research in the context of the task of developing creative competencies of visual literacy can be based on all of Matyushin's research experiences, including his work on the *Color Handbook*.

Equally promising for the development of visual literacy are the aspects that Matyushin emphasized in his "Expanded Vision" experiments and that he used to achieve active perception:

- specially prepared perceptual stimulus (object, dissonance, situation, lighting, sound environment, etc.),
- creative will and motivation to control the timing of perception,
- spatial imagination to "assemble" the image,
- verbal description of the visual impression received.

Each of these aspects can be analyzed and developed to address the practical challenges of visual literacy and creative visual perception research.

Conclusion: Matyushin's Contribution to the Field of Visual Literacy

Visual literacy serves as a fundamental introduction to a visual language, empowering individuals to both comprehend and craft their own visual narratives. In the realm of Expanded Vision, Matyushin focused on the fundamental elements of perception that are utilized in the synthesis of visual images. However, these elements were regarded as impulses that initiate the imaginative process, wherein perceptual experiences are synthesized into an image. Matyushin's projects were not intended to produce a textbook per se, but rather to provide instructions that would aid individuals in developing creative perceptual skills for observing the world around them.

The concept of Expanded Vision, as the ability to govern the imagination through the integration of all perceptual experiences, where visual perception serves as both the impetus and organizing structure, was not comprehensively summarized in a dedicated publication. Understanding this idea requires delving into Matyushin's manuscripts, unpublished during the artist's lifetime, such as "The Creative Path of the Artist" and "The Creativity of the Artist of New Dimension" (Matyushin, 2011), as well as his letters, the work plan of GINKhUK's Organic Culture Department, and two conceptual schemes, which received their graphical and semantic interpretation for the first time in this chapter.

According to Matyushin, Expanded Vision is a creative thinking process in which a vivid perceptual subjective experience is formed. This experience, obtained in the process of creative volitional efforts, is an active agent of thinking and triggers the process of semiosis necessary for "packaging" meaningful experience into the system of intellectual (intellectually mediated) memory. Signs of subjective experience are generated. These signs of subjective experience generate a unique complexity within each person. It is this complexity that serves as an informational basis for human communication, gives birth to new phenomena in culture and art, and acts as a mechanism for the evolution of life.

Although Matyushin himself does not speak of semiosis, his texts with metaphorical interpretations of perceptual experience obtained in the process of experiments with Expanded Vision expressively illustrate this thought complex. The linguistic component of the Expanded Vision system is an integral part of it. But here we are dealing with Matyushin and his colleagues, whose memory is filled with many meaningful visual metaphors, experience of creativity, and a large stock of words. All of this was necessary to make the Expanded Vision experience really work. One could pose the question more sharply. Is it possible to fully perceive the world around us without having the "necessary set of words"? From this point of view, visual literacy is the foundation for building competencies for encoding one's own perceptual experience, for any semiotic activity. And the key factor is the synthesis of visual and linguistic activities aimed at organizing specific competences of visual literacy.

For innovative pedagogy it seems promising to develop teaching models based on the expansion of perception, creating the basis for creative synthesis of the information received. This is another possible technology for activating perception and the whole thinking process. Unexpected and significant results can be brought by research into the developmental effects of Expanded Vision on people of different ages, different cultural competencies, and different mental makeup. The results of such studies can be used for developmental training, self-development, and creative education.

References

Bergson, H. (1914). Collected works, vol. 1. St. Petersburg.
De Witt, A. (2013). *Moral authority, men of science, and the Victorian novel.* Cambridge University Press.
Encyclopedia of the Russian Avant-Garde. (2017). *GINKhUK (State Institute for Artistic Culture).* Moscow.
Gleizes, A., & Metzinger, J. (1912). *Du Cubisme.* St. Petersburg.
Hinton Ch. H. (1915). *The fourth dimension and the era of new thought.* New Man Book Publishing House.
Matyushin, M. (2007). *Colour handbook: The regularity of variability of color combinations.* Publisher Aronov.
Matyushin, M. (2011). *The creative way of the artist.* Museum of Organic Culture.
Organica. The Objectless World of Nature in the Russian Avant-Garde of the 20th Century. (2000). Catalogue of the exhibition at the Gmurzynska Gallery. Cologne. 1999–2000. (Ed. Alla Povelikhin). Moscow.
Ouspensky, P. (1916). *Tertium organum: The key to the world's mysteries.* Forgotten Books.
Pchelkin, R. (2019). *Moscow Museum of Pictorial Culture. History without Bills. Avant-garde. List No. 1.* State Tretykov Gallery.
Tilberg, M. (2008). *The color universe: Michael Matyushin on art and vision.* Novoye literaturnoye obozreniye.

9

THINKING IN PICTURES

Temple Grandin's Contribution to Visual Literacy

Jacqueline Huddle

Indiana University-Bloomington

Biographical Sketch

Temple Grandin was born in August 1947 in Boston, Massachusetts. Early on in Grandin's life, her mother became increasingly concerned about her destructive behavior (Grandin, 2013, p. 3). When Grandin's mother noticed she was also falling behind developmentally, she brought her daughter to a neurologist. Grandin explains that as a child she "showed the symptoms of classic autism: no speech, poor eye contact, tantrums, appearance of deafness, no interest in people, and constant staring off into space" (Grandin & Johnson, 2006, p. 33). When her mother took her to the neurologist, Grandin was diagnosed as being brain damaged (Grandin, 2013, p. 3). Grandin would not be diagnosed as autistic until she was approximately 12 years old. This was due to the relative lack of knowledge about autism in psychiatry at that time. In fact, the diagnosis of autism was only four years old when Grandin was born (Grandin, 2013, pp. 5–9). Autism would not be included in the *DSM (Diagnostic and Statistical Manual of Mental Disorders)* until its third and fourth editions (Grandin, 2013, pp. 15–16).

Today, Dr. Temple Grandin is a professor at Colorado State University. She has been at the university for over 25 years teaching in the Graduate Program for Animal Behavior & Welfare. In addition to her teaching responsibilities, she has also been sharing her research about autism and animal behavior around the world. The driving force of her research has been understanding autism and different ways of thinking, emphasizing the importance of visual thinking. Grandin defines visual thinking as, "the ability to see associated images from your 'virtual memory files' and access

DOI: 10.4324/9781032651781-10

them in different ways to problem-solve, navigate, and interpret the world" (Grandin, 2022, p. 45). This chapter explains how Grandin's personal experiences influence her research, describe Grandin's visual thinking scholarship, draw connections between Grandin's work and visual literacy concepts as well as describe ways her work can impact other fields, specifically education.

Introduction: Recognizing the Importance and Rarity of Visual Thinkers

An influential mentor in Grandin's education was her high school science teacher, Mr. Carlock. In her early education career, Grandin did not excel academically due to her lack of focus. Carlock helped Grandin become a better student by encouraging her personal interest in science. He even helped Grandin build a human-sized cattle chute that she used to calm her anxiety attacks. Grandin, like many other autistic people, experienced severe issues with physical touch. She explains that the anxiety when being touched, "was like a great, all-engulfing tidal wave of stimulation, and I reacted like a wild animal. Being touched triggered flight; it flipped my circuit breaker" (Grandin & Johnson, 2006, p. 58). During a summer visit to her aunt's dude ranch in Arizona, Grandin saw a cattle chute, "an apparatus vets use to hold cattle still for their shots by squeezing them tight so they can't move" (Grandin & Johnson, 2006, p. 4). Immediately, Grandin noticed how relaxed the cattle became from the pressure of the chute. When experiencing an anxiety attack at her aunt's ranch, she decided to try the chute on herself. In her memoir, Grandin describes the experience:

> At first there were a few moments of sheer panic as I stiffened up and tried to pull away from the pressure, but I couldn't get away because my head was locked in. Five seconds later I felt a wave of relaxation, and about thirty minutes later I asked Aunt Ann to release me. For about an hour afterward I felt very calm and serene. My constant anxiety had diminished. This was the first time I ever felt really comfortable in my own skin. (Grandin, 2006, p. 59)

Grandin credits this experience as being one of the first times she realized her connection with how animals see and experience the world. She did not see the connection to science, however, until Carlock helped her build her own chute. After their project was completed, Carlock encouraged Grandin to explore why the machine helped calm her. He not only helped Grandin get a library card and taught her the basics of research, but he also helped guide her to her future career by showing her that learning and studying can be interesting and relevant to her own experiences.

Later in life, Grandin realized that not everyone thinks in images the way she does. She explains that her mind uses words much like a Google image search. "Words serve only as the index tabs on all the visual images in my memory" (Grandin, 2013, p. 3). The more visual memories she has, the more information she has to pull from. During her college years and her early years of working on cattle ranches, she realized her perspective allowed her to understand animals in a way the other ranchers could not.

One of her first design projects included working on a dip vat at a cattle-handling facility in Arizona. Grandin defines a dip vat as, "a long, narrow, seven-foot-deep swimming pool through which cattle move in single file. It is filled with pesticide to rid the animals of ticks, lice, and other external parasites" (Grandin & Johnson, 2006, p. 5). She immediately began researching other existing dip vat designs to inform her approach to engineering an improved dip vat model. Due to her ability to visualize photo-realistic images, she was able to trial-run different design options in her mind. When describing this thought process, she says:

> I started running three-dimensional visual simulations in my imagination. I experimented with different entrance designs and made the cattle walk through them in my imagination. Three images merged to form the final design: a memory of a dip vat in Yuma, Arizona, a portable vat I had seen in a magazine, and an entrance ramp I had seen on a restraint device at the Swift meat packing plant in Tolleson, Arizona. (Grandin & Johnson, 2006, p. 7)

While Grandin's initial design was not perfect, it worked immensely better than the system before it. Cattle were not frightened when they went through the vat, instead, they entered the handling system voluntarily, and this confused and surprised the other ranchers. Grandin could not believe that no one else had ever thought to figure out what was scaring the cattle and making them balk. The ranchers first questioned her design choices and even made changes to her work which caused danger to the animals. Grandin often got into arguments with the ranchers, which caused her to lose jobs early on in her career. At the time she thought the ranchers were stubborn and quite frankly stupid. It was not until she furthered her research into visual thinking that she realized their confusion was due to a lack of visualization skills, an area where she greatly excelled (Grandin, 2006, p. 32).

Grandin's Visual Thinking Research

Different Types of Visual Thinking

From her research, Grandin has concluded that there are two types of visual thinking: object visualizers and spatial visualizers. Grandin summarizes these two types of thinking by saying, "The object thinker builds the computer. The spatial thinker writes the code" (Grandin, 2022, p. 32). She unpacks this description by explaining that the object visualizer sees, "the world in photorealistic images" and the spatial visualizer, "sees the world in patterns and abstractions" (Grandin, 2022, p. 32). Grandin's knowledge of these two types of visualizers was anticipated by the research of Maria Kozhevnikov, a lecturer at Harvard Medical School and a researcher at the visual-spatial cognition lab at Massachusetts General Hospital (Grandin, 2022, p. 31). Through her case study research, Kozhevnikov and colleagues (2002, 2005) found that there are two groups of cognitive styles which include the iconic type, people who, "construct vivid, concrete, and detailed images of individual objects in a situation," and the spatial type, people who, "create images that represent the spatial relations between objects that facilitate the imagination of spatial transformations such as mental rotation" (Kozhevnikov et al., 2002, p. 48). Kozhevnikov was the first researcher to discover different modes of visual thought and for developing a group of questionnaires and skill tests, including the Visualizer-Verbalizer Cognitive Style Questionnaire (VVCSQ) and the Grain Resolution Test. Both tests have become, "the gold standard in studies about spatial and object visualization" (Grandin, 2022, p. 31).

In her newest text, *Visual Thinking: The Hidden Gifts of People Who Think in Pictures,* Grandin further delves into the importance of visual thinking and the specific traits characteristic of both spatial and object visualizers. As her research has illustrated, spatial visualizers tend to excel in subjects such as music and math. These are the people that become, "statisticians, scientists, electrical engineers, and physicists" (Grandin, 2022, p. 32). Grandin herself is an object visualizer. These people tend to succeed at hands-on subjects and/ or visual subjects such as art, woodworking, cooking, and geometry. Object visualizers commonly work as, "graphic designers, artists, skilled trades-people, architects, inventors, mechanical engineers, and designers" (Grandin, 2022, p. 32). Often, people are not fully visual thinkers, as Grandin explains, "It's a verbal-visual continuum, not a binary" (Grandin, 2022, p. 18). In other words, very few people fall completely into the visual or verbal category. Those who do lean heavily to one side of the continuum, like Grandin, tend to have unique abilities and a specific way of processing information.

Visual Thinking and Neurodiversity

In addition to the differences between visualization types and characteristics of visual thinking, Grandin has also helped further connections being made between neurodiversity, genius, and visual thinking abilities. It is important to note that Grandin does not ground her concept of visual thinking in the work of Rudolf Arnheim, writer, art and film theorist, and perceptual psychologist who founded the concept of visual thinking. She also does not reference Visual Thinking Strategies (VTS), a visual analysis methodology co-founded by Philip Yenawine and Abigail Housen. Instead, she focuses on establishing the thinking processes of known visual thinkers and the apparent connection between visual thinking and neurodiversity. Grandin understands the core tenet of neurodiversity as "a new paradigm for thinking about neurological disorders, including dispensing with the word *disorders*. Instead of pathologizing conditions like autism, proponents of neurodiversity advocate that these 'conditions' be looked at as positive differences" (Grandin, 2022, p. 161, emphasis in original). Grandin recognizes the benefits of her autism and has repeatedly stated that her visual thinking abilities have made her successful in her career. Her message involves advocating for the acceptance of all minds, especially within the educational system. She expresses the importance of neurodiverse children being given opportunities early on in life to hone their unique skill sets. She emphasizes the importance of early intervention by sharing her own story and high-lighting the work of famous innovators and inventors who were on the spectrum and who were visual thinkers. This list includes individuals such as Thomas Edison, Albert Einstein, Steve Jobs, and Leonardo da Vinci.

Grandin turns to the work of Thomas G. West to further illustrate the connection between visual thinking abilities and genius. Like West, Grandin sees the importance of paying attention to the thought processes of famous visual thinkers. West recognizes the differences in human cognitive processes and encourages readers to think of these differences in a positive light. He expresses the need for society to understand these "paradoxical patterns of mixed capabilities ..." for there to be "better development and use of a wide range of special talents throughout the population" (West, 2009, p. 24). In other words, neurodiverse abilities, such as visual thinking skills, are a sign of human variance. Grandin strongly agrees with the need for a deeper understanding of different ways of thinking to benefit the development and survival of our society. Research shows we are "facing an unprecedented skills gap at a time when the need for skills is ever more pressing" (Grandin, 2022, p. 96). This lack of hands-on skills has left us with a shortage of tradesmen, and medical professionals during the COVID-19 pandemic (Grandin, 2022, p. 96). This lack of workers in hands-on professions has Grandin extremely worried about the future of our country. She credits this skill gap to the elimination of hands-on classes in schools and experiential learning opportunities within K-12 education. In Grandin's mind and professional opinion, this is our greatest failure in education. If we do not help visual thinkers hone their skills early on, we will suffer from the lack of their contributions to the world (Grandin, 2022).

Visual Thinking and K-12 Education

When it comes to visual thinking, Grandin feels we have "screened out" visual thinkers in the educational system. In her 2010 TED Talk titled, *The World Needs All Kinds of Minds,* Grandin explains, "People are getting away from doing hands-on stuff. I'm really concerned that a lot of the schools have taken out the hands-on classes, because art, and classes like that-those are the classes where I excelled" (Grandin, 2010, 1:16). In all of her publications on autism, Grandin shares the significance of her experiences of hands-on learning, both in and out of the classroom, that have helped hone her talents as a visual thinker. Experiences such as making costumes for school plays, taking wood shop, embroidery classes, working with horses, and sewing taught her responsibility and problem-solving skills that she put toward her future career. To further establish the significance of all types of thinkers, Grandin refers to Howard Gardner's Theory of Multiple Intelligences. Gardner's theory "challenges the classical view of intelligence that most of us have absorbed explicitly (from psychology or education texts) or implicitly (by living in a culture with a strong but possibly circumscribed view of intelligence)" (Gardner, 2006, p. 5). Gardner lists a growing number of human intelligence included in his theory: linguistic intelligence, musical intelligence, logical-mathematical intelligence, spatial intelligence, and bodily kinesthetic intelligence. Grandin refers to Gardner's work as a way to further emphasize the truth of human variance and the need for educators to address the needs of a diverse group of learners in the classroom.

While there is no perfect test to identify visual thinking abilities, Grandin has tests of her own that she likes to use in lectures on visual thinking and autism. For adults, Grandin likes to use the IKEA test which includes the scenario of buying a piece of furniture from IKEA. She then asks people if when they read the instructions, do they look predominantly at the pictures or if they read the words? If you use pictures, you most likely lean toward being a visual thinker because visual thinkers struggle with following sequential directions (Grandin, 2022, p. 17). An exercise that Grandin likes to use when speaking with groups of children and groups of school administrators includes a picture analysis. This exercise includes showing a picture "of a steer exiting a chute, staring at a bright spot of sunlight on the floor. The caption says: NON-SLIP FLOORING IS ESSENTIAL" (Grandin, 2022, p. 21). When she shows this picture to a group, Grandin asks "for a show of hands: How many see that the animal is looking at the sunbeam?" (Grandin, 2022, p. 21). Grandin noticed that there are consistent results across the groups of children and the groups of adults she does this exercise with most of the children focus on the sunbeam while school administrators tend to focus on the caption (Grandin, 2022, p. 21). These results somewhat support the notion that verbal learning is favored over visual learning in the classroom. While some of the children Grandin speaks to have already been exposed to an education system that favors verbal communication over visual communication, some children still embrace creativity and visual ways of seeing the world which allows them to recognize images as having meaning. Administrators have already gone completely through a verbally biased education system which causes them to focus on textual information over visual information.

Grandin's visual-verbal experiments further emphasize the need for a more streamlined approach to adding visual literacy within the K-12 curriculum. While there has been significant evidence given for the importance of incorporating visual literacy within K-12 learning (Anderson et al., 2021; Metros, 2008) there has still not been a universal systematic attempt at doing so. There are many challenges noted within the literature to incorporating visual literacy within K-12 classrooms such as a lack of resources for teachers (including visual literacy training), visual literacy not being included in state standards for education, and visual subjects not being valued as highly as STEM disciplines. However, there has been some success in starting with pre-service educators in an effort to address these challenges and make the incorporation of visual literacy within K-12 learning more realistic (Anderson et al., 2021; Mayall and Robinson, 2009; Metros, 2008).

Impact of Grandin's Research and Advocacy

The contributions of Dr. Grandin's professional career have been vast and interdisciplinary in nature. Grandin has had a considerable impact at Colorado State University (CSU). In 2020, she was named one of the top ten most influential professors by CEOWORLD Magazine (D. DeGroot, 2020). Grandin's work as an activist has influenced the way parents and educators understand an autism diagnosis. Through her activism and the writing of many books on autism, Grandin has shared her story and advice with parents and educators of autistic children. Her memoir, *Thinking in Pictures: My Life with Autism* (Grandin, 2010b) inspired the award-winning HBO movie *Temple Grandin*, which helped expand her reach to a larger audience. Grandin has also been the subject of several children's books, including *How to Build a Hug*, and *Temple Grandin and Her Amazing Squeeze Machine*.

Currently, Grandin's personal story and research have been connected to visual literacy within education and visual learning-related scholarship. In, "Visual Literacy and Art Education: A Review of the Literature," author Scott McMaster references Grandin's (2010a) TED Talk and describes her as, "an autistic woman who learned in a primarily visual way and was able to overcome many of the hurdles autistic people face by embracing her visual way of learning and using it creatively" (McMaster, 2015, p. 27). Grandin has also been referenced within the academic librarianship literature to support the use of visual literacy skills for improving wayfinding in the library (Misenhelter, 2017, p. 3). In the article titled, "Manga and the Autistic Mind," Robert Rozerna cites Grandin's work and shared their own story of being the parent of an autistic child as the foundation for the necessity of including more visual literature within the English classroom. Specifically, Rozerna argues for the inclusion of manga "or Japanese Comics" within the reading requirements because it "seems to hold a special appeal for adolescents with Autism Spectrum Disorder (ASD)" (Rozerna, 2015, p. 60). Rozerna further explains why this specific type of literature potentially appeals to ASD individuals and how the inclusion of manga within the curriculum can better serve the diversity of students as a whole.

Connections to Visual Literacy and Potential Contributions to the Field

In her text, *Animals in Translation,* Grandin explains, "I hope that what I've learned will help people *see*" (Grandin, 2006, p. 26, emphasis in original). Grandin has stated numerous times in her scholarship that her visual thinking abilities are the greatest asset in her teaching, equipment engineering, and animal behavioral analyst careers. At its core, Grandin's research is about understanding the cognitive processes of visual thinkers and educating the world about the benefits of visual thinking as well as how to interact with and support visual thinkers. Her dedication to emphasizing the importance of visual thinking for all learners is directly in-line with current visual literacy research. Visual thinking is a common topic in the world of visual literacy. Maria D. Avgerinou and Rune Pettersson see both visual thinking and visual perception as being pillars of visual literacy (2020). Both scholars are in agreement with Grandin's claim that visual thinking abilities are interdisciplinary skills that can not only benefit visual thinkers but society as a whole. Avgerinou and Pettersson express that, "expecting people to be creative without giving them any opportunity for training in visual thinking seems not only irrational but unfair" (2020, p. 49). As a society, we need innovative and creative thinkers to solve world problems. If we do not provide a prosperous learning environment for all thinkers, especially those who are visually inclined, we will not have the creative solutions we need to survive.

Grandin's research could be useful to visual literacy researchers focused on cognitive theories. Her knowledge about her own brain function through MRI and fMRI (functional magnetic resonance imaging) testing and her research on autistic brain function highlights the importance of understanding the cognitive processing of visual thinkers and neurodiverse people. Grandin uses the metaphor of an office building when describing the different parts of the brain. She highlights the occipital cortex, "responsible for the occipital lobe-the part of the brain that processes visual information," as one of many vice presidents in the office building (Grandin, 2013, p. 25). All parts of the office building (brain) need to communicate through different means in order for things to function properly. However, in a neurodiverse brain, "an elevator might not stop at the seventh floor. The phones in the accounting department might not work. The wireless signal in the lobby might be weak" (Grandin, 2013, p. 26). In other words, different brains have different strengths. This variety of strengths requires different types of communication in order to thrive. Grandin's description and research of the neurology of autistic minds could potentially further inform perception theory research within the field of visual literacy. Perception is:

> Not simply the visual stimuli falling on one's retina, nor the physical sensations gathered through other senses that complete our perceptual process. The brain serves as a central interpreter, organizing and interpreting the data gathered through the senses, making sense of this information and acting according to its interpretations. (Serafini, 2013, p. 31)

In other words, perception is the process by which the brain takes in and interprets visual information. Grandin's research focuses on the importance of visual thinkers' cognitive processes and why the perceptual abilities of extreme visual thinkers matter. As described in the literature, the perceptual process happens in a series of steps, "including the sensing of information, the use of past experience, both real and genetically acquired, and the processing of information along dual pathways" (Barry, 2002; Barry, 2020, p. 3). Grandin's understanding of the neurology of visual thinkers can enhance the knowledge of the perceptual processes of neurodiverse thinkers within visual literacy scholarship. Grandin's scholarly work can not only help perception theory research evolve but can also potentially help reach a larger audience and further highlight the significance of perceptual abilities within academia.

Grandin's focus on the visual thinking abilities connection to neurodiversity has great potential for enhancing current teaching methods of visual literacy. Specifically, Grandin's work on how visual thinkers learn and why it is important to encourage neurodiverse thinkers to hone their abilities early in life can help evolve how and why visual literacy is utilized in the classroom. One framework that Grandin's research could potentially align with is the ACRL (Association of College and Research Libraries) *Framework for Visual Literacy for Higher Education*. This Framework was published in April 2022. The document was created with the goal of further developing the 2011 ACRL *Visual Literacy Competency Standards for Higher Education* as well as being a companion document to the ACRL *Information Literacy Framework* (Thompson et al., 2022). The final framework was established by data collected from an IRB-approved qualitative study completed by the ACRL Visual Literacy Task Force. The resulting document contains four themes for learning visual literacy, each with its own knowledge practices and dispositions. Grandin's work pairs well with the last theme: learners pursue social justice through visual practice. As the *Framework for Visual Literacy* explains, "By building reciprocal relationships with communities, acknowledging the limits of their own knowledge, and seeking to better understand their worldview, biases, and perceptions, as well as those around them, learners can become conscientious contributors to a more just world" (ACRL, 2022, p. 8).

Grandin's approach to sharing her own story and research with large audiences around the world has helped inform different communities about autism and the impact of visual thinkers. Her ability to reach people on a personal level and her knowledge of different ways of thinking would be extremely beneficial to educators' approaches to teaching visual literacy skills. Educators can further reference Grandin's story and research in a way that expresses the need for more inclusive visual representation and teaching methods.

Conclusion: Visual Literacy for K-12 Education

While Grandin's focus on the importance of visual thinkers is somewhat new, her research on autism and animal behavior has been closely tied to visual thinking abilities for years. Even though she has been included in some visual literacy discussions, there is room to go deeper and really examine how she contributes to the field. Grandin's research and activism for autism do show great promise for being utilized in the world of K-12 education, specifically in relation to visual literacy instruction. One challenge for utilizing Grandin's work in this way is that she does not offer practical tools for visual literacy instruction. However, she does explain the characteristics of visual thinking and an understanding of why we need visual thinkers in our world. Grandin's work can be seen as the "why" behind the importance of visual literacy being incorporated into K-12 education. The relevancy of visual literacy tends to challenge practitioners and educators need to address this with administration and colleagues. Grandin offers a bridge over this challenge through her vulnerability in sharing her story and through examining the stories of other visual thinkers who have changed the world. The personal is relevant and Grandin's work is an exemplary example of the relevancy and importance of visual thinking abilities as well as the incorporation of visual literacy within the educational curriculum.

References

ACRL. (2022, April 6). *Companion document to the ACRL framework for information literacy for higher education: The framework for visual literacy.* American Library Association. https://www.ala.org/acrl/sites/ala.org.acrl/files/content/standards/Framework_Companion_Visual_Literacy.pdf

Anderson, E., Avgerinou, M. D., Dimas, S., & Robinson, R. (2021). Visual literacy in the K12 classroom of the 21st century: From college preparation to finding one's own voice. In *Handbook of research on K-12 blended and virtual learning through the i2flex classroom model* (pp. 84–108). IGI Global. 10.4018/978-1-7998-7760-8.ch005

Avgerinou, M. D., & Pettersson, R. (2020). Visual literacy theory: Moving forward. In S. Josephson, J. D. Kelly, & K. Smith (Eds.), *Handbook of visual communication: Theory, methods, and media* (pp. 433–464). Routledge.

Barry, A. (2002). Perception and visual communication theory. *Journal of Visual Literacy, 22*(1), 91–106. https://www.tandfonline-com.proxyiub.uits.iu.edu/doi/abs/10.1080/23796529.2002.11674583

Barry, A. (2020). Perception theory: A neurological perspective on visual communication. In S. Josephson, J. D. Kelly & K. Smith (Eds.), *Handbook of visual communication: Theory, methods, and media* (pp. 3–27). Routledge.

DeGroot, D. (2020, September 8). *CEOWORLD magazine named the top 10 college professors in the United States.* Our Community Now. https://ourcommunitynow.com/news-local/dr-temple-grandin-of-csu-named-one-of-the-top-college-professors-in-the-country

Gardner, H. E. (2006). *Multiple intelligences: New horizons in theory and practice* (Revised, updated edition). Basic Books.

Grandin, T. (2010a). *Temple Grandin: The world needs all kinds of minds | TED Talk.* Retrieved April 19, 2023, from https://www.ted.com/talks/temple_grandin_the_world_needs_all_kinds_of_minds

Grandin, T. (2010b). *Thinking in pictures: And other reports from my life with autism.* Vintage eBooks.

Grandin, T. (2013). My experience with visual thinking and sensory oversensitivity: The need for research on sensory problems. In M. A. Just & K. A. Pelphrey (Eds.), *Development and brain systems in autism.* Psychology Press.

Grandin, T. (2022). *Visual thinking: The hidden gifts of people who think in pictures, patterns and abstractions.* Rider Books.

Grandin, T., & Johnson, C. (2006). *Animals in translation: Using the mysteries of autism to decode animal behavior.* Harcourt.

Kozhevnikov, M., Hegarty, M., & Mayer, R. E. (2002). Revising the visualizer-verbalizer dimension: Evidence for two types of visualizers. *Cognition and Instruction, 20*(1), 47–77.

Kozhevnikov, M., Kosslyn, S., & Shephard, J. (2005). Spatial versus object visualizers: A new characterization of visual cognitive style. *Memory & Cognition, 33*(4), 710–726. 10.3758/BF03195337

Mayall, H. J., & Robinson, R. S. (2009). Investigating visual literacy integration: Lida's legacy? *TechTrends: Linking Research & Practice to Improve Learning, 53*(2), 48–49. 10.1007/s11528-009-0268-8

McMaster, S. (2015). *Visual literacy and art education: Review of the literature.* 10.13140/RG.2.1.4331.2482

Metros, S. E. (2008). The educator's role in preparing visually literate learners. *Theory into Practice, 47*(2), 102–109. 10.1080/00405840801992264

Misenhelter, M. (2017). *Academic libraries and signage: Visual literacy skill to improve wayfinding* [Master's thesis, Emporia State University]. Emporia State Institutional Repository Collection (ESIRC).

Rozema, R. (2015). Manga and the autistic mind. *The English Journal,* 105(1), 60–68.

Serafini, F., & Gee, J.P. (2013). *Reading the visual: An introduction to teaching multimodal literacy.* Teachers College Press. http://ebookcentral.proquest.com/lib/iub-ebooks/detail.action?docID=3544848

Thompson, D. S., Beene, S., Greer, K., Wegmann, M., Fullmer, M., Murphy, M., Schumacher, S., & Saulter, T. (2022). A proliferation of images: Trends, obstacles, and opportunities for visual literacy. *Journal of Visual Literacy, 41*(2), 113–131. 10.1080/1051144X.2022.2053819

West, T. G. (2009). *In the mind's eye: Creative visual thinkers, gifted dyslexics, and the rise of visual technologies.* Prometheus Books.

10

DAVID HOWES

Pioneer of Sensory Studies

Brian P. Kennedy

Brian P. Kennedy Arts Consulting, LLC

Biographical Sketch

David Howes was born in Montreal in 1957. He studied social anthropology at the University of Toronto (1976–1979) and at Oxford University on a Commonwealth Scholarship (1979–1981). After his Oxford degree, Howes planned to carry out field research in eastern Indonesia, but the ongoing tragic war in Timor prevented travel to the region at that time. He returned to Canada and decided to move into law at McGill University in Montreal, where he took two degrees (1981–1985). This proved a detour because he did not want to practice law, and, instead, he took teaching jobs in the departments of religion and sociology at Concordia University in Montreal, before beginning doctoral studies in anthropology at the University of Montreal. In 1990, he decided to do fieldwork on the comparative sensory orders in two societies in Papua New Guinea where some renowned anthropologists had studied, among them, Edmund Snow Carpenter (1922–2011). Carpenter had been one of Marshall McLuhan's collaborators in the 1960s, conducting studies among the peoples of the Canadian Arctic, but also in Papua New Guinea, which is the most linguistically diverse place on earth, with over 800 languages. Howes' doctoral study was published as *Sensory Relations* (1992). Over the next three decades, the ongoing research, teaching and publications of David Howes have distinguished him as a pioneer in the field of the anthropology of the senses, and as an innovative thinker in "sensory studies." Under his leadership, the Centre for Sensory Studies at Concordia University in Montreal has generated a remarkable sequence of innovative conferences, research papers and book publications.

DOI: 10.4324/9781032651781-11

He co-founded the journal *The Senses and Society*, and has served as general editor of the book series, *Sensory Formations* (2003–2009), and the *Sensory Studies* series (2015–), both published by Routledge.

Introduction

As Howes defines it:

> Sensory studies involve a cultural approach to the study of the senses and a sensory approach to the study of culture. It challenges the monopoly that the discipline of psychology has long exercised over the study of the senses and sense perception by foregrounding the sociality of the sensorium. History and anthropology are the foundational disciplines of this field. However, sensory studies also encompasses many other disciplines as scholars from across the humanities and social sciences have, over the past few decades, successively turned their attention to the sensorium. (Howes, 2013, para. 2)

Sensory studies offer an expanded field into which scholarship on visual literacy can be imported to the betterment of both. The continuing emphasis on focal point learning within education systems, using digits and letters as primary means of communication, to the neglect of wider non-textual formats and media, has caused visual literacy studies to remain relatively siloed, despite the current hyper-visual world of mass communication, and to be inattentive to the cognitive potential of the non-visual senses.

Emerging Interest in Sensory Experience

Howes' initial interest in exploring the varieties of sensory experience in history and across cultures, was sparked by attending a lecture in the Senior Common Room of Trinity College by Marshall McLuhan, who was talking about "the laws of media" and their impact on "sense-ratios". McLuhan's books, *The Gutenberg Galaxy* (1962), *Understanding Media* (1964), and *The Medium Is the Message: An Inventory of Effects* (1967), established him as a leading intellectual, although during his later years "the Canadian media guru" was dismissed by many as eccentric and unfocused, until the digital revolution rehabilitated him as a genius who predicted the Internet and its effects on society. McLuhan believed that technology impacted social organization and relationships, and, through its effects on cognition, it encouraged specialization. He promoted the ideas of one world, the world as one, and the "global village". He argued that the way information is conveyed is as important as its content – "the medium is the message".

McLuhan emphasized the importance of the human senses, and regarded communications media as "extensions of the senses" (McLuhan, 1994, p. 4).

This impacted Howes powerfully: "McLuhan saved me from falling for Merleau-Ponty" (Howes, 2023b, interview). At the University of Toronto in the late 1970s, all of the other members of his cohort were reading the French philosopher's classic work, *Phenomenology of Perception* (1962):

> All of the talk was about the phenomenology of perception, the unity of the senses, and the idea that you are the center of the world. But McLuhan brought from [James] Joyce the idea of the *collideroscope* of the sensorium. What an idea! The senses smashing up against each other in a *collideroscope*, always rearranging themselves, and the self in the process. (Howes, 2023b, interview)

Maurice Merleau-Ponty (1908–1961) was renowned for his focus on embodiment (or "embodied cognition"), and also emphasized the sense of vision as the act of looking that opened the body to the wider world. The body is conscious and therefore is both subject and object, seeing and seen (Merleau-Ponty, 1962, 1964a, 1964b). Inspired by McLuhan, Howes quickly saw through Merleau-Ponty, questioning his doctrine of the unity of the senses and (paradoxically) overbearing attention to the visual. Where Merleau-Ponty saw synergy, Howes saw hierarchy, and where Merleau-Ponty focused on vision, Howes surmised that this expressed an unconscious bias, instilled in the philosopher by his culture. In Western thought, vision is at the top of the hierarchy, but in other cultures other senses may come to the fore.

Howes had already begun to develop his own theories about sensory orders. He was suspicious of McLuhan's technological determinism, and wanted to explore what a focus on "techniques of the senses" might yield (as distinct from McLuhan's emphasis on the impact of changing technologies of communication, e.g. writing, print, electronic communication). With the aid of a grant from the Olfactory Research Fund (the research division of the New York-based Fragrance Foundation), he went to Papua New Guinea to research smell and odors while carrying out research into other fields of sense on the side. He concluded that McLuhan had tended to lump oral societies together indiscriminately and oppose them en masse to literate (read: visual) societies. Rather than that, he argued, each society must be approached on its own sensory terms.

Key Contributor to the Sensory Turn

Howes' first book, *The Varieties of Sensory Experience: A Sourcebook in the Anthropology of the Senses* (1991), established him as a key contributor in what was termed "the sensory turn." Sensory anthropology explores:

how the patterning of sense experience varies from one culture to the next in accordance with the meaning and emphasis attached to each of the modalities of perception. It is also concerned with tracing the influence such variations have on forms of social organization, conceptions of self and cosmos, the regulation of emotions, and other domains of cultural expression. (Howes, 1991, p. 3)

Historians of medieval times had been precursors of the sensory turn, including Johan Huizinga (1996 [1919]), who studied not only historical experience but "historical sensation," and Lucien Febvre, who famously proposed that "The sixteenth century did not see first: it heard and smelled, it sniffed the air and caught sounds" (1982 [1942], p. 432). Anthropologists had also pointed in this direction, for example, Claude Lévi-Strauss (1970 [1964]) whose study of Amerindian myths sought to unravel their "sensory codes." During the 1980s, anthropologists and historians began to embrace the senses in earnest (Corbin, 1986 [1982]; Feld, 1990 [1982]), and started to compile a bibliography to counter emphasis on the "visualism" of Western culture. The rise of visual culture and visual studies as academic disciplines, each emphasizing the primacy of vision, deepened the hierarchy of the senses. As Howes explains: "The anthropology of the senses was ... initially inspired by a desire to explore under-investigated non-visual modes of experience. It would later draw attention to the varying ways in which sight is configured in different cultures" (Howes, 2013, para. 7), including Western culture. Technological development assisted this movement, with tape recorders, camcorders, and other devices allowing capture of sights and sounds with higher quality than ever before.

Aroma: The Cultural History of Smell (Howes et al., 1994), was a groundbreaking work, a study of olfaction using multidisciplinary approaches, that has been translated into several languages. Exploring the social role of smell throughout history and society, this seminal publication presented knowledge about "osmologies" (olfactory classification systems) from many parts of the world. It also examined results from psychological and neurobiological laboratory research experiments, which tended to dissociate the senses by examining them one-at-a-time, challenging assumptions and conclusions. In one study, participants were tested with pine-scented tissues which they found to be "fresher" but also "rougher" than unscented ones, even though their consistency was the same. Where did the perception of roughness stem from, the researchers wondered? It should have been obvious that the pine smell triggered an association with the abrasiveness of pine needles. Howes holds this example up as demonstrating how the senses act together with each other, and it is not possible to dissociate them (see the discussion in *Sensorial Investigations,*

2023a, chapter 5, pp. 144–173). For example, he has called the work of visual literacy scholar, James Elkins, in *How to Use Your Eyes* (2000), "profoundly revealing, but at the same time curiously stultifying insofar as the nonvisual senses are concerned" (Howes, 2023c, para. 6).

Howes has long worked in concert with the cultural historian, Constance Classen. They co-authored *Aroma* (with Anthony Synnott), and also wrote *Ways of Sensing: Understanding the Senses in Society* (2013) together. As Mark Smith noted in *A Sensory History Manifesto* (2021, p. 27): "Few historians … have done as much to establish the importance of the senses historically as Constance Classen; no non-historian has done as much to popularize sensory history as anthropologist David Howes." Classen's publications have been at the forefront in the development of academic scholarship in the history of the senses and the anthropology of the senses (1993a, 1993b, 1997, 1998, 2005, 2012, 2014, 2017). She served as general editor for *A Cultural History of the Senses*, an impressive six-volume series "investigating sensory values and experiences throughout Western history and presenting a vital new way of understanding the past" (Classen, 2014, p. xi). The volumes, from antiquity to the modern, take a domain-based approach. Each volume is composed of nine chapters (by different authors), which respectively address the senses in social life, the city, the marketplace, religion, philosophy and science, medicine, literature, art, and media. This approach departs from the conventional "unisensory" (one-sense-at-a-time) approach to writing sensory history (or studies focusing on one sense – visual literacy) by redirecting attention to the interaction of the senses within and across each of the nine domains, and across the six-time periods.

In 2014, Howes edited a special issue of the journal, *The Senses and Society*, on the theme of "Sensory Museology" (Howes, 2014). It documented the emergence of experimental approaches to audience engagement within contemporary museum studies and curatorial practice which take the idea of "bringing the senses back in," as their point of departure, in particular touch – as exemplified by the transition from the "hands-off" to the "hands-on" museum display (Black, 2005; Chatterjee, 2008; Dudley, 2010; Pye, 2007). An early example that Howes noted (Howes, 2014, p. 264) took place at the MIT List Visual Arts Center in Massachusetts. *The Sensorium* exhibition, curated by Caroline A. Jones, showed how new technologies used by contemporary artists had helped develop a hybrid moment where prior segregation of the senses had been upended by a multisensory mix that had transformative implications for society. Exhibits included walls with odors, strobe lights, lasers, along with a singing microscope that invited viewers to a hybrid moment "where modernist segregation of the senses is giving way to dramatic sensorial mixes, transmutations, and opportunities for intensified and playful mediation" (Jones, 2006, p. 2). Howes and Classen have truly broadened the field of sensory museology with publications, including *The Museum of the Senses* (Classen, 2017), building on "The Museum as Sensescape" (Classen & Howes, 2006) and "Museum Manners" (Classen, 2007). These have explored the connections between vision and other sensory inputs, thereby expanding methods of close or slow looking, visual language, and visual thinking employed in museums, especially in art museum educational programs based on concepts of visual literacy.

Recent Publications

Ever prolific, Howes has built on his edited volume *Empire of the Senses: The Sensual Cultural Reader* (2005), with *Senses and Sensation: Critical and Primary Sources* (2018), in four volumes, in which, as editor, he presents key texts for anyone engaging the field of sensory studies. The range of approaches in *Empire of the Senses* (2005) offers much to the field of visual literacy. For example, Oliver Sacks explores "The Mind's Eye: What the Blind See," concluding "… one can no longer say of one's mental landscape what is visual, what is auditory, what is image, what is language, what is intellectual, what is emotional – they are all fused together and imbued with our own individual perspectives and values" (Howes, 2005, p. 41). Constance Classen writes of the visualism of the Desana people of the Amazonian rainforest:

> its emphasis on integrating and animating color energies is surely very different from the visualism of the West, with its emphasis on linearity, detached observation and surface appearance. In fact, the "world view" of the Desana is rather a sensory kaleidoscope, with color shifting into smell and then into flavor and so on. (Howes, 2005, p. 161)

Two of Howes most recent publications aim to shift the axis of academic discourse yet again: *The Sensory Studies Manifesto: Tracking the Sensorial Revolution in the Arts and Human Sciences* (2022), and *Sensorial Investigations: A History of the Senses in Anthropology, Psychology and Law* (2023a). In these books, Howes continues his relentless effort to sensitize fellow scholars to the sociality of sensation and cultural contingency of perception. Just as meaning is socially constructed, so too are sensory experiences: "This is why it is not enough to look at the senses as 'energy transducers,' 'information gatherers' or 'perceptual systems'; they must also be understood as cultural systems" (Howes, 2005, pp. 4–5). He elaborates in *The Sensory Studies Manifesto*:

the vaunted status of vision also smuggled in a certain blindness with respect to the multisensory character of most human experience: vision, being the paragon sense, could stand for all the senses, with the result that the "other senses" were easily ignored or assimilated to a visual model. (Howes, 2022, p. 7)

Howes argues that Aristotle and his contemporaries had a very different understanding of the senses, which was as much cosmological as anatomical. This is given in the way each of the senses was associated with a different element: "Water was the element of sight (because the eye contains water), air the element of hearing, fire the element of smell and earth the element both of touch and taste, which is a mode of touch" (Howes, 2023a, p. 119 quoting Connor, 2015, p. 241). Thus, in ancient Greece, as in ancient China and India, and in many contemporary traditional societies, the senses have been regarded as media (or mediators), not just receptor organs.

Howes vigorously challenges assumptions within Western psychology, demonstrating how people make sense of the world by engaging their senses, how the museum and design world is engaged in manipulating the senses, and how incorporating multiple disciplinary perspectives is necessary to the study of perception (which for too long, in his estimation, was the exclusive preserve of psychology). Rudolf Arnheim's *Visual Thinking* (1969) had advanced "a theory of thinking as a continuation of seeing" that worked well for Western culture, but not, for example, in the "ear-minded" native cultures in Brazil, or the "nose-minded" cultures in the islands of the Indian Ocean (Howes, 2022, p. 11). Whereas in Western culture, the dominance leads to greeting each other with "Nice to see you" and "You're looking good," in the Andaman Islands, the Ongee "will refer to themselves by pointing to their nose and ask 'How is your smell?' when they greet each other. They navigate the forest by sniffing and are careful to 'bind' their smell to their bodies" (Howes, 2022, p. 12).

In *Sensorial Investigations*, Howes demonstrates in ample measure how the degrees he received in law, earned between his academic degrees in anthropology, have provided a rich seam for exploration of the study of the senses. He has argued that "the law" is a cultural system and he favors "cross-cultural jurisprudence." A judge needs to recognize their own cultural biases, as well as the backgrounds of litigants, before making judgment. This is in fact true of everyone who makes judgments, whether in daily life or work. Howes is employed in two universities, as a full-time professor at Concordia University, elevated recently to Distinguished Research Professor (2021), and as Adjunct Professor in the Faculty of

Law at McGill University. *Sensorial Investigations* offers a synthesis of Howes' thinking about the senses:

> The expression that I use now for what I do is 'Lead with the senses,' by which I mean don't start with ideas about cognition, or language, or representation. The latter are all very popular topics with academics, but they deflect attention from the sensuous. The other thing I like to say is 'Don't psychologize.' For the longest while psychology and then neuroscience enjoyed a monopoly on the study of the senses and perception. They lock the senses inside the head, in the brain. What I'm interested in is historicizing the senses. It's the socialization of the senses that ought to concern us first and foremost, and that really runs counter to the way we are so inclined to psychologize things in our society. (Howes, 2023b, interview)

Howes is calling for recognition and appreciation of the overall sensory landscape before concentrating on any one sense. Academic disciplines, including visual literacy studies, can draw from Charles Baudelaire by inquiring into the correspondence of the senses – the poet walking "the forest of symbols," discovering that "sound, fragrances and colors correspond" (Howes, 2022, p. 19).

Other Initiatives in Sensory Research

Visual literacy scholars will find much of interest on the Sensory Studies website (www.sensorystudies.org), which, under Howes' curatorship, has become the leading publicly available resource about its subject, and its detailed sections provide information about: sense-based research being conducted by over 600 scholars throughout the world; guidance for academic faculty in preparing courses related to advancing knowledge of the senses, including syllabi and course outlines from dozens of educational institutions; a bibliography of significant publications in sensory studies from 2007 to date; details about past and upcoming conferences, lectures, exhibitions and other events on the senses, history and politics of perception; a research forum for advanced research, listing recent scholarship, exhibitions, theses, videos, and podcasts.

The Centre for Sensory Studies (established in 2010) located in the Department of Sociology and Anthropology at Concordia University, grew out of and in turn incorporated the "Concordia Sensoria Research Team" (CONSERT), which was co-founded in 1988 by Howes, Anthony Synnott, and Constance Classen. The Centre is currently composed of 18 faculty from 9 different academic departments, and around 40 graduate students.

It otherwise includes, alongside CONSERT, three laboratories: The Laboratory for Sensory Research at the business school promoting and enabling research on sensory marketing; The Concordia Vision Laboratory located in the psychology department conducting psychophysical experiments in human perception and exploring aspects of vision; and a studio lab called labxmodal founded by Chris Salter (now at the University of the Arts, Zurich). The latter two laboratories invite scholars of museum studies and visual literacy to expand their research by creating opportunities for visitors to be immersed in alternately configured environments to the everyday. One series of projects seeks to create "the performative sensory environment." For example, similar to a museum display, but without objects, a space can mix up the senses, with audiences not as passive viewers but active participants who help co-produce experiences. These might involve blindfolds or facemasks, bare feet experiencing different surfaces and textures, aromas of tea wafting from behind a backlit screen, the dipping of hands in paint made from icing sugar, or an acoustic dining experience, blowing bubbles, spilling pasta, and drumming with cutlery.

Howes and Salter first teamed up to add this arts-based research, or "research-creation" component, to the Centre's outputs, and have created many "performative sensory environments" over the years. After their experience of immersion, visitors are interviewed about it and the insights gleaned are woven into research papers. In 2023, the Center for Sensory Studies (2023) held its fourth academic conference in a series titled *Uncommon Senses* with presentations, workshops, and art exhibitions advancing research in the social sciences and humanities and arts on the past and future of the senses. The 2023 conference was subtitled "sensory ecologies, economies and aesthetics".

Conclusion: Impact of Howes' Work for Visual Literacy

It has been asserted that a lot more research has been conducted on vision than on any other human sense (Hutmacher, 2019). Research has shown that people fear the loss of their sight more than any other sense (Enoch et al., 2019). This is often understood within Western culture as the result of the development of philosophies and technologies that privileged knowledge based on visual evidence, offering "observations" and "perspectives" that facilitate a "lens" on history (Smith, 2021, p. 41). The development of education systems founded on reading in silence, using our eyes (often with spectacles) to absorb information, has emphasized the preeminence of vision. The work of David Howes challenges scholars and researchers in visual literacy to situate their work within a wider understanding of the senses. This he describes in *Sensorial Investigations* as an alternative approach that "could

be called *sensitivism* to distinguish it from both empiricism and cognitivism."
He continues:

> Sensitivism involves leading with the senses conceived as both bearers
> and shapers of culture. Sensitivism foregrounds the study of *cultural
> practices* (the techniques of the senses) over physiology (the senses as
> receptor organs). The focus is on the interaction between the senses and
> the world as well as each other rather than on the neural pathways
> leading from sense organ to brain. (Howes, 2023a, p. 118)

In 2014, the year Howes focused an issue of *The Senses and Society* on
sensory museology, I invited him to present a keynote lecture at the 46th
annual conference of the International Visual Literacy Association (IVLA),
hosted by the Toledo Museum of Art (TMA) in Toledo, Ohio. This was the
first time the association (founded in 1969) had held its annual gathering in a
museum. As TMA's director (2010–2019), along with many colleagues,
I implemented a thorough reworking of the institution based on visual
literacy methodologies, leveraging the expertise of the education department
(Kennedy, 2010, 2013, 2019). Howes was impressed by the ways teaching
visual literacy, based on the elements of art and the principles of design, was
leveraged in so many aspects of the museum's activities (Kennedy & Deetsch,
2019). The speakers at the conference included artists, Magdalene Odundo
and Aminah Robinson, and experts on aspects of visual literacy, including
Philip Yenawine, Lynell Burmark, and Stephen Apkon. TMA also introduced
Howes to Kathy Mills, a prominent researcher on multimodal literacy, based
in Australia, and he wrote the foreword for her book, *Literacy Theories for the
Digital Age* (Mills, 2015). In it, he remarked that he had been reading the
book in manuscript form while on the plane to the IVLA conference in Ohio.
He wrote that he was looking forward to the conference due to a remark I
had made in a video available on YouTube (Kennedy, 2013) that "visual
literacy is the key to sensory literacy, and that creating conditions for sensory
literacy should be the goal of the contemporary museum" (Mills, 2015,
p. xv). The exhibitions accompanying the conference at TMA were multisensory and playful, encouraging visitors to engage their senses of sight,
sound, and touch through active participation with works of art (Classen,
2017; Ottney, 2015; Toledo Museum of Art, 2014). The overall visitor
reaction was enthusiastic, with works by, among others, Pinaree Sanpitak,
Magdalene Odundo, and Aminah Robinson, inviting audiences to have a
multisensory experience.

Mills, like Howes, believes that visual skills alone, cannot address the
digital world today. Although academic research and education systems
continue to rely on visual texts (or words with visuals), new sensory-literacy

pedagogical and learning models are needed to promote multisensory literacy. This is a necessary future for research and the IVLA has continued to pursue a more multisensory agenda by holding its 47th conference at the San Francisco Museum of Fine Arts, and its 48th, under Howes' guidance, at the Centre for Sensory Studies at Concordia University, Montreal. The 51st meeting took place at M Leuven, a museum in Leuven, Belgium, that has adopted visual literacy principles in radical ways in its displays and programs (Leuven, 2019). The 53rd IVLA meeting (2021) was a virtual conference, due to the COVID pandemic. It was organized by TMA and the University of Toledo, where a memorandum of understanding, signed between the two institutions in 2018, had led to a campus initiative in visual literacy, available to students in all majors. By 2022, 14% (127) of UT's faculty had opted into the Visual Literacy Group in the university's course management system (Deetsch & Appel, 2022). This type of campus-wide and multi-departmental adoption of visual literacy is exceptional within American universities, but it is likely to become more widespread over time. Howes argues:

> The invention of the concept of visual literacy introduced a momentous rupture into the way literacy had been understood to date, in terms of skill at reading and writing. The arrival of the visual literacy concept shifted the onus from competence in reading and writing texts to competence in creating and decoding images. This shattered the logocentrism of the western tradition. It positioned the visual on par with the textual. This diversification of the modalities of cognition (or what Howard Gardner called "frames of mind") now needs to be extended further, so that other senses can be accorded the status of being literate (which remains a cardinal value). The idea of tactile literacy, olfactory literacy, and above all multisensory literacy (following Kathy Mills) – or sensory literacy, in short, has tremendous potential to open the doors of perception. It all comes down to our senses being the best available means for making sense of the world and other people. (Howes, 2023b)

While it can be asserted that there has been a conspiracy to suppress the importance of visual literacy by textual scholars, in recent times a more collaborative approach has emerged. In a similar ecumenical spirit, David Howes has encouraged an acceptance of sensory approaches and the correspondence between them. Howes understands that there can be resistance to the term visual literacy, but he himself supports it:

> In regard to visual literacy, the people I deal with in education don't like the word literacy. They see it as colonial and so forth, but this is where I

say we've got to use sensory literacy because you are raising the senses to the level of literacy. We need that hoist to be able to go on from there, so we can say there is a literacy of the senses. A lot of visual literacy is about coding and decoding. One of the things about my work is that it defies categories. It's historical and anthropological and that means you can't put it in a box. (Howes, 2023b, interview)

Vision is a vital sense, and visual literacy is essential.

References

Black, G. (2005). *The engaging museum: Developing museums for visitor involvement.* Routledge.

Center for Sensory Studies. (2023, May 6). *Uncommon senses IV: Sensory ecologies, economies, and aesthetics.* https://centreforsensorystudies.org/uncommon-senses-iv-sensory-ecologies-economies-and-aesthetics/

Chatterjee, H. (2008). *Touch in museums: Policy and practice in object handling.* Berg.

Classen, C. (1993a). *Worlds of sense: Exploring the senses in history and across cultures.* Routledge.

Classen, C. (1993b). *Inca cosmology and the human body.* University of Utah Press.

Classen, C. (1997). Foundations for an anthropology of the senses. *International Social Science Journal, 49*(153), 401–412. 10.1111/j.1468-2451.1997.tb00032.x

Classen, C. (1998). *The color of angels: Cosmology, gender and the aesthetic imagination.* Routledge.

Classen, C. (Ed.). (2005). *The book of touch.* Berg.

Classen, C. (2007). Museum manners: The sensory life of the early museum. *Journal of Social History, 40*(4), 895–914. https://www.jstor.org/stable/25096398

Classen, C. (2012). *The deepest sense: A cultural history of touch.* University of Illinois Press.

Classen, C. (General Ed.). (2014). *A cultural history of the senses.* 6 Vols. Bloomsbury.

Classen, C. (2017). *The museum of the senses: Experiencing art and collections.* Bloomsbury.

Classen, C., & Howes, D. (2006). The museum as sensescape: Western sensibilities and indigenous artifacts. In E. Edwards, C. Gosden, & R. Phillips (Eds.), *Sensible objects: Colonialism, museums and material culture* (pp. 199–222). Routledge. 10.4324/9781003086611

Connor, S. (2015). Literature, technology and the senses. In D. Hillman & U. Maude (Eds.), *The Cambridge companion to the body in literature* (pp. 177–196). Cambridge University Press.

Corbin, A. (1986 [1982]). *The foul and the fragrant: Odor and the French social imagination.* Harvard University Press.

Deetsch, M., & Appel, H. (2022). Seeing across disciplines: An experiment in visual literacy across higher education. In J. Lee, S. Beene, X. Chen, W. Huang, L. Okan, & F. Rodrigues (Eds.), *Seeing across disciplines: The book of selected readings 2022* (pp. 54–64). International Visual Literacy Association. 10.52917/ivlatbsr.2022.014

Dudley, S. (Ed.). (2010). *Museum materialities: Objects, engagements, interpretations.* Routledge.

Elkins, J. (2000). *How to use your eyes.* Routledge.

Enoch, J., McDonald, L., Jones, L., Jones, P. R., & Crabb, D. P. (2019, November 1). Evaluating whether sight is the most valued sense. *JAMA Ophthalmology, 137*(11), 1317–1320. 10.1001/jamaophthalmol.2019.3537

Febvre, L. (1982 [1942]). *The Problem of Unbelief in the Sixteenth Century: The Religion of Rabelais.* Harvard University Press.

Feld, S. (1990 [1982]). *Sound and sentiment: Birds, weeping, poetics and song in Kaluli expression.* University of Pennsylvania Press.

Howes, D. (Ed.). (1991). *The varieties of sensory experience: A sourcebook in the anthropology of the senses.* University of Toronto Press.

Howes, D. (2005). *Empire of the senses: The sensual cultural reader.* Berg.

Howes, D. (2013). *The expanding field of sensory studies.* Sensory Studies blogpost. https://www.sensorystudies.org/sensational-investigations/the-expanding-field-of-sensory-studies/

Howes, D. (2014). Sensory museology. *The Senses and Society, 9*(3), 259–380. 10.2752/174589314X14023847039917.

Howes, D. (2018). *Senses and sensation: Critical and primary sources.* 4 Vols. Routledge.

Howes, D. (2022). *The sensory studies manifesto: Tracking the sensorial revolution in the arts and human sciences.* University of Toronto Press.

Howes, D. (2023a). *Sensorial investigations: A history of the senses in anthropology, psychology and law.* Pennsylvania State University Press.

Howes, D. (2023b). Transcript of interview with Brian Kennedy, Concordia University, Montreal, July 27, 2023.

Howes, D. (2023c). *The aesthetics of mixing the senses.* David-howes.com. https://david-howes.com/senses/aestheticsofmixingthesenses.pdf

Howes, D., Classen, C., & Synnott, A. (1994). *Aroma: The cultural history of smell.* Routledge.

Huizinga, J. (1996 [1919]). *The autumn of the middle ages.* Trans. R. Payton & U. Mammitzsch. University of Chicago Press.

Hutmacher, F. (2019). Why is there so much more research on vision than on any other sensory modality? *Frontiers in Psychology, 10*(2246). 10.3389/fpsyg.2019.02246

Jones, C. (2006). *Sensorium: Embodied experience, technology, and contemporary art.* MIT Press.

Kennedy, B. (2010). *Visual literacy: Why we need it! [Video].* YouTube. https://www.youtube.com/watch?v=E91fk6D0nwM

Kennedy, B. (2013). *What is visual literacy? [Video].* YouTube. https://www.youtube.com/watch?v=O39niAzuapc

Kennedy, B., & Deetsch, M. (2019). Speaking visual at the Toledo Museum of Art. In L. Vermeersch, E. Wagner, & R. Wenrich (Eds.), *Guiding the eye: Visual literacy in art museums* (pp. 71–77). Waxmann.

Leuven Museum. (2019). 51st annual IVLA conference. https://www.mleuven.be/en/programme/51st-annual-ivla-conference

Lévi-Strauss, C. (1970 [1964]). *The raw and the cooked: Introduction to a science of mythology, 1.* J & D Weightman, Harper and Row.

McLuhan, M. (1962). *The Gutenberg Galaxy.* University of Toronto Press.

McLuhan, M. (1994 [1964]). *Understanding media: The extensions of man.* MIT Press.

McLuhan, M., & Fiore, Q. (1967). *The medium is the message: An inventory of effects*. Bantam Books.

Merleau-Ponty, M. (1962). *Phenomenology of perception*. Routledge.

Merleau-Ponty, M. (1964a). Eye and mind. In J. E. Edie (Ed.), *The primacy of perception* (pp. 159–190). Northeastern University Press.

Merleau-Ponty, M. (1964b). *The visible and the invisible*. Northeastern University Press.

Mills, K. (2015). *Literacy theories for the digital age: Social, critical, multimodal, spatial, material and sensory lenses*. Multilingual Matters.

Ottney, S. (2015, April 26). *Play time: TMA to host interactive exhibit memorial through Labor Day*. Toledo Free Press. https://toledofreepress.com/play-time-tma-to-host-interactive-exhibit-memorial-through-labor-day/

Pye, E. (Ed.) (2007). *The power of touch: Handling objects in museums and heritage contexts*. Left Coast Press.

Smith, M. (2021). *A sensory history manifesto*. Pennsylvania State University Press.

Toledo Museum of Art. (2014). *Insight: Contemporary sensory works*. https://archive.org/details/insight-contemporary-sensory-works

11

NADA SHABOUT

The Challenge of Visual Literacy in Modern and Contemporary Arab Art

Marty Miller
Louisiana State University

Biographical Sketch

Dr. Nada Shabout was born in Scotland in 1962. She spent her high school years in Baghdad, then traveled to the United States to pursue her post-secondary career. While her undergraduate studies focus on the creation of architecture and painting, with a minor in urban planning, her graduate focus shifted to art criticism, art history, and cross-cultural studies. She added a PhD in the humanities, focusing on criticism and art history, cross-cultural studies, and Arab studies. Currently serving as regents professor of art history at the University of North Texas, her areas of expertise include the historiography of Arab art and Iraqi art, cultural destruction and preservation, identity politics and art, as well as global, postcolonial and feminist theory.

Scholarship, in Shabout's case, consists of more than a publication record. It includes teaching, advocacy, and outreach through presentations and interviews to improve awareness of Arab art's importance in a global art context. Shabout is arguably responsible for bringing modern and contemporary Arab art into the spotlight in the United States. She created one of the world's first university classes on modern Arab art. Her work with and advocacy for Modern Iraqi people has led her to co-found the Association for Modern and Contemporary Art (AMCA) of the Arab World, Iran, and Turkey, a non-profit, apolitical organization that promotes scholarly communication in the field. Her scholarship and advocacy on behalf of Arab art has created a more complete picture of global modern and

DOI: 10.4324/9781032651781-12

contemporary art, and therefore advancing the visual literacy of learners worldwide.

Introduction

It is cliche to say that the study of Arab modern and contemporary art is complex – such a description could be applied to any style or period of art. A more accurate statement would be that it is unfamiliar, unknown, and/or not frequently or fully researched by students and scholars in the Western region. One of the competencies of visual literacy is that learners will understand visual creations as sources of information. To fully assimilate this information into their knowledge base, a learner must be able to 'read' and understand it accurately. Owing to the lack of familiarity with the original context in which Arab artists work, Westerners struggle to develop visual literacy in this area of modern and contemporary art. It is this gap in contextual knowledge that Shabout began rectifying upon publishing *Modern Arab Art*, and has continued to do so through her scholarly activities. This book was groundbreaking not only for its subject matter, but for the obstacles that Shabout overcame to bring it to fruition.

Even before she even considered writing a book, Shabout faced significant challenges in finding research source material on Arab art. In her presentation to the Smithsonian in 2021, she mentions the obstacles she encountered when she began researching this topic for her dissertation. She discovered that Arab art received very little attention in Western art history scholarship, if it was mentioned at all.

> As an international student here in the United States in the 1980s, I was baffled by this absence ... Why is it that no one seemed to know anything about it, but then [were] fascinated by my references to it in my own work, which of course was then perceived as exotic? (Smithsonian American Art Museum, 2021)

This was a glaring omission, particularly when one considers the centuries of contributions by Arab artists.

She goes on to describe the issues she encountered and the reaction of the academic community when she indicated her intent to study Arab art. "But as a student ... I was faced by a number of challenges: starting with, what is ... Arab art and how can it be modern? (Smithsonian American Art Museum, 2021, 21:19). Shabout went on to describe the art history world's history of devaluing and marginalizing Arab art, shoe-horning it into very narrow "either/or" categories. In this environment, she posits:

The 20th century art production of the Arab world can only belong to either Islamic art, a new, but well-established category in western art history, or, a geopolitical, cultural, and anthropological area studies. That signaled the clear problem of recognition and acceptance or lack of. (Smithsonian American Art Museum, 2021, 22:05)

Shabout persevered, but, despite finding a program willing to support her studies, she encountered more obstacles. The most glaring of these obstacles was the lack of scholarship on modern Arab art. Additionally, getting access to archival materials in Arab collections was difficult for a myriad of reasons, including the political climate in some regions. She also encountered problems getting research funds for a topic that was not recognized as a legitimate field of study. "And as I discovered quickly, a problem of methodologies: a language to speak about Arab arts aesthetics" (Smithsonian American Art Museum, 2021, 22:37). Simply put, a method for articulating what the message of an artist's work is meant to convey, or to verbalize the context behind the work, was needed for true visual understanding to be obtained. Modern Arab art, she asserted, required a new language or methodology to achieve visual literacy in Arab art. As we shall see, this means shifting the current language and methodology of studying modern and contemporary art to one that removes Western/colonialistic assumptions of what constitutes 'real' art.

In *Modern Arab Art*, she states that Arab art "cannot find unity" (Shabout, 2007, p. 43). Part of this lack of unity is owing to what the term 'Arab' means concerning identity. It is not bound by clearly defined geographical borders, by specific ethnic or cultural characteristics. The concept of 'Arab identity' came about both because of the Ottoman Empire's dissolution and a need for unifying Arabic-speaking people. Shabout addressed this in her 2019 lecture at the Contemporary Museum of Art in Houston, pointing out that Arab is a blanket term applied to speakers of Arabic. It is not a race, "but rather a very open-ended ethnicity ... that allows for variation within it" (Contemporary Arts Museum, Houston, 2019, 13:57).

There is no uniform style when it comes to Arab art. Shabout points out that the major factor impacting this lack of unity is the nature of contemporary art, regardless of where or by whom it is created. As with any other group of contemporary artists, Arabic-speaking artists represent a wide variety of ethnicities and experiences, all of which result in equally rich and varied forms of artistic expression (Shabout, 2007, pp. 43–44). It is, she states, "governed only by its own rules and defies classification and consistency" (Shabout, 2007, p. 43).

Unpacking the "Other" Status of Arab Art

Until recently, Arab modern art has not been accorded the same respect and attention as its Western counterpart by art historians (Shabout et al., 2010, p. 31). Two main reasons for this lack are an emphasis on a Western canon of modern and contemporary art and the history of colonization. There was, and still is, a tendency to focus heavily on the art of the West, to use its definition of what is visually 'modern,' and to relegate those works that do not fit this definition to the sidelines and/or place them under a single category. Patronizing terms, such as 'Orientalism' and 'exotic' further the 'Otherness' accorded Arab art and artists, thereby assigning them to peripheral roles in global visual history.

The neglect, misinterpretation, and misrepresentation of this subject on a research and educational level are what makes Shabout's entire scholarly record essentially transformative. Beginning with her book, *Modern Arab Art*, Shabout began to unpack the issues that challenged people's understanding of Arab art in general as well as providing a solid beginning point for educating them on the complexities that impact artists of each region grouped under the umbrella term of 'Arab.' By writing *Modern Arab Art*, which was based on her 1990 graduate research, Shabout has stated that her motivation "was to advance an art historical conceptualization of modern Arab arts through understanding its underlying political and ideological motives, within a need for a constructed identity" (Smithsonian American Art Museum, 2021, 34:50). While she acknowledges the contributions that Western art education made to some Arab artists' development, Shabout directs viewers to look beyond the Western canon's definitions of modern/contemporary art, to study and appreciate modern Arab art on its own terms, within its own unique context. She points out that the 'problem' of modern and contemporary art lies with the Western perception that modernity and tradition are "a singular linear continuum … whereby tradition is considered antithetical to change … [This] issue is decidedly irrelevant to the Arab world, and has distorted the understanding of Arab Modernism" (Shabout et al., 2010, p. 39). Much of this perception of 'Otherness,' or outside the Western definition of modernism, lies in the language used to describe and write about Arab art, which still has not been fully decolonized. It reduces Arab artists to imitators of European artists, rather than individuals making independent choices about their works' style and content (Contemporary Arts Museum, Houston, 2019, 15:22–19:32).

A particularly exclusionary concept within art history that must be confronted is the Western concept of Orientalism, a term used to both define and condescend to the art of non-Western artists from Turkey to

Japan and other so-called 'Far Eastern' regions. Arab art was seen as exotic, 'Other,' beautiful but 'lesser' because it did not fit into the Western canon. This is true of contemporary Arab art as well; in her contribution to *New Vision: Arab Contemporary Art in the 21st Century*, Shabout refers to the "persistent politics of representing the 'other' – a newer, friendly version of Orientalism" (Shabout, 2009, p. 14). These attitudes go hand in hand with colonialism, and its marginalization of the people that it ruled for decades, which aided in furthering the Western-centered canon of both history and art history. By doing so, colonialism helped to create an inaccurate and incomplete global visual record.

This flawed view of non-Western art hinders visual literacy, since it renders an accurate understanding of Arab art all but impossible. For example, art history textbooks, both past and present, limit their discussion of Arab art to Islamic art, if they mentioned it at all. This assumption that all Islamic art is created by Arab artists is as inaccurate as saying all Catholic art is made by Italian artists. Shabout explains the difference is a matter of ideals; the goal of Islamic aesthetics is a religious ideal whereas modern and contemporary Arab aesthetics focus on a secularized ideal (Shabout, 2007, p. 35). While the imagery may be rooted in traditional artistic forms, Arab art is ultimately the vision of the individual artists, "representing an innovative means of self-expression formulated in response to Arab artists' psychological and social motivations, as well as their intellectual understanding of the arts" (Shabout, 2007, p. 35).

Art historians, she states, "perform art criticism for the discipline in various forms – and particularly when we dismantle and deconstruct mainstream accepted preconceptions and narratives, when we historicize regions, cultures, and artists who are left out of the canon" (Smithsonian Art Museum, 2021, 7:40). Each Arab country has its own socio-political and cultural individuality that shapes artists' visual language and the content of their work, examples of which will be highlighted later in this chapter. The current dialogue in art history:

> ... is rethinking contemporary art during what it perceives as a global crisis, considering recent geopolitical economic and health emergencies, and their impact on visual culture and artistic practice. Modernism in the arts, as it developed outside Europe, and, or North America, is now an important and growing area of research in art history. (Smithsonian Art Museum, 2021, 13:36)

Shabout, as her scholarship attests, is a participant in this transformative discussion.

Arab Modernism and Contemporary Art: Shabout and the Visual Conspiracy

If learners and instructors are to fully "participate in a changing visual information landscape" (ACRL, 2022, p. 2), and "pursue social justice through visual practice" (ACRL, 2022, p. 2) by inclusion of Arab art in their art historical studies, they must be able to recognize the subjective nature of art historical labels as well as its Eurocentric and colonial biases. One of these biases, Shabout asserts, originates in the Western perception that modernity and tradition are "a singular linear continuum … whereby tradition is considered antithetical to change … [This] issue is decidedly irrelevant to the Arab world, and has distorted the understanding of Arab Modernism" (Shabout et al., 2010, p. 41). She also points out the irony of this European viewpoint, in light of the fact that much of what is visually 'modern' in European art is easily traced back to non-Western traditions (Shabout et al., 2010, p. 41).

To gain a more accurate view of Arab art, the learner must examine how modern and contemporary Arab artists defined modern art. Arab artists, Shabout explained, did not see modern art as a break from earlier artistic periods and styles; it was a conduit to expressing their identities and culture through new forms of visual expression. They would not "accept or practice the European severance with history and found no contradiction between modernity and the past" (Shabout et al., 2010, p. 39), since for them modern art developed organically out of their visual historical record.

This leads to an important difference in the definition of what is modern and contemporary art according to the West versus the Arab art world. For the Western modernist, the expressive possibilities of art are paramount. Free expression, as they saw it, cannot be practiced if it is tied to past forms of art. Shabout describes the Western vision of modernism succinctly, "Modernism was to be secular, and about the new" (Shabout et al., 2010, p. 34). This is in direct contrast to how Arab artists view modernism; they do not make art simply for its own sake. Art, they believe, serves more than one purpose. Shabout writes that modern Arab art, as with the art of other formerly colonized countries, "became an essential tool in the search for, creation, and maintenance of national consciousness and identity" (Shabout, 2007, p. 50). This brings up another important difference in Arab artists' vision of their profession, the "role in maintaining civilization and serving humanity in a global context" (Kholeif et al., 2015, p. 52). To this end, Arab artists believed their purpose was not just to create art but to serve as educators in modern art to the public at large (Shabout, 2020). A visual manifestation of both this need to educate and maintain Arab identity can be seen in the continued use of Arabic script as a design element. Arabic script had historically been used in Islamic art; it would be recognizable to the public and "... could serve as an easy 'subject matter' for a kind of abstraction that would be understood by the public ..." (Shabout, 2020, p. 48).

If the artist is to communicate, educate, and maintain Arab culture for a worldwide audience through art, thereby promoting large-scale visual literacy, then modernism was seen as an absolute necessity for Arab artists to be a part of the global art community. Shabout referenced Egyptian artist, Ramsis Yunan, who argued for modernism as a means of cultural development and advancement. Yuanan's stance was that the interaction of innovation and heritage were necessary for "true Egyptian art" to exist. "Therefore," he stated, "we should not fear any innovation, no matter how extreme it may be, for those who fight innovation under the pretext of protecting our national identity reveal the weakness of their faith in its potential for growth" (Shabout, 2007, p. 27).

Arab art, Shabout has said, has been rejected for its political implications. She and other art historians have been struggling with the current obsession with identity politics, and its implied exclusivity, in the arts, to the point where it threatens to take over all art related discourse. This is particularly challenging, given the shift to a post-colonial era which has allowed Arab artists freer expression. Her approach is to take Arab art out of the issue of 'identity politics' while still addressing the individual political climates which have consistently informed the visual products of Arab artists. "On many levels," Shabout writes in *Sajji: A Century of Modern Art,* "politics provide a space of continuity for Arab art of the twentieth and twenty-first centuries" (Shabout et al., 2010, p. 37). Ongoing conflicts, many of which can be traced back to colonialism as well as conflicting ideas of what it means to be an Arab nation, will naturally have an impact on Arab visual arts (Shabout et al., 2010).

Given that this is the Arab artists' reality, it isn't possible to be visually literate in Arab art without knowing the political climate that the artists were and are working in. Political dissent and rebellion against colonial powers were and are popular subjects. For instance, Palestine and the Intifada have been a consistent influence on Arab imagery. Large-scale armed conflicts between Iran and Iraq, the Gulf wars, and the invasion of Iraq garnered not only global attention but that of Arab artists (Shabout, 2018, p. 41). In Iraq, the Baathist regimes and the war in the early 2000s profoundly changed the art market within the country, as well as sending many artists into exile in the West. This created a visual schism between the two groups, creating new audiences for both. Those who remained in the country lost state sponsorship once the Hussein regime ended and found themselves completely out of sync with artists who left the country and who had been exposed to modern styles and materials (Nusair, 2013).

Shabout advocates strongly for viewing Arab art through the artist's eyes and the scholarship of those who are versed in the Arab visual language and culture. This art cannot be shoehorned into the Western canon. Furthermore, there is a difference between how the artists of the modern period and contemporary artists view the term Arab. For the former, it brought those who shared a common heritage together. In contrast, many in the latter group, particularly those "'globalized' artists of the diaspora" reject the label of Arab as they view themselves as "belong[ing] to a global world that accepts them as artists per se, a category in which identity is not a factor" (Shabout et al., 2010, p. 31).

Conclusion

Scholars and educators, like other professionals, revise, refine, and expand their body of work over time. Sometimes their early scholarship requires major changes, sometimes minor ones. Shabout has stated that her views on modern art have changed since the publication of *Modern Arab Art*. In 2022, she told interviewer Aya Namir that, at the time, she was largely focused on the separation between Islamic art and modern Arab art, which she now thinks looked so significant to her initially because of the lack of background knowledge of the eighteenth- and nineteenth-century artists (Afikra, 2022). She points out that new information has come to light that affects her original scholarship.

This new information came in the form of the translated primary documents that she, Anneka Lenssen, and Sarah Rogers curated in their 2018 publications, *Modern Art in the Arab World: Primary Documents*.

> Now we know more ... based on the primary resources that we're finding what the artists were seeing and thinking and we can sort of detect/decipher what they were subconsciously ... seeing and thinking as well and I think that allows us to reconsider the connection with the Islamic that was perhaps strongly rejected by some on the surface but not necessarily in the practice and now we sort of can untangle the continuity more and understand how that kind of comes together. (Afikra, 2022, 10:01)

Shabout had, in *Modern Arab Art*, asserted that Islamic art and modern/contemporary art were separate visual entities. However, the statements of the artists working with these 'traditionally Islamic' design elements suggest that this separation is not as clearly defined as she originally thought. Here Shabout is modeling how to apply the themes of participating in a changing visual information landscape and practicing visual discernment and criticality (ACRL, 2022, p. 5, 7). Based on these recently available primary sources, she has concluded that the Arab view continuity in art history discussed previously in this chapter is more inclusive of Islamic art than was originally perceived.

Her involvement with the international Arab art community has been and continues to be highly impactful. She has been active in the quest to recover the lost works of the looted Iraqi Museum of Modern Art. In an interview with author Isis Nusair, she discussed her work with The Modern Art Iraq Archive, which "displays the work in an open format that invites worldwide use, including by the Iraqi National and expatriate communities, and encourages users to help identify and understand individual pieces" (Nusair, 2013, p. 124). Upon embarking on this project, her motivation centered on documenting the collection of the lost works. There was no documentation or archival system in place for "the intellectual output of the twentieth century." Since all archives had been lost or destroyed or were incomplete due to the Iraq war, she acted upon the suggestion of her colleague, Saleem al-Bahloly, to map "out modernity in Iraq through text," she expanded the project "to include newspaper and journal articles, exhibition catalogs, and all relevant publications." She decided upon a cut-off date for art works and text in the 1990s, she posits, which marked the shift in Iraqi art from modernism to postmodernism (Nusair, 2013, p. 125).

Shabout has impacted both teaching and course creation with her scholarship. In 2020, Dina Ramadan of Bard College, wrote that the publication of *Modern Art in the Arab World: Primary Sources,* edited by Shabout, Anneka Lenssen, and Sarah Rogers, enabled Ramadan to create her course, *Art, Aesthetics and Modernism in the Arab World.* This course "was primarily intended to introduce students to the intellectual and cultural history framing the debates and discourses that shaped the development of modern art in the region from the 1900s to the 1970s" (Ramadan, 2020, p. 92). She states that such a class would not have been possible previous to this publication, owing to issues of accessibility, linguistic and physical, to the documents in this collection. She further praises the breadth of the collection, which includes letters, exhibition texts, manifestos, diary entries and other documents, while also "affording space to understudied artistic movements" (Ramadan, 2020, p. 92). Ramadan also cites *Modern Arab Art* as an excellent source that can be appreciated by a wide audience and have applications across the humanities and social sciences (Ramadan, 2020).

Shabout's scholarship and instruction activities as well as her organizational activities benefit a range of disciplines, art history being the most obvious. As she has stated in both her interviews, presentations and writing, this is an area of art history that has been marginalized and misunderstood for decades. Shabout has pointed out, as quoted previously in this chapter, that Modern and contemporary Arab art does not need to be 'rescued,' it does need to be respected and receive broader attention in academic art instruction (Smithsonian American Art Museum, 2021, 15:15). That said, visual literacy, as we know, is not confined to the study of fine arts. There are other fields that would gain from her work. These include, but are not limited to, Middle Eastern studies, international politics studies, and colonial history (in the international sense). Some of Shabout's writings are included in dual language publications which are useful tools for students in the process of learning the Arabic language.

Shabout has spent her career charting the path to a fuller understanding and acceptance of Arab art in the modern and contemporary periods. She has sought out and supported living artists, supported recovery and preservation efforts in Iraq, co-founded an international organization, created a robust publication record, won numerous awards, all while teaching art history at a state university. Shabout's assertion that Arab art cannot be separated from its creator's reality is pivotal to the learner's ability to achieve visual literacy. Without it, learners risk acquiring a distorted view of a significant part of the global visual record. Arab artists' contributions have transformed the face of art history by advocating for Arab art and artists to take their rightful place in the global study of art history. To exclude these artists from thoughtful, unbiased, informed visual study is to render visual literacy in modern and contemporary incomplete, if not impossible to achieve.

References

Afikra. (2022, April 21). *Nada Shabout: Contemporary Arab art, conversations [Video]*. YouTube. https://youtu.be/wsQmw9GKMBQ
ACRL. (2022, April 6). *Companion document to the ACRL framework for information literacy for higher education: The framework for visual literacy.* American Library Association. https://www.ala.org/acrl/sites/ala.org.acrl/files/content/standards/Framework_Companion_Visual_Literacy.pdf
Contemporary Arts Museum, Houston (2019, January 31). *Beirut and the Arab world: Modernism, art and culture [Video]*. YouTube. https://youtu.be/_hMQzFVEAbg?si=1tRI4cNoiMwZcwAX
Kholeif, O., Stobbs, C., & Shabout, N. (2015). *Imperfect chronology: Arab art from the modern to the contemporary: Works from the Barjeel Art Foundation.* Whitechapel Gallery.
Lenssen, A., Rogers, S., & Shabout, N. (2018). *Modern art in the Arab world: Primary documents.* The Museum of Modern Art.
Nusair, I. (2013). The cultural costs of the 2003 US-led invasion of Iraq: A conversation with art historian Nada Shabout. *Feminist Studies, 39*(1), 119–148. 10.1353/fem.2013.0012

Ramadan, D. A. (2020). Teaching modern art: Situating aesthetic debates within Arab intellectual history. *Review of Middle East Studies, 54*(1), 92–96.

Shabout, N. (2007). *Modern Arab art: Formation of Arab aesthetics.* University Press of Florida.

Shabout, N. (2009). Contemporaneity and the Arab world. In H. Amirsadeghi, S. Mikdadi, & N. M. Shabout (Eds.), *New vision: Arab contemporary art in the 21st century* (pp. 14–20). Thames & Hudson.

Shabout, N. (2018). Modernism, Palestine and the Arab world. In N. ʿAnānī & N. Shabout (Eds.), *Nabil Anani – Palestine, land and people* (pp. 39–47). Saqi Books.

Shabout, N. (2020). Mediating abstractions through the Arabic letter. In S. Takesh & L. Gumpert (Eds.), *Taking shape: Abstraction from the Arab world 1950s–1980s* (pp. 40–49). University of Chicago Press.

Shabout, N. M., Al-Khudhairi, W., & Chalabi, D. (2010). *Sajjil: A century of modern art.* Skira.

Smithsonian American Art Museum. (2021, October 21). *Clarice Smith distinguished lecture: Nada Shabout [Video].* YouTube. https://youtu.be/MHMddgjBM4o

INDEX